Animals & Men 1-5:

In the Beginning

Issues 1 – 5 of *Animals & Men* magazine

April 1994 – April 1995

Animals & Men 1-5: In the Beginning

© 2001 CFZ Communications

ISBN 0 9512 872 66

Printed & published by CFZ Communications

- an imprint of the Centre for Fortean Zoology

15 Holne Court, Exwick, Exeter, EX4 2NA, England

email: cfz@eclipse.co.uk

www.eclipse.co.uk/cfz

TEN YEARS OF
THE CENTRE FOR FORTEAN ZOOLOGY:

It's hard to believe that the CFZ is nearly a decade old! I became a professional monster hunter more by luck than by judgement. Like everything else in my life it happened almost by chance. After a serendipitous chat in 1994 with a representative of one of the better-known Sunday newspapers about the "Beast of Exmoor" and the subject of cryptozoology - the study of unknown animals - a subject that had been my hobby for many years, I was quite surprised to read that I was "one of Britain's foremost cryptozoologists".

In a 2001 interview with the Yorkshire UFO Society I was asked how I first became involved in the subject:

"I've been interested in this stuff all my life. My interest probably started when I was a little boy. I was brought up in Hong Kong surrounded by all sorts of weird and wonderful animals anyway. Every week my mother used to get me library books and one week when I was about seven years old she got me a book called "Myth or Monster" which introduced me to the wonderful concept that there were real monsters like the yeti, the loch Ness monster and sea serpents in the world around us. I was immediately hooked and I've been interested in cryptozoology ever since."

Cryptozoology is the study of hidden or unknown animals, and such creatures, belonging to a species wholly or partly unknown to science, are usually collectively referred to as 'cryptids'.

Many researchers, myself included, are interested in a related category of mystery animals often termed the 'pseudo-cryptids'. These are animals which are out-of-place: known species which by accident or artificial introduction (or sometimes both) live in a geographical area where one would not normally expect to find them. An example being big cats on British moorlands.

But the third category - the one that interests me the most are zooform phenomena. These are not animals at all, but are entities or apparitions which adopt or seem to have animal or part-animal form. This is where we, at least partly, enter X Files territory. In many ways, these elusive and contentious entities have plagued the science of cryptozoology since its inception - and tend to be dismissed by mainstream science as thoroughly unworthy of consideration. Zooform phenomena seem to be a mysterious blend of paranormal manifestation and mythological icons.

As I became more deeply involved in the study of zooform phenomena I began to realise that you could no longer study these 'creatures' in isolation. In many cases, zooform phenomena are inextricably linked with a wide range of other paranormal and fortean phenomena, most especially crop circles and UFOs.

It was because of this curious dichotomy of definition that my ex-wife and I finally decided to found the Centre for Fortean Zoology in April 1992. We were staying with friends in Derby and discussing the problem of my being a cryptozoologist who didn't necessarily want to study cryptozoology per se when my friend Dave said, "Well, I guess you need to start a new science then."

I had to agree with him. I was already a devotee of the work and philosophy of Charles Fort, the American researcher who had given his name (unwittingly and one suspects unwillingly) to the study of anomalous phenomena and so the name Fortean Zoology really found itself.

No, that's not entirely true.

I originally wanted to name my nascent scientific discipline 'anarchozoology'. Taking the political philosophy of anarchism, rather than the popular interpretation of the term, my concept of anarchozoology was to be a discipline where one made up one's own rules, and then stuck to them, rather than being bound by the rigid dogma of the preconceptions of someone else's scientific world view. It seemed to me then that the omniverse was such a strange and bewildering place that it was only by fusing the two apparently disparate concepts of 'discipline' and 'anarchy' that one could make any sense of it all. It still seems like that to me today.

I had been working as a freelance writer and researcher for some years, and it seemed to me that the time was ripe to formalise my research, and to form an institution through which I could share my research with others working in similar disciplines.

However, this was not the full reason. Because of the very nature of mystery animal research, and especially when one is considering the subject of zooform phenomena, which in itself is a strange and disturbing discipline, there is a tendency for some sectors of society to treat you like a bloody lunatic because you date to show an interest in things that are away from the norm. Perhaps the fact that at the time I was a drug addled hippie didn't really help, but I felt that I needed all the spurious credibility that I could get if we were going to have any chance of being taken seriously researching into such diverse subjects as frogfalls, Cornish Big Cats, animal mutilations, and the Owlman of Mawnan (all of which we looked into before the CFZ was a year old).

Although when it started the CFZ consisted of Alison, me and my mate Dave from Derby, after a couple of years it seemed a logical move to start expanding our horizons. Serendipitously, at the time I had recently made friends with a lady called Jan Williams from the North of England who, together with Trevor "Beast of Exmoor" Beer was running a short lived organisation called S.C.A.N - (The Society for Cryptozoology and the Anomalies of Nature). I became a regular contributor to their magazine, and when after four or five issues, Jan and Trevor went their separate ways I asked Jan, diffidently, whether she fancied helping me start up a Cryptozoological magazine. I wanted to call it *Animals & Men* after a line in a song by *Adam and the Ants* from their unjustly ignored debut album *Dirk Wears White Sox*. Remember at the time I was still a bloody hippy and my writings and methodology were horribly imbued with references to anarchic politics and obscure rock records. Much to my eternal gratitude Jan agreed and the magazine (and thus the CFZ proper) was born.

The rest is history!

Alison and I were practically bankrupt at the time that the first issue of Animals & Men was published in the early summer of 1994. We hitchhiked to London and gatecrashed the first ever *Fortean Times* Unconvention with our complete stock of two hundred of these magazines. Much to my surprise I sold the lot and sat at the bar feeling rather please with myself

At the bar was a middle aged Irishman with a bodrhan, wild staring eyes and attitude. He was Tony "Doc" Shiels, and he and I soon got talking and drinking. Within an hour we were firm friends. A journalist from The Guardian came up to me and asked me and my companion for an interview. We were both pissed and slightly belligerent. He asked who we were. "Doc" threatened to curse him, and I replied in my most pompous ex -public schoolboy voice. "Dear boy, I'm Britain's best known Cryptozoologist"......Of course I wasn't any such thing, but they printed it anyway, and if it's in the papers it must be the truth 'cos seven years later I'm still here and we've just published issue 25 of *Animals & Men*. Funny old world innit?

By the end of the weekend we had well over a hundred subscribers and our future was secure. We continued publishing magazines at roughly three monthly intervals but it wasn't until issue three that we had our first proper break.

Also at the 1994 Unconvention I met Dr Karl P. N. Shuker, someone with a REAL claim to be Britain's greatest cryptozoologist at the time, and someone else who has, over the years, become a good and dear friend. He was lecturing and during his lecture he told the fascinating tale of some alleged monster footage that had been taken at Lake Dakataua on the Island of New Britain off the coast of New Guinea. This story galvanised the entire British cryptozoological establishment and we dedicated many pages of the next few issues to the story until just after issue 4 we managed to get hold of a copy.

We were the first people in the UK to get a copy, and indeed (sorry to those awfully nice fellows at Tokyo Broadcasting Company TBS) but as far as we know all the video copies currently circulating in the UK originally came from us. Unfortunately for cryptozoology as a whole the pictures turned out to be of salt water crocodile(s) but fortunately for us, not only did it take some time for this fact to be discovered but it was one of our researchers, Darren Naish, who discovered the fact and first published it in our 1997 Yearbook.

In 1995 we decided to start a second publication, the annual Yearbook. This 200 plus page collection of longer research papers has been published annually ever since.

Unfortunately in 1996 Alison and I separated and were divorced after long, messy and painful legal proceedings a year or so later. My old friend and colleague Graham Inglis whose main qualifications for the job were that he was:

a. An old mate
b. Had some knowledge of administration and computerised office procedures
c. Had worked with me on a number of projects over the years
d. Could party like it was 1999 when it was only 1996

came on board to fill Alison's roles as administrator and general partner in crime.

Even now, five years after the split I look back at those months with horror and I can truthfully say that if it had not been for the strength and fortitude of Graham and my many other friends in the CFZ around the UK I don't think I would be sitting here now writing this story. I would probably be dead. And I mean that.

In the mid 1990s the Carribean island of Puerto Rico was plagued by an outbreak of animal mutilations.

These were blamed on El Chupacabra (Spanish for The Goat Sucker - also a derogatory term for prostitutes of the lowest order).

The reports described attacks on a wide range of domestic livestock and there were even disturbing reports of attacks on human beings. Researcher Conrad Goeringer wrote in 1997 that:

"Believers in the chupacabras say that the beast is a hybrid creature, in appearance something which resembles a cross between a giant dog and a lizard. It is said to walk upright on two feet, is capable of flight, and sinks its fangs into victims and kills them by drinking their blood. News reports of chupacabras sightings come from mostly rural areas; and while the mysterious creature seems to prefer farm animals like sheep, goats, and chickens, it has been alleged to attack humans."

A researcher at the Centre for Fortean Zoology, who shall remain nameless described the animal (most famously depicted by Puerto Rican researcher Jorge Martin) as a cross between a kangaroo and Sonic the Hedgehog (a computer game character) on acid! By 1996 the attacks had spread to Mexico, Guatemala and even the mainland United States.

The reports continued and in September 1997 we were approached by AVP Films, an independent company to take an expedition to Puerto Rico, Mexico and Miami in the hope of tracking down some witnesses and discovering the truth about the creature.

The resulting adventures are told in the Channel 4 Film *The Fearless Vampire Hunters* and in my book *Only Fools and Goatsuckers* which was belatedly published by CFZ Press in 2001.

On our return to the UK, Graham and I were only too aware that if we were to expand our activities we needed to take someone else on board. At that time we had been corresponding on and off with a geezer called Richard Freeman for several years. He had co-authored an article on Dog Headed Men with me for the third volume of *Fortean Studies* and we had collaborated on a number of short TV shows. He, too, was a party animal with a stupid sense of humour, but unlike Graham or me he had proper zoological qualifications. He had followed up a City and Guilds in Animals Management and he had studied zoology at Leeds University.

We asked him whether he wanted to join us at the CFZ. He did and he is still here three years later. All the pieces were now in place. By the end of 1998 we were all living in slightly bohemian squalour at my house in Exeter. The CFZ was now in place and all were present and correct.

One of the best parts of my job is that occasionally I get invited to various parts of the world to appear at conferences as a guest speaker, and so, just in this guise I was in the United States during the summer of 1999. I was lucky enough to be out in the middle of the Nevada desert and to meet many friendly and kind people who took me out into the desert on exploration trips. During my sojourn in Nevada I met several people who told me stories of a broadly cryptozoological and fortean nature that I want to follow up as soon as finances and time allow. These include:

a. People who claim to have seen the giant Thunderbird - the mythical bird icon of Native American folklore which is still seen occasionally to this day.

b. Stories of strange animal carvings on remote hillsides out in the Colorado desert which are reminiscent of the Thunderhorse of Native American legend

c. Reports of giant eels seen in remote desert springs and oases

d. People with first hand experience of mysterious were-coyotes.

However, I also discovered possibly the most intriguing mystery that I have ever encountered. Whilst I was in Nevada I met Dr Lloyd Pye, a charming man, who showed me a specimen that affected me more than any of the other strange things that I have seen during my cryptozoological career. It was a skull - apparently humanoid, but so unlike that of a human that in all my years as a researcher I have never seen anything like it. According to Lloyd in about 1930 "an American girl of Mexican heritage in her late teens (15 to 18) was taken by her parents to visit relatives living in a small rural village 100 miles southwest of Chihuahua, Mexico. The girl was forbidden to enter any of the area's numerous caves and mine tunnels, but like most teenagers, she went exploring.

At the back of a mine tunnel she found a complete human skeleton lying on the ground's surface. Beside it, sticking up out of the ground, was a malformed skeletal hand entwined in one of the human skeleton's upper arms. The girl proceeded to scrape the dirt off a shallow grave to reveal a buried skeleton smaller than the human one and also malformed. She did not specify the type or degree of any of the "malformations".

Before I became a professional monster hunter and cryptozoologist I was, for many years, a qualified nurse in a succession of hospitals for the Mentally Handicapped in south Devon. Whilst doing my training I had the opportunity to study people with a wide range of physical and mental disabilities including people who suffered from genetic syndromes of disability that these days are unknown!

This puts me in a unique position amongst fortean investigators, because I am in the position to be able to refute any claims that this skull is merely that of someone suffering from gross deformities. There are so many differences between the morphology of this skull and that of a 'normal' human that I am convinced that an embryo exhibiting such a wide range of deformities would not be carried to term.

However it appears that according to some analysis at least that the skull is of a sub adult!

It should also be noted that in every syndrome of mental and physical handicap of which I am aware the deformities are very obvious. The strangest thing about this skull is that it is perfectly symmetrical - it is as if the skull is meant to be the way it is.

The initial DNA tests have been inconclusive, but many observers, including me, are convinced that Lloyd has in his possessions something very special indeed!

Because it has large, saucer shaped eye-sockets, and because the foramen major is positioned in such a way that some people have suggested that this is a creature evolved for a low gravity existence, many folk who actually believe that Lloyd Pye is telling the truth about this remarkable specimen have claimed that it is the skull of a hypothetical alien-human hybrid.

Well, I may believe in monsters I don't believe in humanoid aliens, but the skull most definitely exists. I have seen it. I have held it. Lloyd has also unearthed evidence that there may be two more of these artefacts in a monastery near Cholula in Mexico. It is ironic but I drove right past the very same monastery when I was hunting for vampires, and I am determined that one day I shall go back to find out (if I can) what these bizarre skulls really are.

On my return to the UK I was thrown into a particularly unpleasant situation. I had been employed by Top Events Ltd of Tarporley in Cheshire – a company owned by a bloke called Roy Bird - to edit their magazine, *Quest*. During that time I commissioned a large amount of work from various friends and colleagues throughout the fortean community. Unfortunately, after a few months it became obvious that Bird was a crook and had a record of fraud and misappropriation of funds.

Many people including all three of the main CFZ faculty members, Jon's own father, and a lot of the major players in the fortean community ended up being owed a lot of money as a result of this short lived liaison with Bird and his company and I resigned at the end of November 1999.

However this liaison did me a lot of harm on a personal level. As a result of my relationship with Bird I lost my publishing deal with Domra books and fell out with many people whom I had considered friends. The whole episode left a nasty taste in my mouth.

At the end of 1999, however, we were approached by NM News of Solihull to work on their new project - a national Sunday newspaper with an ethical 'green' remit. From the start I had grave reservations about the project and felt that it was too idealistic to succeed. However we were all willing to try and our brief sojourn with the project (which only lasted eight or nine issues) finally gave us enough money to set the CFZ up properly. From being a rather grubby and sordid bachelor pad, we invested time and money, acquired a housekeeper and eventually made some semblance of order out of the ongoing chaos. We also used some of this new found wealth to promote our first annual convention, which was a great success.

Unfortunately the year 2000 was in all other respects a particularly horrible one. Toby, the CFZ Dog and a very dear friend to us all died in June, and over the year various friends, pets and projects painfully passed away. I battled unsuccessfully with ill health, and Graham's ex-girlfriend Tracey killed herself. Money, emotional and health problems proliferated until none of us knew what the hell was happening. I was pretty well bed-ridden and worse, I had become completely addicted to the medication I had been prescribed. I was a junkie, Graham was incoherent with grief and Richard, poor fellow, was the only one who held us all together. It seemed to us that all our years of hard work had come to nothing.

Then, as always seems to happen, someone came to the rescue. Hong Kong based TV Production Company Bang Productions took Richard out to the rain forests of northern Thailand in October in search of a legendary giant snake called The Naga. His adventures, and the ensuing publicity carried us forward until the end of the year. For the first time in years all three of us celebrated the advent of the New Year separately, and I am sure that none of us looked back upon the death of the old year with anything but undisguised loathing.

However, with 2001, a new year was dawning and we slowly began the long, slow job of clawing ourselves back towards some sort of equilibrium. By the time of writing things are looking pretty rosy with new books, new expeditions and new projects peppered all over the horizon and even a new CFZ doggie asleep on the carpet in our sitting room.

We've had the good times, we've hit the bad times, and now we've got another decade to look forward to. The next ten years looks like its gonna be fun.

Jon Downes
Exeter
2001-07-22

Issue I
April 1994

Issue I April 1994

Issue One of *Animals & Men* was unique. It was only ever intended as a speculative venture and when I first formulated the idea I never thought, in my wildest dreams, that it would still be being published eight years later. It was the only issue not to be typeset on a computer, and was put together in the best traditions of back bedroom fanzines using a typewriter and copious amounts of glue. My ex-wife and I had been publishing music fanzines for some years and had a certain amount of experience in the small press world, but it was the first time that we had ever attempted anything on this scale.

The Centre for Fortean Zoology, which had been founded a couple of years before, still wasn`t anything more than a grandiose concept with very little substance to back it up. When we first teamed up with Jan Williams, who had been the co-founder of the now defunct Society for Cryptozoology and the Anomalies of Nature [SCAN], we inherited about thirty of their members and several articles which had been intended for SCAN News, but the vast majority of the debut issue was written by Alison and myself. My articles were mostly excerpts from a failed boom project called "The Mystery Animals of the Westcountry" and, looking back upon it, the whole issue was a little parochial. Nevertheless, it was a brave effort and as events proved, from little acorns...........

ANIMALS & MEN
THE JOURNAL OF THE CENTRE FOR FORTEAN ZOOLOGY
ISSUE ONE

Is the legendary Mapinguari a surviving Mylodontid Ground Sloth? ... Frog Falls ... Mystery Martens ... Golden Frogs ... Relict populations of Asian Rhinos ... The Surgeons Photo is a hoax ... News.

This Magazine is published by Spanish Train Publications a branch of STP Communications an independant media arts organisation that has been operating in the Exeter area since 1987.

For more information please write or telephone:

THE CENTRE FOR FORTEAN ZOOLOGY
STP (UK)
15 Holne Court
Exwick,
Exeter
Devonshire UK
EX4 2NA

Telephone 0392 424811

****
This issue was put together by the following hard working Zoological nutcases:

Editor   : Jonathan Downes
Newsfile   : Jan Williams
Birds   : Alison Downes
Contributors : Nick Maloret
             ' Bill Petrovic
Cartoons   : Lisa Peach
             : Jane Bradley
Cover by Lisa Peach
Typeset by Jon

****

Many thanks to:

Karl Shuker, Trevor Beer, Stephen Shipp, John Allegri, John Jacques, Graham Inglis, and above all to Bernard Heuvelmans without whom none of this would have been possible.

****

SUBSCRIPTIONS

A Four issue subscription is:

Six Pounds Sterling   (UK/EIRE)
Seven Pounds Sterling   (EEC)
Eight Pounds Sterling   (Non EEC Europe)
Ten Pounds Sterling   (OZ,NZ,USA,Canada
                         Surface Mail)
Twelve Pounds Sterling (OZ,NZ,USA,Canada
                         Air Mail)
Twelve Pounds Sterling (Rest of World
                         Air Mail)

We intend to come out roughly four times a year but in an uncertain world full of Fortean Phenomena and with the inevitable glitches in the space-time continuum which will certainly ensue we don't guarantee anything as predictable as a strict three month release schedule.

ADVERTISING

Small Ads (up to thirty words) are a pound each for subscribers. Trade ads are by arrangement.

CONTENTS

THE GREAT DAYS OF
ZOOLOGY
ARE NOT DONE....

This is a magazine predominantly about unknown animals but it is not purely a magazine about Cryptozoology or the study of completely new species. We also aim to cover out of place animals, animals that have been declared extinct that suddenly prove their existance and even, to a certain extent Fortean phenomena that involve animals when the editorial team feel that such an article would be either interesting or appropriate.

Computers are both the answer to the Forteans dreams and the banes of their lives. They are wonderful tools for data storage and information processing and they are unwieldy mazes of electronic tat in which evil gremlins can lurk and from whence they occasionally emerge to play havoc with your life. This magazine is produced on a number of computers and over the last three months a lot of things have gone wrong with several of them which is why this debut issue is not only about a month late, but is not up to the standard of typography that we would otherwise achieve. We unreservedly

apologise for spelling, grammatical and typographic errors which may have sneaked past us. Don't judge us too harshly because of them.

This is a non profit making project from a publishing team who have steadfastly failed to make a profit in the seven years we have been in operation. Donations of time, money, equipment and expertise are always extremely gratefully received. If you want to contribute articles, reviews, eyewitness reports, photographs or any other evidence please do.

This is a completely non partisan publication. There are too many painful schisms within the science of Cryptozoology and its allied disciplines and we have no intention of adding any more. We want to provide a forum for discussion and good natured controversy, and we hope that with this, our debut issue we have managed to make a good start. The views expressed in each article are those of the author and not necessarily those of the Editorial Team, who usually in any case, take opposing viewpoints on each and every subject.

Please give us your support because in our own little way we actually think we are doing something rather important.

Best Wishes,

Jonathan Downes.

NEWSFILE..

Compiled by Jan Williams with occasional irrelevancies from The Editor.
(Let's face it, Jan would never use the word 'groovy')

SURGEON'S PHOTOGRAPH A HOAX

The famed Loch Ness Monster photograph, supposedly taken by Colonel Robert Wilson on 19th April 1934 has been declared a hoax. Loch Ness researchers David Martin and Alastair Boyd claim that Christian Spurling, who died last November, confessed to making the monster from plastic - wood and a toy submarine. Spurling was the step-son of film producer Marmaduke Wetherell who was hired by The Daily Mail to track down the monster. Prints supposedly found by Wetherall in December 1933 proved on examination to be hoaxed - probably made by a Hippo-Foot Umbrella Stand. Ridiculed by Fleet Street, Wetherell asked Spurling to produce a monster. Wetherell's friend Maurice Chambers, suggested Harley Street Gynaecologist Robert Wilson as 'front man' and Wilson was provided with four photographic plates to take to an Inverness Chemists for processing. Overwhelmed by the resulting publicity, the co-conspirators decided to keep quiet. All involved are now dead and the model - sunk by Wetherell - probably still lies on the bed of Loch Ness. (Sunday Telegraph 13/3/94, Daily Mail 14/3/94).

MYSTERY CATS

Cornwall.

The British mystery cat scene has been dominated in recent months by The Beast of Bodmin, star of stage, screen and SUN newspaper. Brown, black, and spotted big cats have been seen in the vicinity of Bodmin Moor for many years, but attained 'beastly' status in October '93 when Jane Fuller of Cardinham was knocked unconcious whilst walking her dogs late at night, and awoke to find a black animal crouched growling nearby.

Visual evidence for the existance of at least one large black cat on the moor formed the centrepiece of a BBC South West documentary, later shown nationally on BBC2. The video, shot by farmer Rosemary Rhodes shows a leopard like cat approximately four feet long.

Less impressive was a photo of 'The Beast' which appeared in The Sun on the seventh of January. Taken by Keith Farmer at Fenton Pits, this photo shows a black cat like animal in a most unusual stance, almost as if its tail is nailed to the floor. (Sun 1/7/94).

An alsatian sized black cat seen by motorist Alan Smallbone near the poetically named Praze-an-Beeble, South Cornwall, in November, was 'explained' by The West Briton newspaper as 'Mister Man', a black half-Persian cat belonging to Colin and Dawn Sharpe. (West Briton 25/11/93, 2/12/93).

Isle of Wight.

Are the island's mystery cats Servals? Naturalist Martin Trippett suggested in The Sunday Telegraph that three young Servals which escaped on the island in 1973 could explain many of the 'big cat' reports. The Sun, rapidly becoming essential reading for mystery cat afficianados - printed a photograph of a cat shot near Brading seven years ago, and identified by the experts as a Serval or Ocelot. Markings and ear-shape suggest that this particular mystery cat is actually an Asian Leopard Cat (Felis bengalensis). (Sunday Telegraph Jan 94, Sun 11/1/94, Isle of Wight County Press 14/1/94).

Somerset.

A huge cat was seen in Love Lane, Burnham, in early February. Witness Phil Gamblin said "It was black with a long tail but I wouldn't say it was as big as a panther". (Weston Mercury 4.2.94).

Midlands.

The Wolverhampton Express and Star (1/2/94) reported that a Great-Dane sized black cat attacked cat hunters Nick Dyke and his un-named companion in a lonely churchyard at Inkberrow, Hereford and Worcester. Inspired by reports of a leopard-like cat in the area, Mr Dyke and his companion were trying to bait the animal with dead chickens when it leapt from under their feet into a nearby tree. According to Mr Dyke, the cat hit his head and shoulders, sending him flying backwards, then reared up and lashed out at his friend, gashing her rib cage before running away. (Wolverhampton Express and Star 1/2/94).

A panther-like cat was seen in Tividale Road, Tipton, West-Midlands in the early hours of February 4th, and later the same day Mrs Eileen Rudd spotted a similar animal in the back garden of her home at Ashenhurst Rd, Dudley. It had a smooth black coat, and a thick tail which curved at the end. (Wolverhampton Express and Star 5/2/94, 7/2/94).

Greater London.

Police with loud hailers warned residents of Winchmore Hill, North London to stay indoors on the 11th March as they searched the streets for a Lion. A helicopter was drafted in and London Zoo supplied a tranquiliser gun. The initial report by David Booth was followed by seven others during the day, describing a golden-fawn animal two foot to two and a half feet high in The New River area. The search was called off after Douglas Richardson of London Zoo examined a photograph taken by Lia Bascock and declared it to be a domestic cat - later identified as Bilbo a ginger tom from Elsiedene Road. A nice tidy conclusion to the mystery - but Winchmore Hill lies three miles from Cuffley and Goff Oak to the north and Finchley to the south west - all noted for big cat reports in previous years. (Daily Mail 12/3/94)

South Yorkshire.

A huge, black cat with piercing yellow eyes shocked a man walking his labrador in Todwick when it crossed the bridleway in front of him. He said that it left pawmarks three times the size of the dog's. (Yorkshire Post 15/1/94).

Lincolnshire.

A four foot long puma-like cat was seen in Stapleford Woods by driver Paddy Morris in January. The cat stared at him for several seconds before disappearing over the hedge. (Yorkshire Post 15/1/94).

Derbyshire.

The Peak Panther - reported in areas around Edale Moor for many years - was seen on two successive days in January by the same witness. Dennis Morley was walking his dogs near Chapel en-le-Frith when the animal appeared. He described it as 4 to 5 feet long, with a black, glossy coat, long, drooping tail, and small ears. (Yorkshire Post 21/1/94).

County Durham.

Possible puma droppings found last year and frozen for preservation by mystery cat investigator Eddie Bell are being sent to experts for analysis.

Scotland.

Reports of a huge, black cat roaming Glenurquhart prompted the SSPCA to loan a large cage trap to Mr and Mrs Ronnie Moffat whose cottage overlooks Loch Ness. The cage was set up in December but the cat seems to have avoided it so far. (Press and Journal 13/12/93)

Northern Ireland.

Residents of Belfast were warned to stay indoors on 12th January whilst soldiers, police, and a helicopter crew searched for an Indian Tigress believed to have escaped from Bellevue Zoo. The 17 year old tigress was found dead in the moat surrounding her enclosure the following day. (Daily Mail 13/1/94)

OTHER EXOTICS

Kent.

Four Argentinian Peccaries (Tayassu pecari), were released by vandals from The Brambles Wildlife Park, at West Blean in mid February. Three were recaptured fairly quickly, one even wandering back into its enclosure, but the last one remained at large for a week. According to the newspapers he attacked two dogs, an eleven stone Bull Mastiff and a Rottweiler, but according to the park themselves he was an innocent victim of canine aggression. The four Peccaries were named Dozy, Beaky, (the one that remained out for longest) Mick and Tich. (God only knows what happenned to Dave Dee). Afficionados of the late lamented Frank Zappa however would agree that it would have been far groovier if one had been named Gregory. (Daily Mail 28/2/94 1/3/94).

Kent.

Wild Boar hunting has been revived in Kent - three hundred years after the species became extinct. A 200lb Boar was shot at Wittersham in early March and hunting parties are tracking a sounder of around sixteen of the animals in woods in the vicinity of Tenterden, Benenden and Biddenden. The Wild Swine are accused of damaging vines at Tenterden Vineyard and two cars have collided with the animals. Kent Police say they are aware of the existence of these creatures in the Tenterden area but it is not a major problem. (Daily Mail 16/3/94).

Oxfordshire.

Bears were kept at the royal palace of Woodstock until the thirteenth century, but revivalists will be intrigued to hear of a brown bear roaming Chadlington, a few miles away. First seen by farmer John Blackwell in September 1992, the bear has made several appearances since - on one occasion causing a bus driver to swerve as it reared up in the road in front of him. The rusty-brown animal leaves huge prints showing long claw-marks, and makes a hooting-howling noise. No livestock attacks have been reported but the bear seems to be partial to goldfish. (Daily Mail 24/1/94)

Merseyside.

Liverpool's famous Liverbird has been joined by Liver-sharks. To the stonishment of Scousers Scyliorhinus canicula, the lesser spotted dogfish shark, has taken up residence in the polluted waters of the River Mersey. The sharks, which grow to a maximum length of about three feet are largely harmless, but they do have a venomous spine in their dorsal fin. Anyone going across the Mersey therefore should stick to the ferry (Sunday Telegraph 9/1/94).

WORLDWIDE

THE CREATURE FROM CLEAR LAKE
Catfish or primitive whale?

In September 1993, fisherman Lyle Dysin hooked what may turn out to be the catch of his life in Clear Lake, Northern California. And - you guessed it - he threw it back.

Dyslin's action was prompted by compassion for the creature, which reminded him of his "little dachshund". Before returning the 'fish' to the water Dyslin. carved his initials into its forehead (seems an odd way to show compassion), and took photographs, which have been sent to scientists for computer enhancement and analysis. Initial reaction was that it was probably a mutant catfish - but is this really the case?

The head of the animal resembles that of a dog, albeit without the ears. Dark and crowned, it slopes to a round-ended nose, with whiskers like those of a catfish. The pectoral fins are fleshy and the back bears bony plates, similar to the diamonds of a sturgeon. But the most suprising feature is the broad, flat tail which is not vertical - as in all fish - but horizontally set like those of whales and dolphins.

It is possible that this is not the only such creature caught on the North American Continent. In Fortean Times (No 70), Mike Dash referred to William Hagelund's reported capture of a "baby Cadborosaurus" in 1968. The accompanying sketch shows a creature which differs from Dyslin's catch in having only pectoral fins, but shares the crowned, blunt nosed head, the whale-like tail and the dorsal plates. Hagelund also released the animal, moved to do so by "strong compassion for that little face staring up at me".

Discussing Canadian Lake Monster Sightings (Searching for Hidden Animals - DOUBLEDAY 1980) Roy P Mackal makes a persuasive case for the survival of primitive toothed whales - Basilosaurus or Zeuglodons in the region. Mackal states that the vertical flexure reported for Naitaka or Ogopogo, suggests horizontal tail flukes - a mammalian feature. Some reports of the Naitaka refer to plate scales on the creature's back, and to sparse hairs around the head. Plate scales have been found in association with Basilosauridae skeletons and hair or bristles around the head are common in many types of whales.

Comparing a 30 inch 'mutant catfish' with a huge serpent-like extinct whale may seem ridiculous but Terry Knight, fishing guide at the 8 million year old Clear Lake, says he receives calls every year from fishermen who claim to have hooked a giant fish which pulled their boat around the lake. Do any baby Zeuglodon fossils exist? (San Fransisco Examiner 3/10/93)

NEW CRAB SPECIES

Cilunculus Battenae a new species of crab from the USA was named after its discoverer, Sonia Dawn Batten, a Marine Biologist from Southampton University. BBC Ceefax 15/1/94

AMBULOCETUS - A MISSING LINK?

Ambulocetus - a fifty million year old fossil discovered in Pakistan - is a whale with legs, and provides the link between land dwelling ancestors of the whales and early marine whales with vestigial legs. Hans Thewisson of the Northeastern Ohio Universities College of Medecine says swimming would have been its main mode of locomotion - its front feet pointed outward, making walking awkward, and on land it probably rested its body on the ground. (New Scientist 22/1/94)

HONG KONG MERMAID

A crowd of people gathered on the Hong Kong waterfront in early October 1993, after a fisherman radioed in to say that he'd caught a mermaid. He described it as having a pointy face, human like hair and no arms or legs. Sadly the fishing boat never arrived with the strange haul (BBC Ceefax 14/10/93)

Newsfile Correspondents: Phil Bennett, Ben Chapman, Louise Cook, Andrew Greig, Nick Maloret, Steven Shipp, Dr Karl Shuker, Samantha Yardy.

Giant Ground Sloths in Amazonia?

by Jan Williams

Do Giant Ground Sloths still roam the jungles of Amazonia? David C Oren of the Museu Paraense Emilio Goeldi is searching for proof in Acre state, West Brazil.

The fossil record shows three families of Ground Sloth: **Megatheriidae**, **Mylodontidae** and **Megalonychidae**. Some were massively built animals exceeding the size of elephants - others just a few feet tall. The vegetarian ground-sloths had molar teeth, well developed tails, and powerful fore claws, and were capable of rising up on their hind legs to pull down branches from trees.

It is assumed that ground sloths went extinct about 8,500 years ago, but the possibility of their survival into modern times was queried during the late nineteenth century. Argentinian paleontologists Ameghino and Moreno collected Patagonian legends relating to a nocturnal, ox sized creature with huge claws, and a piece of hide, encrusted with small bones which resembled that of the fossil Mylodon. The hide appeared fresh and other remains, both of Mylodon and of men, were found in the cave from which it came. Additionally, explorer Ramon Lista claimed to have encountered a gigantic creature resembling an Armadillo, but with long hair, which seemed impervious to bullets. On this basis Ameghino postulated the survival of a species of ground sloth and named it **Neomylodon Listai**.

When mylodon dung from the cave was tested using the Carbon 14 technique it proved to be at least 10,000 years old. Expeditions to the area failed to find any evidence of living ground sloths and it was suggested that the apparent freshness of the hide was due to conditions inside the cave.

In a paper (1) published in August 1993, David C Oren suggests that Amazonian legends of the 'Mapinguari' are consistent with the expected characteristics of a remnant ground sloth, which may still survive in western Brazil.

Local lore describes the **Mapinguari** as human sized with long reddish fur, a monkey like face, very tough skin, and feet which are 'turned backwards'. It is generally assumed to be either mythical, or as suggested by Heuvalmans, (2), an unknown primate, like the **Didi** of Guyana or the disputed **Ameranthropoides loysi**. Oren himself originally believed the **Mapinguari** to be mythical, until his attention was drawn to reliable contemporary accounts of encounters with the creature.

Witnesses gave Oren remarkably consistent descriptions, both of **The Mapinguari** itself and of the tracks and faeces it left behind. These descriptions, he believes, match the expected appearance and behaviour of a small forest dwelling Mylodontid Ground Sloth. The reddish fur is consistent with mummified remains, and ground sloths walked with their claws curved towards their body, which could explain the feet being 'turned backwards'. The size is small for a ground sloth, but, as Oren points out, forest dwelling mammals tend to be smaller than their savannah cousins.

The only vulnerable parts of **The Mapinguari** are said to be the eyes, the open mouth, and the navel region. Fossilised skins of South American Mylodontids are formidably armoured with layers of dermal ossicles on the shoulders, back and thighs, and fossil skeletons show some Ground Sloths had ribs which were very close together, providing further protection.

The Mapinguari is reported to twist Bacaba Palm trees to the ground in order to feed on the fruits. Leaves and stems are often recognisable in the creature's faeces which resemble those of the Tapir and the Horse. Oren has examined samples of Ground Sloth faeces and states that these also resemble those of horses.

According to legend **The Mapinguari** has one eye located in its belly. Oren suggests that this may be a specialised gland, capable of producing a noxious gas, which allows specimens to escape. (3).

Could such an animal have survived undetected? Oren points out the difficulty of observing a creature of crepuscular and nocturnal habits in tropical rain forest, and that remains would rapidly decay. Amazonians avoid contact because of the fear it engenders, and eye witness accounts are ignored because of its mythical status.

David Oren hopes that his expedition will provide evidence to show that the Ground Sloth still exists in Amazonia. First hand **Mapinguari** reports have become less frequent in recent years. If Oren is correct in his beliefs, let us hope that we have not consigned **The Mapinguari** to legend a few years too soon, and missed the chance of conserving this survivor from the Pleistiocine.

REFERENCES

1. **OREN David C:** Did Ground Sloths survive to Recent times in the Amazon region? **Goeldiana Zoologia No 19 (Museu Paraense Emilio Goeldi 1993).**
2. **HEUVELMANS** Bernard: On the Track of Unknown Animals (Rupert Hart Davis:London 1958)
3. **New Scientist** No 1909 (22/1/94).

My Thanks to David C. Oren for kindly providing me with a copy of the above paper.

feathered folklore

A story that I first heard from my mother has now passed into the realms of Urban Folklore/Modern Myth.

The "Penguin in the Bath" story has been popping up all over the place in different forms. The essentials of the story are that a person/child of doubtful age/sanity picks up a penguin at a zoo/wildlife park and takes it home to put in the bath.

My mother swore that this happenned to a friend of a friend's mentally handicapped son on a school trip to Paignton Zoo, but the story has since turned up from many other sources and refuses to die.

Another story which has all the hallmarks of a piece of feathered folklore in the making is the legal battle in India between two families who both claimed that they owned the same pet parrot. The judge showed Solomon like restraint and persuaded the sagacious fowl to recite the names of the children of the family who really owned him. This story has also been repeated on several occasions and seems likely to take its place alongside the other well known piece of parrot lore about the parrot who flies in through the bars of a prison cell and squawks 'I can talk can you fly?' at the understandably annoyed inmate.

The only real puzzle when dealing with these stories of hyper intelligent Psitticiforms is how come my parrot, (A Lesser Patagonian Conure named Socrates) does nothing more Fortean than mumble 'Good Boy' while he is not shouting abuse at all and sundry in what I suppose must be fluent Parrot Language.

Birds eh?

Alison and Jonathan Downes.

RESEARCH PAPERS.

EVIDENCE FOR THE HITHERTO UNSUSPECTED SURVIVAL OF TWO RARE MUSTELIDS
IN THE SOUTH WEST OF ENGLAND TOGETHER WITH A REAPPRAISAL OF THEIR
TAXONOMIC STATUS

By JONATHAN DOWNES

INTRODUCTION

In 1977, Langley and Yalden discussed the status of the Pine Marten (Martes martes) and The Polecat (M putorius) when they surveyed the decline of the rarer British Carnivores in an eponymous paper for The Mammal Review,(1) and they concluded that both species were long extinct in the southern parts of Britain. There is, however evidence to suggest that they may have been premature in their conclusions especially in the South Western Peninsula, and therefore it seems reasonable to re-evaluate the current status of both species.

PART ONE: THE POLECAT (Mustela putorius)

Langley and Yalden place this species as having been hunted to extinction by 1887 (Devon), 1890 (Cornwall), and 1910 (Somerset) but a number of later records suggest that the species survives at least in Cornwall to the present day.

SOMERSET

There are three Somerset records from the earliest part of this century the most recent being in 1919.(2).

DEVONSHIRE

Writing in 1968, H.G.Hurrell whose name crops up again and again in this discussion, recorded this species from the Modbury area near Kingsbridge in 1925, and noted another pair which were killed in the same area in 1935 as well as noting an animal seen by his cousin crossing the Dart in 1910.(3) There are a number of North Devon records from the first part of the Century.(4). One was killed by dogs in a cornfield in September 1937, and there was a specimen caught at Coombe Martin in 1906. Hurrell (who obviously didn't know about the 1937 record), stated that the 1935 records were quite possibly the last English records as the animal was by then (1968) confined to Wales and

Scotland. St Leger-Gordon and Harvey (5) give another record from 1930 of four creatures 'larger than stoats' which were seen playing amongst boulders at Bellever, but conclude that it is "probably correct to regard the species as extinct in the region".

CORNWALL

The animal was found in Cornwall well within living memory.(6) Writing in 1970 Rennie Bere said: "The Polecat..is known to have been present in the Budock Valley near Falmouth up to 1914." The Institute for Cornish Studies have a number of records (7) including two from Penryn in 1908 and 1919, early 20th Century records from Boscastle, Tintagel, Chacewater and Lands End, as well as 19th Century records from Liskeard and St Ives and records from the valley below Budock School near Penryn, and from Sennen before the first world war.

The most recent Cornish records are from Goonhaven in 1934 and an animal which was seen on a number of occasions near Camborne in 1942, which was probably the same animal as the 'Coarse furred,black bellied ferret' found drowned near Gwealavellan the same year,which Dr Turk described in 1959 as 'Possibly the last surviving Polecat in the County'.

Writing about the status of the Polecat in Cornwall, Rennie Bere says that there are large numbers of what he describes as cross bred Polecat-Ferrets (although the term can be used to describe ferrets with Polecat colouration) living wild in the County. This scenario is used repeatedly by a number of authors to explain sightings of wild looking animals in areas where the wild animal is no longer found. One wonders however from where the wild population that the escaped domestic animals are supposed to have interbred with actually came from.

This excuse is therefore the least effective way of proving that a wild population no longer exists that I have ever heard. A more likely theory, but one which smacks of desperation and an ineffectual attempt at making facts fit the theories is Genetic and can be used to explain the West Country sightings of both Polecats, and Wildcats (F silvestris). This is that a well established feral population of the domesticated race of the animal in question, or the domesticated race of a close specific analogue of the animal in question exists. When the animals were first liberated then they interbred with the remnants of the original wild population before the original wild population disappeared, but every now and then a genetic pattern producing characteristics unique to the wild strain comes to the surface and animals of one species are found which exhibit characteristics found only in another species.

As recently as 1985 (8) Porter and Brown wrote that the precise taxonomy of the Mustelidae was uncertain, especially as regards the Weasel Family. The Ferret is generally regarded as a domesticated sub species of the common European Polecat. They admit, however that it is not only extremely hard to differentiate between certain strains of Ferrets and wild Polecats, but that the knowlege of biochemical and genetic differences between the two animals is so sketchy that true 100% differentiation is impossible. The methods used to differentiate between the two animals are arbitrary in the extreme, (mainly down to differences in the markings of the facial mask-and there is an enormous range of colouration morphs in the wild Polecat let alone the domesticated Ferret). The REAL problem is that the Mammalogical establishment have the intransigent attitude that because they believe that Polecats are extinct therefore all Polecats seen in the wild are actually Ferrets.

We have already discovered one blatant example of this from the South West. Here is another. Rennie Bere writes:(6) "A Polecat-Ferret that I saw near Launceston in March 1969 was unusually dark for a Ferret..." and HERE is the punchline.."but it could not have been mistaken for a Polecat." Why? Many, if not most eminent zoologists state that the two animals are indistinguishable. It has been claimed by several sources including popular wildlife author Phil Drabble (9) that although the skull of a domesticated ferret is generally considered to be smaller and thinner than that of a wild Polecat , if a 'polecat' was fed on soft food-bread and milk for example-from the time it was weaned and a 'ferret' was flesh fed in an open pen with plenty of room for exercise, the differences would be reversed.

I have two animals in my collection which are undoubtedly of domestic ferret ancestry,but which appear to be of entirely different species. One has the 'typical' polecat build and shape,but is,whilst not an albino extremely light in colour, whereas the other specimen is tiny boned and 'ferret' like whilst having the colouration of a wild Polecat,and looks identical with one of the Sutherland subspecies of the Polecat whose skull was apparently indistinguishable from that of a ferret. (This subspecies is presumed to have been driven to extinction in the years immediately previous to the First World War). Even if one is to accept the explanation that the Polecat-Ferret is a smaller, and lighter coloured beast than the Wild Polecat, animals are still seen in the region, that do not fit in with ANY of the currently accepted models of the taxonomic zoology of the region.

On the 12th April 1992 a pair of animals were seen by Mrs Barbara Holt at Luddock Wood in Cornwall. She described them as eighteen inches in length with a long bushy tail, the back was dark whereas the face had a very distinct mask over the eyes and a white muzzle.They came out of a hedge at about 4.00 PM playfully chasing each other. Mrs Holt looked at pictures of Polecats, Polecat-Ferrets and Ferrets and unerringly described them as the former.(11). There is no doubt that some Ferrets have gone wild in the region, but to my mind there is very little doubt that many of these feral beasts have interbred with the last wild Polecats and that the so called extinction of the species in the county is just another manifestation of Scientific short sightedness.

PART TWO:
THE PINE MARTEN (Martes martes).

Although Langley and Yalden (1) state that this species was hunted to extinction by 1834 in Surrey and between 1830-50 in Hampshire there has been a well documented series of sightings in Surrey over the past thirty years or so, and this relict population has even been the basis for a popular childrens book (12) and in a brief account of the fauna of the New Forest the author notes that "occasionally someone thinks they see a Pine Marten"(13). The further west we go, the more doubt is cast upon their results. They state that the species was extinct in Dorset between 1800-50 and in Somerset, Devon and Cornwall between 1870-80. Although I can find no firm records from Dorset later than 1848, (The only other Dorset records, a posible New Forest animal from 1916 and a creamish coloured animal, from Abbotsbury in 1951 (14), which appears to have been a Ferret), the county records for Somerset, Devon and Cornwall, some of which are indeed cited by Langley and Yalden only to be summarily, and somewhat unfairly dism issed paint a more optimistic picture.

CORNWALL

Miss S.B Andrews saw an animal that she identified as a Marten in a tree at Tehidy Park in Cornwall during the summer of 1932.(15). Whereas, in the light of new evidence which was not available to Langley and Yalden I am prepared to accept the Devonshire records which follow, this sighting is unique at least as far as I am aware, and is not corroborated by further anecdotal or archival evidence.

SOMERSET.

A 1851 report placed the species within the Mammals of Somerset (15) and there was a record of 'something that appeared to be a Pine Marten' from Luckwell Bridge on Exmoor during the winter of 1924 (16). This, again seems on the surface of it to be an isolated incident, but we shall return to the Martens of Exmoor later in this paper.

DEVONSHIRE

There is no shortage of historical evidence for the existance of the species within the County but unlike the neighbouring counties, there is a great deal of evidence to suggest that this species survived well past 1900. A comprehensive rundown of Devon sightings from the first half of this century was made in 1953 (17) by the renowned Devonian naturalist H.G.Hurrell, a character who assumes pivotal importance in this narrative..

"Mr Rossiter of Paignton tells me he is convinced he saw a Pine Marten near Paignton about 1918. Another reliable observer, Mr Prior of St Albans claims to have seen a Marten in Piles Copse, Dartmoor, about the middle of May 1932. One was seen very clearly at Noss Mayo, River Yealm in June 1952 by Major Brenda Gough. Several times an animal was glimpsed at night at Brentmoor House during 1952. There are reasons for thinking it may have been a Marten. Mrs Weeks of Yelverton and her son suspect that they saw a Marten in a high fir tree at Maristow in April 1953".

Three years later Hurrell wrote again:(18)

"Mr V Almy has come across references to this species at Puslinch, Yealmpton in 1843 and 1860 . Mr O.D.Hunt reports that his sister saw one at Gnaton near Newton Ferrers on July 11th 1955. It crossed the road in front of their car".

One was seen at Combeinteignhead on 26.11.72. Another Pine Marten was seen at there a year earlier, implying that this cryptic animal may well have been well established in the area at that time.(19):

"Boxing Day 1971. I saw a Pine Marten on top of my Budgerigar Aviary having been attracted by the noise of the birds. The Marten ran off at my approach. Its identification is not in doubt because I have kept Mink and can state positively that the animal was a Marten"

Another Marten was seen by R.M.Jewson in 1973:(13)

"Denham Bridge,River Tavy 8.9.73: I was fortunate enough to spot an animal moving through the top branches of a high oak tree and then to some more oaks. At first I naturally suspected a squirrel but it was far too big for a squirrel while the tail was too bushy to be a Mink.Also it was dark brown or red certainly not black. It took flying leaps from tree to tree with great agility. Having seen HGH's (Hurrell's) ranch bred Pine Martens when they were allowed to climb trees in a wood at Wrangaton I concluded that the animal I saw was indeed a Pine Marten.The leaps from tree to tree were quite considerable and it was fascinating to watch its performance".

More recently is a report from Wembworthy on the 20th February 1978 made by Mr P.M.Stark:(17)

"8 a.m An animal was seen in the trees of a coniferous wood running along the branches and going from tree to tree by jumping from the end of one branch to the nearest branch of the next tree. I could not see its colour against the light but it definitely had a bushy tail and appeared to be decidedly larger than a squirrel so I felt bound to conclude that it must have been a Marten. Knowing that size can be difficult to estimate I have carefully reconsidered my assessment, but I still feel it was definitely too big for a squirrel".

An animal which looked very much like a Pine Marten was seen ten years later in August 1988 by Mr Flemming of Exeter. He was driving his family towards Fingle Bridge for a days outing when they got hopelessly lost in the sunken Devon lanes. Suddenly an animal the size of a large cat jumped into the road in front of them and ran up the road before them with the car following at about the same speed. Mr Flemming is interested in Natural History,and was confused at what he saw as he knows that Pine Martens are not found in Devonshire. He described a long, sinuous dark red-brown beast which undulated sinuously along the road before him. On a visit to Wales soon afterwards he visited a Wildlife Park and compared what he had seen with every animal that he could find including Pine Martens and Polecats,and he was convinced that what he had seen was a Marten. His only misgiving was that the

animal had not seemed to have the ubiquitous fawn throat patch or bib,and had seemed to be a uniform colour all over. This, as we shall see is nowhere near as negative a piece of evidence as it would at first seem.

Three years later on the 4th October 1991 Mr Nettley, of Bag Tor House, Ilsington heard his wife call him to see a strange animal that was climbing a tree at the end of his drive.The animal had disappeared by the time his wife had taken him to the tree in question but she gave a clear description of a long thin squirrel like animal about two feet in length, and coloured reddish grey, which she immediately identified as a Pine Marten from one of the families books on British Wildlife. Mr Nettley spoke about the matter to a number of people who all told him that what she had seen was a squirrel, except for his Father in Law,an ex Policeman who told him that a Pine Marten had been shot by a farmer protecting his chickens, somewhere near Honiton sometime since 1960.

Mr Nettley also asked me if I could solve another mystery that had been puzzling both him and several of his friends. Apparently a number of them go shooting in the thick deciduous woods in the immediate area, area (near where Mrs Nettley saw her mystery animal), and they occasionally hear the "bangs and crashes" of a fairly large but seemingly invisible beast apparently chasing something in the branches above them.These noises are regularly punctuated by the sound of the creature (if it is a creature) plummeting to the ground and are then followed by silence. He has experienced this somewhat eerie phenomenon regularly over a period of some years, as have a number of his friends and acquaintances, and he was extremely interested in finding out what could have caused them. According to H.G.Hurrell, (1968), (3) this is the sound made whilst a Marten is hunting a Squirrel from tree to tree, a hunt which culminates with a crash as hunter and hunted fall to the ground.I have reports of similar sounds from several sights within a ten mile radius of the 1991 Pine Marten sightings at Ilsington,and they can only be considered as positive evidence.

The details of behaviour recorded by all these observers are also too similar to be coincidental. There are other interesting aspects of the reports as well. The report of the 1973 sighting was particularly significant. Mr Jewson gave his own reasons why the two animals most commonly reported as Pine Martens, the Mink and the Red Squirrel are really only superficially similar. A well known North Devon Zoologist who has asked to remain anonymous has told me that there is a small but flourishing colony of Pine Martens, some of which he has observed personally in a densley wooded valley on the edges of Exmoor. At least two other wild populations appear to still exist in the county; one outside Teignmouth and the other in the densely wooded areas of southern Dartmoor but are these animals the survivors of the original wild population?

Harvey and St Leger-Gordon noted in 1953 (5) that escapes of Pine Martens did indeed occur at various Fur Farms on Dartmoor and not all of these animals have been recovered.however they also note that from the escape records the male and the female of the species have never been at large together and so a chance of reestablishing this animal as a breeding population has not occured". The same year H.G.Hurrell remarked: "There have been two or three escapes from Wrangaton since 1940 and one from Chudleigh in 1921. It is unlikely the 1918 Marten could have been an escape but those seen subsequently may have been". I suspect that this is not actually the whole truth. Hurrell, (a naturalist for whom I have the highest regard) had a charming and childish enthusiasm for the species. He wrote a book about his pet ones, and he mentions them enough in all of his other books to show that he was a vociferous supporter of the species. I consider it highly probable that he helped the process of recolonisation along a little by releasing specimens from his own captive breeding programme to bolster up the fading wild population.I know that if I had been in the same position I would have done exactly the same thing!

Paul Blight at the Zoology Department of Bristol University said: "I am convinced that there has been no natural population since the war",and he agreed with me that any specimens still in the

area were probably descendants of animals liberated by Hurrell. Kelvin Boot the Devon Naturalist is also interested in the species but he tends to discount the Devon sightings since about 1950 as being a mixture of misidentification and over eagerness by the Mammal Recorders for the Devonshire Association,who were all members of the Hurrell Family. He told me however that Hurrell had indeed attempted a reintroduction programme on Forestry Commission land in the 1950s and 1960s but that it had been unsuccessful.I would suggest that from the evidence I have presented, and from evidence that keeps on coming in, that the reintroduction programme was in fact a success, although whether or not Hurrell himself knew this I would not like to say.

On the 17th July 1992 the situation was further complicated when The Animal Liberation Front announced that they had liberated a pair of Pine Martens stolen from Paignton Zoo at an undisclosed site in the County.

PART THREE:
OTHER MARTEN SPECIES IN THE SOUTH WEST OF ENGLAND?

Ian Linn of the Zoology Department of Exeter University,and also a distinguished Mammalogist, agreed with my tentative theories about Martens in Devonshire but added a bombshell of his own when he said that he believed that the animals kept by Hurrell,which are probably the ssource of most if not all contemporary Pine Marten reports in Devon were not the native Martes martes but the North American Martes americana,a closely related but entirely different animal. Another report from 1979, only served to confuse the matter further:(17)

An extremely puzzling corpse was found on the road between Exeter and Exmouth where it had obviously been run over by a car. It was originally identified as a Pine Marten but it was eventually found to be a Beech Marten, (Martes foina), a species that is not supposed to have existed in these Islands since before the last Ice Age. Despite the identification of the mystery corpse as being Martes foina that was given in the Transactions of the Devonshire

Association, Kelvin Boot is convinced that the animal was an American Marten which ties in neatly with what Ian Linn has already told us. MAFF, however agree with The Devonshire Association and have it on their files as M foina (2). The preserved corpse has, as is so often the case, dissappeared so the matter must remain unsolved, for the moment.

Ian Linn, knows of another escapee Beech Marten,this time from a much earlier period, probably during the Second World War, which escaped from a private collection and lived wild in the area for several years before being found dead in a barn belonging to a farmer living in the immediate area of the animals original owner. There is no reason why Martes foina should not live quite successfuly in Devon. It is very similar to its better known relative, and there are very few morphological differences. Is there any reason to believe, however, that the animal was ever resident here? The answer,suprisingly,is "Yes". Prior to 1879 it was believed that both species were endemic to the British Isles and the species now known as M foina was generally regarded as being the more common of the two species. In 1879, however Edward Alston (21) reexamined all the specimens he could find in Museums and concluded that M foina did not exist, and indeed had never existed in the British Isles and that all specimens that had been identified as such were merely misidentified Pine Martens. He then immediately contradicted his own theory by pointing out that a specimen of M foina HAD been killed in Northern Ireland during the nineteenth century. Something Alston only mentioned in passing however, but something that has turned up repeatedly during my investigations into the 20th Century geographical status of Martens in Britain is that they are extremely cryptic beasts and ones which even in 1879 had an uncanny habit of turning up where they were least expected in areas where they had been presumed to have been long extinct.

Utilising Heauvelmans' cryptozoological methodology it becomes clear that for a number of reasons, prior to 1879 both scientists and laymen considered the two species to be endemic to Britain and that the two animals were seen as clearly seperate species. A paper on the

Mammals of Devon written for The Devonshire Association in 1877 (22) includes the following species of the Mustelidae as resident in the county:

P.putorius (Linn) The Polecat, Martes martes (Linn) The Pine Marten and as a distinct species:

Martes foina (Buffon) The Marti (sic)

"This species is now, I believe, nearly extinct as a systematic war is waged against it by preservers of game. Mr P.F.Amery informs me that the last he has heard of was killed near Ashburton about six years ago".

Writing in 1897 Brushfield described the status of the Pine Marten as vermin in medieval (and later) Devonshire:

"MARTEN: There are but few entries on the Parish Accounts of their destruction and all varieties are included under one term. According to Bellamy 'Marten Cat' is one of its names in Devonshire. At Okehampton a 'martyn' was killed in 1780, and a 'marteil' in 1787. Two were paid for at Wellington in 1609 and one ('Marting') in 1700. In each instance 1s was paid. In 1744 '3 Marts Heads'are entered in the Ecclesfield Accounts but from the context they are probably Foumarts".

There are so many pieces of corroborative evidence in the preceeding paragraph it is difficult to know where to start. It is clear not only that a variety of different names were used, (even two animals killed in the same town only a few years apart were called by different names), which implies that two separate species are being discussed, but it is obvious from the way that Brushfield himself describes the animals that HE considered them to be of two different species. In a late nineteenth century paper on the Mammals of Dorset two species of Marten are again described (23):

GENUS MARTES

Marten Cat, (Martes Foina)

The Rev William Chafin in his 'Anecdotes of Cranborne Chase', records Marten Cats as one of the animals hunted there but believs them (1816) to be nearly extinct, their skins are too valuable for them to be allowed to exist. In 1836 one was caught alive near Stock House by the Rev H.F. Yeatmans hounds but biting the Huntsmans Hounds severely was kept alive for some little time. The paper then examines the status of M martes in Dorset and not only places TWO species of Marten within the fauna of Dorset but names M foina as the more well known one.

The main external difference between the two species is that M foina has a white patch or bib rather than a cream patch on its chest. There are also minor osteological and dentition differences as well as genetic ones, and it is interesting to note that even in areas where there is no doubt that the two species co-exist, for example across much of mainland Europe, the two species do not seem to interbreed. The naturalists (and indeed the politicians) of the late Victorian and early 20th Century eras are renowned for their arbitrary creation of new species, and their equally arbitrary 'lumping together' of different species in order to make life easier for the taxonomist. It seems therefore an indisputable fact that until the last century TWO species of Marten DID exist in Britain where only one has survived into the history books. As we have seen, however the current status of either species in the area is doubtful in the extreme, although I would not like to rule out the possibility of both species having survived. It looks extremely likely as if the accepted Mammalology of this country contains at least one glaring mistake.

The history of the taxonomy of the British Mustelids is a complicated one and several species which are no longer recognised have been described. The Irish race of the Stoat, for example seems to be markedly different from the main body of the species and the marked sexual dimorphism in the Weasel has lead to some 19th Century observers concluding that there were in fact two separate species, and the white winter colouration of the Stoat has also prompted the inclusion of a separate species, The Ermine, into a few early handbooks on mammals. One should not create new species on the basis of tiny physiological differences and it would be extremely unwise to consider the Irish Stoat, the Lesser Weasel or the Ermine as separate species, the taxonomic situation of the British Beech Marten is an entirely different matter. We are not dealing with tiny differences but with an entire species that coexists with The Pine Marten across most of its European range. The nineteenth century naturalists who recorded M foina from the region clearly identified the two species of Marten as being entirely separate, and until someone comes up with any evidence to the contrary I see no reason to disagree with them, and am convinced that even if they are now extinct, within the past two hundred years M foina was a resident of the South Western peninsula.

It seems therefore that there are, or have been, three distinct species of Martens (M martes, M foina and M americana, at large in the Devon Countryside. The sightings continue but which of the species they belong to or whether they are hybrids remains to be seen. Despite the undoubted probability of my confusing the matter further there is a fourth species of Marten which may be responsible for some of these sightings. The Sable (Martes zibellina) is a common animal of northern Eurasia. It is also the unfortunate posessor of the most valuable pelt in the genus Martes. It is a common resident of fur farms and has been bred widely. In the years before the multitude of different forms of legislation which now control the fur industry were introduced the South West was a popular site for small, unlicensed fur farms. It is not impossible that some specimens of this species which is a hardy and succesful animal escaped into the wild. (The animal seen by Mr Flemming in 1988 was darker than one would have expected a Pine Marten to be and had no distinguishing throat patch. An exact description, in short, of a Sable).

CONCLUSION

It seems certain that M martes did not become extinct in the mid Nineteenth Century as has often been claimed. There have been too, many sightings in the years prior to 1950, for this to possibly be the case. It is also certain that although their antecedents, and indeed even their exact species remain uncertain several colonies of these rare, elusive and beautiful small mammals still exist in the wilder parts of Devonshire. It also seems very likely that, at least in the past two hundred years, Devon had two species of native Marten instead of the one that is generally recognised. The statement by Alston in 1879 that all British Martens were in fact of one species was based on scarce (and now vanished) source material without the benefit of technology now available to contemporary scientists and is not borne out by anecdotal or folkloric evidence which tend to oppose his theory.

Potentially, the puzzle should be quite easy to solve. The Dorset accounts show that the animals were killed for their pelts and it seems likely that preserved specimens of both species exist in museums and in private collections. In the 1990s we have access to subtle forms of genetic and biochemical analysis undreamed of by the Victorian Scientists who could arbitrarily create or destroy species at the stroke of a pen. The true situation is less encouraging. The mounted Pine Martens in West Country Museum Collections are few and far between. The specimen which was 'once in the collection of the Plymouth Institution' was wild caught, its precise origin is unknown, although it has been suggested that it was killed on Dartmoor.(5). The specimen in Truro Museum is of Cornish Origin but is also without documentation.(7). The specimen in the Plymouth collection was presented by H.G.Hurrell, which would suggest that it was not of wild origin, the specimen in the Royal Albert Museum is labelled as a 'Continental specimen which lived wild having escaped from Hurrells collection, and subsequently been presented to the collection by Major Vickary', and the specimen in the Ilfracombe Museum, according to the 1935 report of the Ilfracombe Natural History Society (4) was... "Given in 1933 by Mr W.J.Parsons, of Combe Martin and was shot at Lynton 'many years ago'". Daphne Hills (16) of the Mammal Department at the British Museum (Natural History) informs me that there are no West Country specimens of either The Pine Marten or the Polecat in the National Collection and she repeats the currently accepted party line that "there are no specimens attributed to M foina from any part of Great Britain". The present state of Mustelid taxonomy is so confused that it seems unlikely that even if we were able to capture a living specimen of one of the mystery martens, that its precise identity could be discovered without DNA typing. (The members of the Marten family are all very closely related, indeed several authorities have suggested that the entire family be regarded as a single species and the eight species, four of which we have seen may have been members of the Devonian zoofauna be demoted to sub specific status).

If I am correct in my assumptions and Hurrell did introduce new blood into the ailing Devonian Pine Marten population, and if as Ian Linn has suggested the new blood was actually of transatlantic origin we have an appalling taxonomic mess. If M zibbelinna has also escaped/been deliberately introduced into the area, then matters can only get more complicated. Several scientists who are well recognised as being eminent men in their own specific field have told me that although the technology needed to solve the riddle of the Mustelid taxonomy once and for all through DNA analysis undoubtedly exists, in these days of draconian funding and manpower cuts, there is little hope of such research being carried out. Lack of money, lack of resources and lack of interest has condemned my researches into the Martens of the West Country to an unsatisfactory conclusion.

REFERENCES

1. Langley and Yalden:The Decline of the Rarer Carnivores in Britain (Mammal Review £7 1977)
2. Baker et al:Escaped Exotic Mammals in Britain (1980)
3. Hurrell:Wildlife tame but free (1968)
4. Palmer:Mammals of the Ilfracombe District p3
5. Harvey and St Leger-Gordon:Dartmoor (1953)
6. Rennie Beer:Wildlife in Cornwall (1970)
7. Institute of Cornish Studies pers corr (1992)
8. Porter and Brown:The complete book of Ferrets (1985)
9. Drabble:Phil Drabbles book of Pets (1976)
10. Harrisson Matthews:Mammals of Britain (1953)

11. Stella Turk Pers Corr 1992
12. Monica Edwards:Fire in the Punchbowl
13. Whitlock:Wildlife of Wessex (1976)
14. Proceedings of the Dorset Natural
    History and Antiquarian Field
    Club 1952 p114
15. Baker:The Somersetshire Fauna
    (Proceedings of the Somersetshire
    Archaeological and Natural History
    Society 1851)
16. Daphne Hills (Pers Corr 1992)
17. Transactions of The Devonshire
    Association Vol 111 210-211
18. Transactions of The Devonshire .
    Association:Vol 89 p 259
19. Transactions of The Devonshire
    Association:p230 Vol 104
20. Transactions of The Devonshire
    Association:Vol 106 p280
21. Alston:On the specific Identity of
    the British Marten (1879)
22. Transactions of The Devonshire
    Association:Vol 9 p325
23. Transactions of the Devonshire
    Association Vol 113 p193

"There are Marten Cats and Badgers
and foxes in the Enchanted Woods"

W,B Yeats
"Celtic Twilight"

ASK NOT WHAT THE CENTRE FOR FORTEAN
ZOOLOGY CAN DO FOR YOU, BUT RATHER WHAT
YOU CAN DO FOR THE CENTRE FOR FORTEAN
ZOOLOGY.........

Obviously you are interested in the
weirder side of the Biological Sciences
or you would not be reading this
magazine.

Would you actually like to get involved
to a greater extent? This is NOT a club
or organisation. It is also not a
publically funded foundation for
scientific research, but as always seems
to be the case when one deals with
subjects of Fortean interest it is
something in between.

We need representatives in as many
countries, counties and even districts
as possible. If you want to take on the
added headache of being an accredited
representative of The Centre for Fortean
Zoology then please get in touch. The
job is (obviously) both hard work and
completely unpaid but we need people to
liase with their local newspapers, to
liase with their local councils, to
interview eyewitnesses, collect
specimens and to run up appaling
telephone bills whilst engaged in long
night time conversations with Jon and
Jan.

We are planning a cuttings library open
to all. Please send us any cuttings or
photocopies that you come across.
Remember to mark them with where they
came from. Within the next few months we
hope to be able to circulate a catalogue
of cuttings available and for a nominal
fee to cover ONLY photocopying costs and
postage we will send copies of anything
we have to anyone who wants it.

We are also planning a permanent Museum
of Cryptozoology as soon as we have
enough exhibits and somewhere where a
permanent display could be kept. We have
several ideas in the pipeline on this
one and we hope that, like the
Conference of Fortean Zoology, another
of our ongoing projects something
concrete will be achieved this year. It
is time for us to reclaim this branch of
Zoology from the people who would have
it become just another, rather tedious
science.

•• •• ••

FROGFALL FEATURE

It seems appropriate that the debut issue of a magazine edited by someone who is closely involved with a musical ensemble called 'The Amphibians from Outer Space' should feature a whole mescalleny of articles on, or apertaining various strange and out of place tailless amphibians. As I was typing up this paragraph I caught a glimpse of something moving across the carpet. It was a medium sized frog which does not appear to be of the species usually found in Exeter. His name is Harold and he now sits, happilly gulping away and eating crickets in one of the Centre for Fortean Zoology vivaria until someone can decide what to do with him.....

A FROG OR TOAD FALL DURING THE 1950's AT PORTSMOUTH IN HAMPSHIRE.

by NICK MALORET

In April 1987 I went to interview a lady living locally regarding a falling object that had torn a hole in her conservatory roof. After examination at the Geology department of Portsmouth Poly this object was identified as probably being a lump of foreign runway tarmac that had lodged in an aircraft tyre. However my dissappointment at not having discovered a fall in the Fortean mould or even an honest to goodness meteorite was tempered by a comment from Mrs Nash, the witness. She recalled, I was fascinated to learn, a friend mentioning having experienced a frog or toad fall at Fallington, just north of Portsmouth, some years previously. Mrs Nash told me that she would try and contact her friend and perhaps try and arrange a meeting.

Sorry to say I never did hear anything further about the Farlington story, but nothing daunted, decided to write to the Portsmouth News asking readers for information about the event. Much to my suprise I received two telephone calls and four letters describing a whole series of these frog-toad falls. Intrigueingly three of these letters appeared to relate to the same event and a very local one at that. All the witnesses describe this frog or toad fall (none were certain of the species) as occuring in the 1950s and according to one, possibly around July 1954. The locality of the event in all these reports is Copnor in central Portsmouth. This is a denseley populated residential district so that the number of witnesses to this happening may not be suprising.

The first account is from Mrs Pat Potter of Portsea:

"On reading your letter in the paper today. I had the same experience when I was a girl living at Copnor. I am forty two now and when I was about nine, my mother and I went to the evening "pictures" at the old 'Tivoli', now a garage in Copnor Road. We came out of the pictures at about 10.00 at night and it was pouring with rain. We crossed Copnor Road and went into Keswick Avenue to cross the bridge called White Stone Bridge, as we lived in Dover Road at the time. Anyway in Keswick Avenue millions of baby frogs or toads came down with the pouring rain. I was laughing all the time. I scooped up loads of them with my mum, and took them home, and put them in the garden. To this day, I have always remembered it, and told the event many times, but people do not believe me, especially my four sons (all grown up now)".

Mrs Potter later confirmed to me on the telephone that the frogs or toads were very much alive, and were falling all over her as they came out of the sky.

The second witness is Mr Harfield of Denmead, Hants. He was situated (again sometime during the 1950's), near the 'Airspeed' playing fields at Copnor. It had just stopped raining after a cloudburst and the time was between 8.00 and 8.30 PM when he noticed hundreds of small frogs or toads littering the playing fields and the 'White Stone' pedestrian railway bridge nearby. Estimating the time somewhat earlier than Mrs Potter Mr Harfield is quite adamant that the fall occurred earlier in the evening. Were there two seperate falls that evening I wonder? Again the frog-toads were alive and fully developed-lacking tails.

Two witnesses were involved in the final report; Mr and Mrs Howe, still resident in Copnor. The following is Mrs Howe's description of the event.

"Having seen your article about toads falling from the sky, we are sure that you will be interested in a similar incident experienced by ourselves. Many years ago, having visited our parents in Redcar Avenue, Copnor, we left the house (on foot) and before we reached the end of the road, a very heavy rainstorm overtook us. Imagine our suprise when we saw an increasing number of tiny frogs spreading across the road. They slithered about on the wet road and multiplied by the dozen as we stood there fascinated! They had to be coming down with the heavy rain, and we stood for a couple of minutes, amazed and intrigued. Unfortunately we were getting very wet and had quite some way to go before we would get home, so we left the scene bewildered and very puzzled. It is difficult to remember when this happenned but it would be somewhere around the 1950's.

There was nobody else around at the time and so we were probably the only people to see the strange phenomenon. The frogs (or toads or whatever), were no more than a couple of inches long, perhaps even less! Your newsletter has brought the memory back to us. We were very young at the time, and we can well remember trying to tell our friends about the incident. They thought we were telling a shaggy dog story!"

Hoping to find some reference to this July 1954 (?) frog-toad fall, I checked the archives of the Portsmouth Evening News for the period and although I found no mention of the event, one or two things turned up that may be relevant.

Firstly it was reported that June 1954 was the wettest for thirty years, with farmers and church fetes generally having a hard time of it. Mention is also made of a solar eclipse on the 30th June, and earlier, on the 23rd June there were three independant sightings of a UFO seen at night above Portsdown Hill. One witness described the object as shaped like a rotating spinning top and that it dissappeared towards the east 'like a flash!'

There also seemed to be an ongoing debate in the letter page of the paper regarding the strange weather, with correspondents variously blaming God, The Russians, and Intergalactic Warfare

Lastly I should mention an odd coincidence in this report. Mrs Potter's address is "Curzon Howe", and two of the witnesses were also named Howe. How indeed?

Three further apparently isolated cases of frog-toad falls:

Yorkshire 1930's. Probably a Sunday 2.30 PM.

Mr C Campbell was motorcycling with a friend on the Thirsk to Scarborough Rd and was caught in a heavy cloudburst. They sheltered under a wall. When the rain ceased they made to continue their journey and were amazed to see 'thousands' of Small, Live frogs or toads scattered on the ground.

Brownsdown, Gosport, Hants. Easter 1930's.

Small frogs or toads littered the ground after a cloudburst. Caller omitted to leave name.

Tunbridge Wells, Kent. Probably 1950, late July or August.

Mrs D.F Yates was staying with relatives in Tunbridge Wells, and whilst walking with them on Rustall Common experienced a shower of 'hundreds' of small live frogs. There was no sign of wind and rain.

THE GOLDEN FROGS OF BOVEY TRACEY

The story of the Golden Frogs of Bovey Tracey (1) is essentially one of those quasi religous medieval allegories which are in themselves garbled survivors from a pagan tradition. The story goes that a poor woodsman lived with his equally destitute family in Bovey Tracey. Their child was suffering from an unspecified illness and was not likely to survive the night. On top of this farrago of misfortune there was a severe thunderstorm. There was a knock on the door and a mysterious lady entered demanding (in a querulous voice) shelter and food. Despite their many misfortunes the woodsman and his family welcomed the mysterious lady, gave her milk and food (which they could ill afford) and a seat by the fire. She then blessed the ailing infant who was miraculously cured, and before vanishing (up a road called to this day Mary Street) she said that so that her benefactors would know this wasnt a dream not only would the child be forever cured but that the next day the family would discover a new spring full of crystal clear water and bright golden frogs.

The religous significance in this charming tale (excepting the frogs) is obvious, and I would hazard a guess that the story probably predates Christian times, and that the Marian details were added to a pagan story about Isis, Demeter, Gaia or any Earth Mother of your choosing. The thing, however that sets this story apart from a myriad of other B.V.M. Visitation legends is the odd vignette of the golden frogs. Just a tiny piece of medieval whimsy? Possibly not.

These frogs were said to have populated the area for many years. If so, what were they? The concept of brightly coloured amphibians inhabiting the English countryside is not as unusual as one might suppose. In a series of newspaper stories covered in Fortean Times one of the events in the aftermath of the falling of 'North African' Desert Dust upon Gloucestershire recently was the appearance of several small PINK frogs, one of which is pictured in the article. Whether there is any connection remains to be seen by future inquisitive Herptologists both in the Dartmoor and Gloucester areas. The article went on to describe specimens of a North African desert Locust which had also been carried by the wind to this country and which had appeared all over the south of England including Plymouth and St Austell, (Incidentally a similar falling of Sahara Dust, also pink was reported from Devon on the First of July 1968) and presumably has happenned on various occasions during the past.

(Other pink frogs have been recorded over the years from Sussex and The Cotswolds, and although there is a well known red phase of the common Frog (R temporia), these animals were definitely not it). (3).

It is not inconceivable that at some time in the past (the BVM visitation took place during an exceptionally violent thunderstorm), a similar collection of desert dust which contained yellow (or golden) frogs dumped its amphibious passengers deep in the heart of the Devon countryside where they established themselves for a short while with some success. Such a fall of yellow mud in rain happenned throughout the region in January 1902 and again on the 22 February 1903. (2). The phenomenon also happened on the same day in Dorset (23):

"During the early part of Sunday morning, February 22nd 1903 with a South West Wind a strangely yellow fog prevailed at Corfe Castle but towards noon some drizzling rain fell and deposited some yellow dust-or rather mud as it was then on the surface of the earth and by 12.30 p.m or perhaps a little earlier, the perculiarly yellow appearance was no longer seen in the atmosphere. Similar falls occurred in various parts of the world and there seems little doubt that all this dust that was deposited at about this time was carried in winds from the North African Desert, the Sahara in which sandstorms not long before had been observed and recorded. It was stated in the Dorset County Chronicle that this deposit of yellow dust was very noticeable on the pier at Swanage for some days after the fall took place".

Charles Fort was also interested in falls of 'Sahara Dust' (it is interesting that the Sahara explanation was also prevalent when Fort was writing in the early parts of this century), and he was similarly unconvinced by the North African explanation. He pointed out that apart from everything else, the desert sand of the North African Wastes is silvery yellow rather than red, (4), yet these sky falls sometimes accompanied by animate and inanimate objects have been going on for millions of years. If we are to believe the official explanation that the pink frogs seen all over the south west of our country during the nineteen eighties were brought to England in clouds of pink dust blown from North Africa,then I feel that the existance of yellow (or Golden) Frogs in Bovey Tracey could be explained in the same way. As we have seen the clouds of yellow dust have appeared .on several occasions and it seems possible that the mystery behind the delightful legend of the Golden Frogs of Bovey Tracey may have after five hundred years been solved.

David Bolton of the Albert Memorial Museum in Exeter suggested to me,half joking that the well attested phenomenon of North African locusts of varying species which arrive almost annually in the South West may also be responsible for the story of the Golden Frogs of Bovey Tracey. After all, he said with a wry smile, proving once and for all that it is not only Cryptozoologists that form ludicrous theories from the most flimsy of evidence, they are both yellow and they both hop.

REFERENCES

1. Coxhead:The Legends of Devon
2. Transactions of the Devonshire Association Vol 35 p81
3. Fortean Times 56
4. Fort:The Book of the Damned (1919)

POSTSCRIPT

In February 1994 local and national newspapers (for example the Daily Mail 3.2.94) were full of the story of Jaffa a three year old Frog discovered in a garden in Truro. Jaffa was, as his name implies bright orange. The Westcountry TV News carried a story about him which said that he, and a similarly coloured mate had been released in a secret location. We contacted Mark Nicholson of the Cornwall Trust for Nature Conservation and he revealed to us that far from being an isolated occurence these oddly coloured amphibians are popping up all over the place. Ranging in colour from bright orange, through yellow to pale cream, these creatures have been reported from all over the county and even from elsewhere in the UK although they appear to be much rarer.

The only explanation that they have come up with is that the colour changes are something to do with the excessive levels of radioactive Radon gas in the county, but they stress that this is only a theory. These animals appear to breed true to type, but as yet nothing is known of their genetic makeup or their position within the ecosystem. Jaffa, himself has been released into a safe habitat, but it is hoped that more specimens (including some of the mysterious cream coloured tadpoles that have appeared in recent years) will be obtained soon. Hopefully we shall obtain some specimens soon as well and when we do, be assured that we will tell you as much as we can. For the present however, it is fairly clear that the charming medeival legend of the Golden Frogs of Bovey Tracey might not be so far fetched after all.

AND IT MAKES ME WONDER...

According to the BBC Teletext service CEEFAX (1/3/94) which in recent months has been a veritable fount of knowlege for fortean zoologists hundreds of fish, 2-5 cm long were found flapping on roads in an (unfortunately) unnamed rural district of Australia. Zoologists (also unnamed) blamed the phenomenon on storms which had swept fish eggs, which had been dormant for a year or two into the clouds where they hatched and fell. Me, I reckon Rolf Harris took them with him when he was climbing his stairway to heaven.

RECOMENDED READING

We are not the only UK Magazine which specialises in the subject of unknown beasts. Craig Harris is the editor of:

CRYPTO CHRONICLES
5 Willow Court
Droitwich
Worcestershire
WR9 9HL

FROM OUR FILES.

THE GOSPEL ACCORDING TO ENID BLYTON.

"The children began to run-but before they had gone very far, they slowed down in suprise. The lane was absolutely full of small frogs! They covered the road, they hopped from the ditches, they made the wayside quite dark with their hopping bodies!.....

....A lady came past on a bicycle. She too was astonished and tried her best to ride without squashing the crowd of little frogs."It's frog-rain" she called to the children. "It's raining frogs° That's where they are coming from!"

The children looked at her in astonishment, forgetting the rainstorm. They looked up into the sky to spy frogs coming down but the rain was too hard for them to keep their heads up—and all the time more and more frogs filled the road till it really seemed that they must be falling with the rain...

....'Never believe stupid things without making sure first that they are right' said Tammylan', This idea of frog rain comes up every year-but if anyone really thought about such a thing they would know there couldn't possibly be such a thing".....

> Enid Blyton
> The Children of Cherry Tree
> Farm pp 107-9 (1940)
>
> Contributed by Petrovic the
> cynic.

CREATURE FALLS IN THE WEST COUNTRY

To date our own files on Fortean Zoological Phenomena are mainly concerned with events in Devon and Cornwall,but we have a few items on file which are relevant to the above articles:

Several large Pipefish were found dried and dessicated by the children of a friend of mine who astonished me by telling how they had found these remarkable corpses in their garden.The fish, though dead,had no apparent injuries and so the obvious explanation of them having been caught by seabirds and then dropped by mistake would not seem to apply. Anyway the odds against any seabird dropping three or four of the same (fairly uncommon) species of fish in exactly the same place would seem to be rather astronomical.(The house was about four miles from the sea).

Amongst the many examples of mysterious falls of animals from the sky collected by Charles Fort (1), there are several from the West Country: "Small snails of a land species had fallen near Redruth, Cornwall, July 8th 1886 'during a heavy thunderstorm'; roads and fields were strewn with them so that they were gathered up by the hatful; none seen to fall by the writer of this account: snails said to be 'quite different to any previously known in the district'.."

Another item from Fort's collection: (1) Originally from The Times 14.4.1837:

"That in the parish of Bramford Speke, Devonshire, a large number of black worms, about three quarters of an inch in length, had fallen in a snowstorm".

These are not isolated occurences. There are two records of what appear to be heavenly showers of hundreds of 'dirty black larvae' of an unknown species on the 26th November and again on Christmas Eve 1913.(2) It is certainly interesting, and may indeed be significant that these incidents always seem to happen in the wintertime. Indeed Similar records of larva falls have been recorded from The Valley Bend district of Randolph County, West Virginia on several occasions during the winter of 1898, and again In Switzerland in 1922 (3).

REFERENCES

1. Fort:The Book of the Damned (1919)
2. Transactions of the Devonshire Association Vol 39 p 79
3. Calkins et al: Mysteries of the Unexplained (1982)

FROGFALLS etc

EYEWITNESS REPORTS

Each issue we shall print reports of zoological phenomena and armed only with some wild guesses we shall attempt an explanation

◆◆ ◆◆ ◆◆ ◆◆

STRANGE SNAKES IN NORFOLK

A couple of years ago, farmer Heather Thurgar was riding with a friend in the village of Aslacton, Norfolk when a large snake slithered across the lane in front of the horses. It disappeared into the grass verge, then returned to the road and reared up aggressively, frightening the horses. The snake was about five feet long and did not look like either an adder or a normal Grass Snake.

Back in 1961, two Italian Grass Snakes were reported in Lowestoft, twenty miles from Aslacton. The Italian Grass Snake is vivid green in colour, grows larger than the British variety, and is more aggressive. Could they be breeding in Norfolk?

A much older report concerning unusual snakes in Norfolk is recorded by J Wentworth Day (2) in 'Ghosts and Witches' (Batsford 1954). He quotes the 'Norfolk Chronicle', September 28th 1782, as follows:

"On Monday the 14th Inst. a snake of enormous size was destroyed at Ludham in this county by Jasper Andrews of that place. It measured 5ft 8 inches long, was almost three foot in circumference and had a very long snout. What is remarkable there were two excrescences on the forepart of the head which very much resembled horns. The creature seldom made its appearance in the daytime but kept concealed in subterranean retreats, several of which have been discovered in the town"...

Wentworth Day also mentions a story of two snakes, each six feet long, which attacked a man at Dereham, and speculates that all these creatures were foreigners which had escaped from ships at Yarmouth.

JAN WILLIAMS

The Italian race of the Grass Snake (Natrix Natrix)

"Thousands, literally are offered for sale every spring in pet stores all over the country, and I have even seen them sold from market stalls. These are mainly imported from Italy, and may differ in minor ways from those that are native to Great Britain...."

> C.H.Keeling: 'Unusual Pets' (Foyle 1958)

Prior to the CITES legislation of 1983 large numbers of European Reptiles of a number of species were imported as pets and it is not particularly suprising, if the much larger Southern European race of N natrix which is bright green with yellow throat patches should have become established in Norfolk.

There are various species of snakes that boast two large horns but they are mostly from the tropics as well as being very poisonous. Wentworth Day's snakes are a real mystery and without any more information I wouldn't like to hazard any guesses.

◆◆ ◆◆ ◆◆ ◆◆

GIANT "RABBITS" IN DEVONSHIRE

Mike Davis saw what he thought was a giant rabbit in the woods near Starcross.

"I was chestnutting in the woods when I heard a twig snap. I thought that perhaps it was a gamekeeper warning me off his land. I saw a large rabbit or hare in the sit up and beg position. It must have been about three foot high. If I could have got close enough to it I reckon it would have come up to the top of my leg. I chased it a fair way into the wood and it went into the undergrowth. This is the only time I have ever seen it. I mentioned it to a guy who goes rabbiting there. He agreed that there were some big ones in the area."

Another anomalous giant rabbit, which this time provoked exactly the opposite diagnosis was reported from Westward Ho in January 1985.(4)

William Phillips discovered a great number of footprints in his garden in Beech Rd. He was convinced that they were made by a wallaby because they were long,deep and in pairs which indicated that they were made by an animal jumping with two feet together. These mysterious paw prints were examined by an animal welfare expert summonned by the local newspaper (and bear in mind that this usually means that the person in question was in charge of the cake stall at the RSPCA summer fete and wouldn't know a wallaby if it was placed in front of him on a silver platter with a sprig of Holly behind each ear),who identified the tracks as those of a large rabbit.

Heuvelmans categorised some of the 'Giant Rabbit' sightings in the unexplored centre of Australia as cryptic marsupials (1) so I shall follow his example and do likewise. There have been wallabies kept on a farm near Holcombe for many years. They have been known to escape. When Mike was at school in about 1981 one escaped but as far as I know was soon recaptured.

The Dawlish Wallabies are the property of Joyce Butler of Holcombe. (2) who has kept wallabies since the mid 1960s. In 1991 she had 41 of them and admits that during the 1970s they had a problem with falling trees due to Dutch Elm Disease. She says that some of her animals may have escaped then,one certainly escaped in May 1985 when it was tranquilised and returned to her from where it had been found in Teignmouth (4), and no doubt other animals have escaped from her collection over the years,although she is convinced that other people in the Dawlish area also keep Wallabies. Mike Davis' giant Rabbits seem to suggest that she is correct.

When I spoke to the Ministry of Agriculture, Fisheries and Food in Starcross in the early spring of 1992 they admitted that there had been a number of feral wallaby sightings from the area over the years,but insisted that they were all traceable to Mrs Butlers collection, and, that these accounts were all of isolated specimens that there was no reason to suppose that they had been breeding.

In July 1986 a lone wallaby was seen apparently waiting for a bus,at a bus stop in Teignmouth. (3). At around about the same time another wallaby was killed in a road traffic accident on Haldon Hill. In 1988 another unfortunate marsupial was killed by a car outside Torquay, and in 1991 The Exeter Museum received the corpse of an animal which had been killed by a car near Lydford on the Western edge of Dartmoor, a place notorious for being the haunt of far more less benign quasi fortean beasts than harmless and herbivorous wallabies.

REFERENCES

1. Heuvelmans: On the track of Unknown Animals (1956)
2. Exeter Weekly News 27.5.91
3. Teignmouth Post 24.7.86
40. Fortean Times 45

****

MURDER SHE WROTE?

Has anyone else any examples of Bird Euthanasia? I keep a mixed collection of birds and recently a male Chinese Painted Quail of mine was taken suddenly and severely ill. It was obviously terminal and so I left it in peace only to find that when I returned a few minutes later that his mate, (a shy and retiring little bird) had finished his suffering and pecked him to death. Whether this was 'Murder','Euthanasia' or even 'Cannibalism' I'm not sure but the female has shown no other signs of aggression either before or after this incident.

Rickard and Michell,in Living Wonders (1983) wrote about bird battles and even bird courts where a creature who had transgressed against the rules of the other members of its social group was apparently 'tried' by a group leader and then sentenced either to ostracism or in some cases to death, but the concept of Avian Mercy Killings is a new one to me. It is difficult however when one is dealing with ones own pets to know where Scientific reasoning ends and Anthropomorphism begins.

ALISON DOWNES

CRYPTO A-Z

PART ONE

Jan Williams deserves the Cryptozoological version of The Purple Heart for services above and beyond the call of duty for even considering undertaking this mammoth task: An annotated list of unknown beasts worldwide in alphabetical order...........

ABU SOTAN: Carnivorous beast marked with black blotches or stripes, living in mountains near the River Rahad, Sudan. There have been similar creatures reported in Ethiopia.

AGOGWE: Small Tanzanian man-beast with russet fur. It has been suggested that these animals represent a surviving relict population of Australopithecines.

AHOOL: Also known as The Athol, this is a large bat like creature with a twelve foot wingspan that has been reported from Java. This grey furred creature has a monkey like face, backwards pointing feet, and feeds on fish.

AMAROK: Enormous wolf known to Eskimos in Greenland. According to Dr Karl Shuker in 'Extraordinary Animals Worldwide' (Robert Hale 1991), a specimen was shot in the Nineteenth Century and the skin sent to Copenhagen Museum.

AMERANTHROPOIDES LOYSI (De Loys' Ape): Photographed by Francois de Loys during an expedition on the Columbia-Venezuela border in 1920. Ameranthropoides has been the subject of much controversy. De Loys described the animal shot on the banks of the Tarra River as tail-less, five foot and one and three quarters inches in hight, and with thirty two teeth (not thirty six), in which respect it differs from all known South American primates. Sceptics suggest that de Loys was either mistaken or deliberately fraudulent, and that the creature is actually a Spider Monkey. Support for de Loys comes from Indian sightings of similar animals in this region and in many other parts of South America.

ANACONDA (GIANT): Persistent rumous from Brazil speak of Anacondas reaching lengths of seventy foot plus - more than twice the accepted maximum length for this species.

ANDEAN WOLF: In 1927, animal trader Lorenz Hagenbeck bought the pelt of an unknown animal from an Argentinian collector who said that it came from The Andes. The long, thick fur varied from black to dark brown in colour, and the neck hair extended to form a mane. German zoologist Ingo Krumbiegel connected the skull with an unusual canid skull in his collection, also from The Andes and in 1953 named the creature Dasycyon hagenbacki (Hagenbeck's thick haired wolf). No further evidence has been found.

ANGEOA: Monster of Dubawnt Lake, Canada, with huge fin. Eskimo legend states that the bones of a great beast were once found on the shores of the lake.

ARASSAS: Creature with the body of a lizard and the head of a cat legendarily found in the French Alps.

ATLAS BEAR: Small sub-species of the Brown Bear, apparently extinct by the end of the 19th Century, but still occasionally reported from the Atlas Mountains of Morocco.

AYPA: Guyanan aquatic creature with head like a tiger, very large teeth and a body covered in scales.

THE NERVOUS TWITCHER

Twitchers are the train spotters of Ornithology. They travel hundreds of miles to see a rare bird that shouldn't have been there in the first place. Alison Downes, our very own Nervous Twitcher presents a regular column on all that is most peculiar amongst our Fortean Feathered Friends.

OUT OF PLACE AND OUT ON A LIMB

Many interesting bizarre stories have come to light recently in the Avian World. Twitchers have been excited by the visit of a rare **Black Throated Thrush (Turdus ruficollis)**, usually seen in India and Pakistan to the River Stour, near Bournemouth just after the New Year. (1) More recently, at the end of February a **Ross Gull** caused a stir by spending a period near the River Wear in Sunderland rather than in its native Kolyma Delta in Siberia, (2) but all of this is as nothing compared to the birth of a perfectly healthy 4 legged Emu in Texas, on a ranch belonging to Mike Hobbs. (3) (I wonder what Rod Hull would make of that?) From four legged birds to one legged birds - a reward has been offered to anyone knowing the whereabouts of property developer Malcolm Keller who dissappeared allegedly owing four million pounds, and took with him 'Hoppy' his one legged Toucan. (4)

SEABIRD DISASTER

More serious and disturbing news is the plight of the seabirds along the Northern coasts of Great Britain. Many birds normally die during the winter months but numbers have been far greater this year. An estimated 67,000 have died of starvation in the past few weeks. Experts looking into the situation cannot decide whether this has been caused by severe winter storms, making it difficult f.or the birds to fish or by overfishing or pollution by man. The debate continues. (5)

THE PARTRIDGE FAMILY'S GREATEST HITS

A Partridge presumed to be critically endangered if not extinct has reappearred. **David's Tree Partridge (Arborophila davidi)** aka **The Orange necked Hill Partridge** has not been seen in the wild since 1927, but two sightings have recently been reported from Vietnam. (6) To continue on the Partridge theme, a new species, not belonging to any existing genus has been discovered in the Udzungwa Mountains of Tanzania. The discovery was made by five scientists from the Zoological Museum of Copenhagen University lead by Dr Lars Dinesen. The new species named **Xenoperdix udzungwenis** lives in evergreen forests in an area rich in unusual birdlife. It appears to be plentiful and the scientists believe they may be descendants of a species which used to be common along the East African coast and into Asia. (7)

TURNING JAPANESE

Scientists in Japan are aiming to restore Japans Crested Ibis. They have a few problems because although there may possibly be a few left in the wild there's only one pair in captivity and they're too old to breed. When the birds depart for that great aviary in the sky, they plan to freeze them, and then try to recreate them by planting Ibis DNA in the egg of another bird. (Shades of Jurassic Park).

REFERENCES

1. Teletext on Three 8/1/94
2. Teletext on Four 28/2/94
3. BBC 2 Teletext (Newsround) 28/1/94
4. Cage and Aviary Birds 26/2/94
5. Today 1/3/94
6. Cage and Aviary Birds 22/1/94
7. Cage and Aviary Birds 26/2/94
8. BBC2 Teletext Newsround 2/2/94

Alberto Lopez Acha from Barcelona wrote to us asking for information about the relict population of The Javan Rhinoceros which was discovered in Vietnam in 1988. The Javan Rhinoceros is a well known, if exceedingly rare animal and we thought that this would be an easy question to answer. Not So. Our researches into the current status of the two species of Asian Forest Rhinoceros proved the aptness of Oscar Wilde's maxim that the truth is never pure and seldom simple'

In 1988 a female Javan Rhino (Rhinoceros sondaicus) was shot by a local tribesman in the jungles of Southern Vietnam about eighty miles northeast of Ho Chi Minh City (formerly Saigon). (1). This was doubly suprising because not only is R sondaicus one of the world's 12 most endangered species of mammal it had generally been supposed to have been confined to the Indonesian island of Java since the 1940's. Or had it?

Hans Hvass (1956) wrote that the animal was confined to Malaya and Java (2) , The Illustrated Encyclopaedia of Wildlife (3) said (1990) that the species was confined to Java with 'possibly a few hanging on in the remoter parts of Indo-China', Grzimek (1988) (4) wrote that the species was completely confined to one National Park in Java (and went on to say that 'reports of sightings in other locations are more than twenty years old and were considered unreliable even then') and the Illustrated Encyclopaedia of Animal Life (1952) merely stated that it had been 'exterminated over much of its previous range'.(5)

These conflicting status reports were too much for us so I did what any red blooded Cryptozoologist would have done under the circumstances. I telephoned Jan Williams who telephoned Karl Shuker who said, (much to my horror) that such discrepencies between major reference books were common and that the material in such books was often out of date and sometimes wildly inaccurate.

Karl went on to say that The Javan Rhinoceros had indeed been thought to have been confined to Java since the 1940's and that the discovery of an apparently healthy population in Vietnam was therefore incredibly good news for the survival of the species.

HELP !

The HELP Section of this magazine has two functions. Firstly we act as a fairly traditional magazine 'Questions and Answers' page but we also publish requests from you, the readers for help with your own researches.

If you can help with any of these queries, or if you have queries of your own, please write to :

HELP, Animals And Men
The Centre for
Fortean Zoology
15 Holne Court
Exwick,Exeter.

Something that everyone seems to have overlooked however is that the two populations of this, undoubtedly the rarest large land mammal in the world, may actually be different sub species. According to Khan (1939) (6) and Nowak (1991) (7) until about 150 years ago there were actually three different sub species widely distributed over South East Asia.

R s inermis: Eastern India, Bangladesh, Assam, Burma
R s annamiticus: Vietnam, Laos, Cambodia, Eastern Thailand
R s sondaicus: Tennaserim, Malay Peninsula, Sumatra, Western Java

Still earlier, perhaps until the Sixteenth Century, other populations lived in the Chinese provinces of Sichuan and Hunan (Rookmaaker 1980) (8). These Chinese subspecies were certainly wiped out four hundred years ago and it seems almost certain that the sub species inermis is also extinct. It seems likely, however that the newly discovered population in Vietnam are of the subspecies annamiticus whereas the Javan specimens are R.s sondaicus and therefore in the interests of genetic purity the suggestions that have been made about interbreeding specimens from the two populations in order to enrich the gene pool may not be such a good idea after all.

Karl Shuker (1) also wrote about a small population of the hairy Sumatran Rhinoceros (Dicerorhinus sumatrensis) that was discovered in a remote valley in Sarawak in 1986, and so whilst we are on the subject of the Asian Forest Rhinos I thought that it might be useful to include a short piece on the subject of the current status of this, possibly the most peculiar looking of the Rhinos.

There are three sub species: (7)

D.s lasiotus: Formerly found in India, Bangladesh and Burma, there may only
                    be six or seven specimens left in Burma.
D.s,harrisoni: Borneo. Only about 30-50 left. These include the survivors in
                    Sarawak discussed earlier, and various relict populations in
                    Sabah, which were noted by British Army personnel in the mid
                    sixties when they weren't meant to be there either. An
                    acquaintance of mine who was involved in these clandestine
                    military operations told me that although he had never seen one
                    several members of his unit had found droppings and footprints
                    which suggested that the species may, (at the time) have been
                    more widespread than was otherwise supposed.
D.s.sumatrensis: This is the most widespread of the subspecies with about 100
                    specimens still living in peninsular Malaya and 400-700 on
                    Sumatra itself.

The biology of both species is relatively little known both because of their rarity and because of their geographical inaccessibility. They co-existed over much of their former range because in areas where both species existed (4) the Javan Rhino lived on the wooded floodplains of large rivers whilst the Sumatran species lived in the more mountainous regions.

It is a good sign for the general progress of both species and of Cryptozoology as a science that such a large species can live undiscovered in an area not only just eighty miles from a major city but that was moreover scarified by defoliants such as Agent Orange in what was probably one of the most ecologically unsound wars in history.

One final snippet of interest that I discovered during my rhino researches. During the aforementioned military campaign in Borneo during the sixties one Britsh Army Unit reported that their camp had been systematically destroyed by a herd of elephants. 'Nonsense' said the wise men at GHQ in Singapore. 'Elephants don't exist in Borneo'. Apparently, however one feral herd, the descendants of a number of AFRICAN elephants presented to o ne of the Sultans of Brunei still roams the jungles, the only wild African Elephants in Asia.

REFERENCES

1. Dr Karl Shuker: The Lost Ark (1993)
2. Hans Hvass: Mammals of the World (1956)
3. Woodward and O'Leary (Ed): The Illustrated Encyclopaedia of Wildlife Vol 6
4. Grzimek: Mammals of the World Vol 4 (1988)
5. Drimmer (Ed): The Illustrated Encyclopaedia of Animal Life Vol 6 (1952)
6. Mohd Khan Bin Momin Khan: Asian Rhinos: an action plan for their conservation. (IUCN)
7. Ronald Nowak (Ed): Walkers Mammals of the World Volume 2 (1991)
8. L.C.Rookmaaker: The distribution of the rhinoceros in eastern India, Bangladesh, China and the Indo Chinese region (Zool Anz Jena 205:253-268)

HELP! WANTED

Animals and Men subscriber, **Richard Muirhead**, of Salisbury wants information on the following subjects:

1. Large Bats in The Forest of Dean.

2. Albino Foxes

3. Something that looked like a Duck Billed Platypus which was killed sometime in the 1700s in the Earl of Tylney's park, near Wanstead in Essex.

4. A wolf killed by a car in West Suffolk during the 1970s, (mentioned in The New Statesman Fortean Column 21.2.94)

Alberto Lopez Acha from **Barcelona** wants information on the Vu Quang Ox. Apart from the references in Karl Shuker's 'The Lost Ark' (1993), I have very little information. Apparently there was an article in a recent issue of 'BBC Wildlife'. Photocopies anybody?

The Editor of this august journal is always interested in information about the following subjects:

1. The wildlife of Hong Kong, especially its Herptofauna.

2. Sligo's Salamander, and any other out of place Megalobatrachius species.

3. Any reports about Mustelids.

4. Living specimens of any species of Amphiuma, Mudpuppy, Siren or Caecelian. Please scrutinise any pet shops you visit and give me a ring if anything turns up. I have an extremely large and lonely Two Toed Amphiuma looking for a mate.

Paul Garner writes:

'There is a well known photograph of a decaying carcass which was hauled up by Japanese fishermen near Christchurch, New Zealand in April 1977, which some speculated might have been a modern plesiosaur. I have read somewhere that analysis of fibres from the carcass revealed the prescence of Elastodin, a protein found only in sharks.

I would be interested to have any further information on this case. Can anyone shed any light on exactly when the initial discovery was made - some reports specify the 10th April, others say the 25th. Also, have the results of the fibre analysis ever been published, if so where. I hope somebody out there can enlighten me'

NEXT ISSUE: Green Lizards which aren't Green Lizards and Sand Lizards which may be. A Round up of queries and historical oddities.

Reviews Section

THE LOST ARK (New and Rediscovered Animals of the 20th Century) by Dr Karl Shuker (COLLINS). Price 14.99.

This is one of those few books where the words 'Exhaustive' and 'Definitive' can actually be used without the reviewer resorting to hyperbole.

I hate to think of the hours of painstaking research that must have gone into this book. It catalogues the Zoological discoveries of the 20th Century.....all of them.

Most books, especially Cryptozoological ones, are content to recycle the relevant chapter of 'On the Track of Unknown Animals' but this book is an exception. Such Zoological Obscurities as The Pygmy Otter Shrew and Bulmer's Fruit Bat rub shoulders with such well known creatures as The Golden Hamster and The Neon Tetra, and it is a tribute to this remarkable piece of scholarship that Shuker makes the stories behind the discovery of well known household pets as rivetting reading as the more arcane zoological titbits on offer.

He sticks his neck out by including such Cryptids as Homo pongoides and Ameranthropoides loysii amongst the creatures he describes, but he writes with such entertaining conviction that even hard boiled sceptics like me are won over. One cannot disagree with Gerald Durrell when he writes that "This fascinating and encouraging book should be part of every naturalist's library".

JONATHAN DOWNES

MY HIGHLAND KELLAS CATS by DI FRANCIS (Jonathan Cape) Price 14.99.

Many Cryptozoologists have been less than impressed with some of Di Francis's hypothoses in the past. Many people considered her first book, theorising that a hitherto undescribed species of indigenous British Big Cat roamed the highlands of Great Britain, to be ridiculous and although I believe that if Cryptozoology is not to become as hidebound as most of the rest of the natural sciences there must be room for apparently absurd theories, like most other Cryptozoological types I found the parts of her second book which put forward the possibility that the Genette Tate dissappearance could be laid at the door of a passing leopard both sensationalist and revolting.

Much to my suprise, however this new book, although it breaks little ground scientifically is rather a heartwarming little tale of a woman and a number of cats on their own against the forces of hidebound scientific intransigence in the shape of the British Museum (Natural History) in general and the Mammal Department in particular. The Centre for Fortean Zoology has had dealings with this department in the past and can therefore sympathise. As a book, however although it is not an essential addition to the Forteans library it is an interesting and pleasant read and with a few reservations it comes with the Petrovic seal of reccomendation. BILL PETROVIC

ISSN   1354-0637

Price One Pound and Fifty Pence

Issue II
July 1994

Issue II July 1994

With Issue Two the immense level of support that we received from the first issue began to pay dividends. We had never realised how much of an interest there was in Cryptozoology in the UK. For years, I had felt like a lone voice crying in the wilderness, and had believed that my life`s interest was something that no-one else really cared about. It was my father who pointed out, after having read issue one, that a magazine that had mostly been written by the editor or his wife was not that professional looking a publication. Luckily, we never had that problem again. With issue two we began to get articles submitted to us.

However, we were still drawing upon the legacy of SCAN and also from my abortive book project. The biggest news of the year was that doubt had finally been cast upon the Surgeon`s Photograph – possibly the most enduring piece of cryptozoological iconography. Then as now, I believed that the explanation that the whole thing had been faked with the aid of a toy submarine and some `plastic wood` should be taken *cum grano salis* and I pointed out that there was more than a little coincidence in the names of several of the alleged conspirators being the same, or very similar, to those in a long series of books by the renowned science fiction author Robert Heinlein. It was the beginning of the magazine`s long love affair with lexilinking and surrealchemical word games..........

Animals & Men
The Journal of The Centre for Fortean Zoology

Mystery Bears in Oxford and Morocco
Medieval Wildmen, Nessie, The Tatzelwurm,
Bantam Behaviour, Aberrant Lizards, News and reviews

sue Two   One Pound and fifty pence.

'Animals and Men' is published by STP Communications, an indipendantly funded media arts organisation which has been operating in the Exeter area since 1987. This issue was put together by the following Zoological malcontents.

Jonathan Downes: Editor
Jan Williams: Newsfile Editor, A-Z and Shoulder to Lean on.
Alison Downes: Cryptoornithology, Special Projects. and administration.
Graham Inglis: Video.
David Simons: Software Jockey
John Jacques: Sole Representation.
Jane Bradley: Cartoons
Lisa Peach: Front Cover.
Ian Wright: Pianist without Portfolio.

CONTRIBUTORS TO THIS ISSUE:

Ben Chapman, Stuart Leadbetter, Roger Hutchings, 'Paterfamilias'

REGIONAL REPRESENBTATIVES.

LANCASHIRE: Stuart Leadbetter
SUSSEX: Sally Parsons
SPAIN: Alberto Lopez Acha.

ADVERTISING RATES

Small ads are free to subscribers (up to thirty words per issue) and trade ads are by arrangement. We can also distribute leaflets for you at an extremely reasonable rates.

The Centre For Fortean Zoology,
15 Holne Court, Exwick
Exeter, Devonshire UK
EX4 2NA

Telephone 0392 424811

SUBSCRIPTIONS

'Animals and Men' appears quarterly in April, July October and January although we make no promises as to the exact date of publication.

A four issue subscription costs:

United Kingdom/Eire: £6.00
EEC: £7.00
Europe non EEC: £7.50
OZ, NZ, US., Canada: £9.00 (surface mail)
OZ, NZ, US., Canada: £12.00 (air mail)
Rest Of World: £10.00 (surface mail)
Rest of World: £12.00 (air mail)

Payment should be in UK Currency or by IMO, Eurocheque or cheque drawn on a UK bank. Republic of Ireland Postal orders are NOT acceptable. All cheques made payable to A&J Downes if you please.

CONTENTS

This magazine was printed by Catford Copy Centre from a Master provided by the publishers. It was typeset on an Amiga 500 and a Star LC24-200 printer using Pagesetter 2 DTP and Penpal Word Processing software.
Copyright STP/CFZ 1994

The Great Days of Zoology are not done!

Dear Friends,

The response to the first issue of 'Animals and Men' was overwhelming and we have doubled our initial subscriber base in only three months. I would like to thank everyone for their enthusiasm and help. I promised in the last issue that by this issue the magazine would be properly typeset. So it has been but the gremlins which lurk within my cryptozoological cyberspace have not entirely left us, and amongst other things my spellchecker programme has almost entirely ceased to function (leaving me with only the 'spellchecker' to whom I have been married for nearly ten years), and one whole section of the magazine was jeopardised when in attempting to transfer an Ascii file from a Word Processing programme to a DTP one I managed

to delete all the "Is", and "Ls" which is a little tricky when the article you are typesetting is about 'Plesiosaurs', but such minor technicalities apart this magazine is going from strength to strength and we sincerely hope that you will continue to support us. Our eventual aim is to be monthly, A4 and glossy but we have a long way to go before we can achieve this although we feel that this is a reasonably attainable objective.

We are still looking for regional representatives to join the intrepid band listed on the title page and we would love to hear fromanyone foolhardy enough to get involved.

Above allwe hope that you ENJOY this issue, we certainly had a good time putting it together for you.

Best Wishes,

EDITOR

NEWSFILE

Edited and Compiled by **Jan Williams** with the occasional interjection (and tedious jokes about catfishes) from The Editor and with no assistance whatsoever from The Lakelands Tourist Board!

MYSTERY CATS

Devonshire.

The Beast of Salcombe Regis- focus of the East Devon 'Cat Flap' in spring 1993 returned to the village in March. Neighbours Jane Stevens and Arthur Longbottom spotted the Puma like black cat in the steeply sloping field behind their homes. Jane took a photograph of the animal but it was too far away for identification. The cat bounded up the field and into woodland, taking only six leaps to cover a distance of seventy feet.*(Sidmouth Herald 19.3.94)*

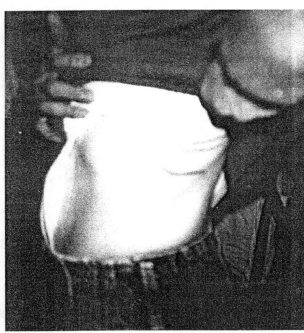

"Sally Dyke displays her wounds" Pic Copyright Craig Harris

Midlands. Sally Dyke (left) stated on "3D" (ITV 21/4/94) that she was attacked by a huge black cat in a lonely churchyard at IInkberrow, Worcs. Sally and her husband baited a path with dead chickens in December 1993. Returning to check the bait Nick Dyke stumbled onto the cat which was feeding in long grass. They say the animal lashed out at Sally, ripping through her waxed jacket and scarring her chest. They did not report the incident at the time - Sally, a veterinary lecturer, cleaned the wound herself and took antibiotics to prevent infection.

STOP PRESS; We have just received reports that film of a mystery 'puma' in Norfolk was recently shown on Anglia TV. We have no further details. If anyone has a video can they let us know?

Essex.

A large panther-like creature was reported to police at Walton-on-the-Naze in May. Witness David Shearing said the animal was "all black, very sleek, and much longer than a cat. It had a very long tail". *(Wolverhampton Express & Star 17/5/94)*

Isle of Wight.

Casts of large pawprints taken in a garden at St John's Wood Road, Ryde, were sent by naturalist Martin Trippett to Dr Karl Shuker for identification. The prints measured 4" by 4.5" and showed no claws. Karl identified the prints as canine rather than feline, and Ryde police were able to confirm that a Great Dane had been reported missing in the area on the previous day. Which confirms yet again that presence or absence of claws on prints cannot be used as a definite indicator of their origin. *(Isle of Wight County Press 6/5/94, 13/5/94; Wolverhampton Express & Star 6/5/94)*

Norfolk.

Farmer and broadcaster Chris Skinner of Caistor St. Edmun saw a cat-like animal in early May. Chris was driving home at 2.35am when he caught the animal broadside on in car headlights. Seconds before the sighting he had had to swerve to avoid a black labrador running down the road, and the 'cat' was the same length, but slimmer in build, with a small head and thick, downswept tail which curved up at the end. The colour was a uniform dark sand, with a darker tip to the tail. From photos of a dozen cat species, Chris identified the animal as a puma.

The sighting followed the appearance of a trail of unusual prints on Chris' farm during heavy snow in February. The prints were about two and a half inches across, with pronounced claws and with tail drag apparent between prints. The dead-straight trail showed the animal had made bounds of between 6 and 11 feet and leapt to the top of an 8 foot wall.

Scotland

Twelve year old Robert Clark reported a black panther in woodland near Craithie Church, Grampian, close to the royal estate of Balmoral, in early April. He described the animal as 3 to 4 times the size of a domestic cat, with pointed ears, a long tail, and dark brown patches on the sides of its face. Robert says the large cat walked towards him, snarling and hissing. When it was about 7 feet away, Robert turned and ran. The tabloid press with their typical obsession with sensational and tactless 'royal stories' inferred that this cat was responsible for the dissapearance of Prince Charles' dog Pooh. *(News of the World 24/4/94)*

Fox Attacks Child in Nottinghamshire.

A fox's savage attack on a sleeping child has mystified wildlife experts in Nottingham. The fox entered the house in Dale Road and bit and scratched four year old Renee Prater, asleep in her bedroom upstairs. Renee's mother has Donna heard screams and rushed upstairs to find the fox sitting quietly on the bloodstained bed. She rushed outside with the terrified child and took her to a medical centre.

When they returned three hours later, the fox was still sitting on the doorstep. Urban foxes are common in the city but are normally wary of people. An attack of this kind is unheard of although a selection of similar stories 'FROM OUR FILES' can be found on the inside back page. *(Daily Mail 24.5.94)*

REDISCOVERY OF PARDEL LYNX COLONY.

One of our Spanish Correspondents Alberto Lopez Acha has written with news of the rediscovery of two populations of the Iberian or Pardel Lynx *(Lynx pardina)* between 1980 and 1982. One in Zamora, only 249 km from Madrid and another one in Valencia, 352 km from Barcelona. *(Quercus No 3.)*

GIANT MUNTJAC IN VU QUANG

Close on the heels (or should that be trotters?) of The Vu Quang Ox, another new large mammal species has been discovered in the Vu Quang Nature Reserve, Northern Vietnam. Rumours of an unknown species of deer in the reserve were confirmed when Dr John Mackinnon and Shanthini Dawson of the joint Vietnamese - WWF survey team examined skull trophies in a native village. Genetic analysis showed the skulls belonged to a new species of deer.

Scientists are calling the deer the 'Giant Muntjac'. Some of its features are unique to muntjacs; large canine teeth, two bony ridges forming a sharp 'v' on top of the face, and 2 glands; but it has much longer brow tines, and longer antlers which are bowed rather than recurved. It also lacks the crest of hair found on the brow of muntjac species, and with an estimated height of 80 cm, and weight up to 50kg, the Giant Muntjac is 50% larger than others. Villagers hunt the animal for meat and up to 20 individuals were trapped in the 6 months prior to January 1994, suggesting that the species is relatively common. Unconfirmed reports suggest the species may also exist in Laos. *(BBC Wildlife 12/6/94)*

BIGFOOT ON THE BOX.

Discerning readers will, no doubt watch the excellent U.S Sci Fi series *'Quantum Leap'* in which the only Samuel Beckett not to be a tedious Hibernian playright has most excellent adventures often with a Fortean theme. The episode screened on BBC 2 on May 24th 1994 featured a rather convincing Bigfoot. The Roger Patterson film of Bigfoot is also featured in the TV advert for 'TAB Clear' a particularly nasty soft drink which in the opinion of the editor tastes a little like a mixture of Tizer and washing up liquid.

COAL EATING TRANSPARENT SHRIMPS

Time is running out for scientists trying to study a colony of crustacians which have been found deep inside the flooded tunnels of Monkweir Mouth Colliery. They are reported to live

off coal dust and the occasional fragment of Miners sandwich. Although experts believe that they are a whole new subspecies (sic) the mine was due to close in May and so the chance to study these surreal creatures will be lost forever. *(BBC Newsround Teletext 17.5.94)*

IT WASN'T ME GUV DEPARTMENT.

Recently there have been a number of hoaxes of interest to crypto pundits (if only to prove that some people; and even some crypto type sill believe anything!) Panic swept through Yaounde, the capital of The Cameroons when a radio station warned of a lion loose in the city. People locked doors and windows and a truckload of police were sent out. It turned out, however to be an April Fool day hoax by the radio station. *(BBC Newsround Teletext 1.4.94)*

Another April fool day hoax and one which (much to the suprise of everyone at CFZ Towers) even had quite a few people believing in it was perpetrated by 'Today' who claimed that a flying rabbit had recently been disacovered by persons unknown. Several people wondered if it could be a phenomenon allied to the well known mutation which causes 'winged' cats but the accompanying photograph showed what looked like a cute looking bunny crossed with a stuffed seagull. (Today 1.4.94. There was even less documentary evidence for 'Tizzie Wizzie" the legendary flying hedgehog of the lake district which unfortunately turned out to be a figment of the imagination of some bright spark in the publicity office of the local tourist board.

COOL FOR CATS.

Munir Viriani of the Sokoke Scops Owl Project believes that African Golden Cats *(Felis aurata,* exist in the Arabuko-Sokoke Forest on the Kenyan coast. On several occasions he has seen cats which correspond to the Golden Cat in size and appearance. Twice the animals were accompanied by cubs. *(East African Natural History Society)*

IGUANA IN NORFOLK.

Rollerskaters nearly ran over a young Green Iguana on a Norwich industrial estate. The eighteen inch lizard (now named 'Lucky') was taken to 'Rons Reptiles' in the city, where the owner, Ron Wells placed him in his colony of Iguanas. Noone seems to know where he came from...except for Lucky and he's not saying. *(BBC Newsround Teletext 1.4.94)*

ARACHNOPHOBIA

The latest 'sport' in pubs at Sparkhill, Birmingham, is Spider Fighting. Bets are placed on fights to the death between poisonous 6" Golden Baboon Spiders and the larger Bird Eating Spiders. RSPCA officials and police are investigating reports. As a lifelong arachnophobe, I'd rather not think about the possible consequences of this one!

ON THE TRACK OF THE FATHER OF CRYPTOZOOLOGY.

Bernard Heuvelmans, the man without whom, quite literally there would be no science of Cryptozoology wrote to us very recently saying nice things about 'Animals and Men' and exclusively revealing that the ten volumes which comprise his complete Cryptozoological writings are being published IN ENGLISH over the next few years, starting with 'On the Track of Unknown Animals' in September this year (complete with 'a new preface resuming half a century of Cryptozoology') and with the others ('even those not yet published in French') following at a rate of 'two or three a year'.

ALMOST TOO GOOD TO BE TRUE?

I think that we are the first UK publication to print a potentially astounding newsstory revealed for the first time in this country by Karl Shuker at The Fortean Times Convention on 19th June. Roy Mackal, the legendary Cryptozoologist has just returned from Papua New Guinea with what is apparently good quality film footage of a serpentiform marine creature that he has conditionally identified as a surviving Zeuglodon. The film was shot during January this year (the rainy season) at Lake Niu Gini, by a Japanese TV film. The creatures which are known to the native population as 'MIGAU' (suprisingly similar to 'MIGOU' the Sherpa name for The Yeti) live off water birds because the volcanic lake has no fish population. It is this idiosyncratic diet which forces them to feed on the surface of the water and has hence made them ideal targets for cameramen. The films have been shown on Japanese and U.S Television but as yet have not been seen by anyone in Britain. We await further developments with baited breath!

LAST BUT BY NO MEANS LEAST....

Readers of Karl Shuker's excellent book 'The Lost Ark' will have been as excited as we all were by the photographs of extraordinary humped elephants from Nepal. Colonel John Blashford-Snell, who took the photographs of what everyone is hoping may be surviving Stegodonts, is going back to Nepal in February 1995 in search of these marvellous beasts and wants volunteers (who can cover their own costs) to

accompany him. Interested? You should be! Write to The Scientific Exploration Society, Expedition Base, Motcombe, Near Shaftsbury, Dorset. SP7 9PB for details (and tell him we sent you). Afficianados of the writings of the man whom Fortean Times compared favourably with Indiana Jones are referred to the next issue of this magazine which amongst other things will contain a piece by Colonel Blashford Snell about his search for giant Monitor Lizards in New Guinea.

Newsfile Correspondents.

Bernard Heuvelmans, Colonel John Blashford-Snell, Alberto Lopex Acha, Angel Morant Fores, Ben Chapman, Craig Harris, Stephen Shipp, Dr Karl P.N.Shuker.

The Woodwose or Wild Man in Britain

by Ben Chapman

During the course of this century, a great interest in tracing a 'missing link' in the chain of evolution of Homo sapiens has proved popular with archeologists, scientists, folklorists and cryptozoologists alike. Reported sightings of remnant hominids are sure to feature in the headlines of the worlds press, be it in China, South East Asia or the North and South American continents.

Europse and particularly Britain has long enjoyed associations with 'wild men' or as he is more often referred to in England, The Woodwose. The term Moodwose, Wedewasa, Wodwos or Wodewese can be traced back in Britain to the early twelfth century. In medeival art he is usually depicted as a big, strong individual covered in hair, animal skins or leaves and brandishes a huge, rustic club or tree branch. He is often represented in combat with some other creature, a lion, a wyvern or a fellow woodwose.

Sub Species or Forest Dweller?

To place the origins of the British Woodwose in perspective, we must first consider the socio-economic conditions prevailing during the end of the Dark Ages and early medieval Britain, i.e population, the natural environment, harsh laws, and the bucolic nature of many occupations and crafts. In these current enlightened times of plastic, concrete and a great abundance of other man made materials, we trend to forget the importance of wood which was the mainstay of the early medieval economy, culture and very way of life.

Housing, vehicles, kitchen utensils, handles and hafts for weapons and tools, fuel, enclosures for livestock and furniture, all relied on wood of which then Britain had in abundance. With timber playing such a predominant role in the lives of the people, many occupations and ancilliary services were wood intensified. Carvers, builders, sawyers, wheelwrights, charcoal burners, bowyers, furniture makers, boat builders, tool and impliment builders, and suppliers of fire wood for cooking and heating the home to name but a few, not only worked with wood but in many cases lived in the woods and the dense forests which provided them with their livelihood. During this period Britain was stillrelatively densely forested before the great forests were denuded of their timber by a rapacious ship building campaign of the Tudor Monarchs.

Such solitary individuals clad in old working clothes augmented with animal skins, who did not venture far from their sylvan environments, could be regarded as *'odd'* or *'wild'* by their contemporaries who dwelt on farms or in villages or towns. As well as those who lived and worked with wood in these forests, were others, social outcasts, the disenfranchised peasantry, and those with severe medical afflictions who were spurned by their neighbours. Add to these the people fleeing from unjust taxation, crimes committed for survival such as poaching or stealing food, such crimes invoked severe retribution including mutilation and death. Another major factor for causing people to seek out solitude away from their fellows was the arrival in Britain in 1348 of The Bubonic Plague or Black Death. Forests proved the ideal place in which to lose oneself and to escape this terrible pestilence. Naturally these latter forest dwellers, like their predecessors, would be wary of strangers and hide themselves.

Over the years their clothing would be replaced by more simple garb like animal skins or coarsely woven grass. Their progeny would know no other lifestyle and would develop fully acclimatised to this basic way of living. Hygene and washing, never a social grace in medieval times would be totally lacking and these hirsute forest dwellers would appear and stink like true animals or 'wild people' which in all respects they actually were!

Conversely they are not a *'missing link'* or different sub species of *Homo sapiens*, simply a group of individuals who, through choice or conditions beyond their control have adopted a way of life unique to that of their fellow men.

Even today we read in newspapers of the plight of some hermit or local eccentric living in a simple hut or a similar structure in a wood or quarry fighting off the beaurocrats in defence of his chosen lifestyle, simply because they consider him out of kilter with society, and they know best!

The medieval woodwose or forest dweller who lived in a 'wood house' or forest, would naturally defend his territory and way of life. It is highly probable that there were 'no go areas' in many forests, which were assiduously avoided by the local populace hence the origins of many popular folk tales concerning the evil deeds of wild men and giants. These areas could prove fatal for the unwary traveller, dissappearances adding credence to the stories surrounding these almost legendary beings. Fee Fie Fo Fum etc!

Homo silvestris.

Though the wodwose references to wild men and women in Britain are comparitively 'modern' in the context of the historic time scale, many early references to wild men abound in ancient literature.

The celebrated Roman writer Pliny (23-79) mentions *Sylvestris Homines* as inhabiting what are now known as The Himmalayas who 'wander about indiscriminately like wild beasts'. This like many other early references such as the dog faced Cynocephali are probably apes or baboons.

A reference which compounds the theory of wild men as being workers or other human denizens of the forest can be found in *Ars Poetica* by the Roman lyric poet Horace (65-8 BC) who uses the words *Sylvestres Homines* in its classical sense to refer to foresters or uncivilised men.

In the British Museum there is a lamp of the first century AD depicting a hairy man holding along knobbed staff. References to the many curious beings in The travels of Sir John Mandeville published in 1449 are all gleaned from classical sources. It is now thought that Sir John Mandeville is a fictitious character.

The popular medieval image of the woodwose as a coarse, hairy individual weilding a knotted branch for a club can be traced back to a French Bestiary of 1300.

Many examples of the woodwose clad in skins or leaves have found their way into Christian iconography, and are to be found in abundance in many churches and cathedrals in both Europe and Britain especially on misericords. Fine examples can be seen at St Mary's Beverley, Chester Cathedral, Whalley Abbey, Ripon Minster, Holy Trinity, Coventry (in combat with a lion), Lincoln Minster, Exeter Cathedral, St Mary Faversham, Manchester Cathedral (two mounted woodwoses in combat), Beverley Minster (fighting a dragon), and Westminster Abbey.

Typical of the medieval romances is the story of Valentine and Orson They were two brothers who were seperated at birth. Valentine was raised at court with all the priveliges of a gentleman and a knight, Orson was brought up by bears in a forest and developed into a formidable wildman. The King, troubled by stories of a giant killing and terrorising his subjects sent Valentine to seek out and slay this giant. When he at last confronted the giant Valentine was disarmed and about to be killed when a wildman appeared and dispatched the giant with a mighty club. The wildman was indeed Orson and the brothers were reunited. Valentine took Orson back to court with him, where his brother became his champion and protector.

The Woodwose in Heraldry.

The science of heraldry boasts many a woodwose or wildman as a supporter to a coat of arms, he is also quite a common charge and is often encountered as a crest.

The heraldic woodwose is usually blazoned as being wreathed about the temples and loin with leaves, mainly oak leaves and carries an eradicated tree or wooden club, or occasionally another weapon such as a sword or axe.

He is to be found supporting the arms of the Duke of Fife, and the families of Douglas, Menzies, and Carr. The arms of Poulett are unique in having; *dexter a savage man and sinister a savage woman*. The crest of the family Walton has a standing woodwose holding in his right hand a trefoil and over his left shoulder an eradicated tree. A savages head is borne on the arms of the families Eddington and Gladstone.

'A carving from St Mary's, Beverley, Yorkshire'
Copyright **Chapman Misericord Library.**

THE CHAPMAN MISERICORD LIBRARY
Ben Chapman has a large archive of misericord photographs of
mermaids, wildmen and many other medieval creatures. Anyone
interested in this particular subject contact him at 10
Young Street, Withernsea, Esat Yorkshire HU19 2DX

Near Lizard...but not near Enough!

by Stuart Leadbetter

During the summer of 1993 and the hype surrounding the coming to Britain of the film *Jurassic Park* the Loch Ness Monster was twice seen and photographed. With all the talk of dinosaurs in the press it was only natural that journalists would group Nessie together with the extinct giants in the resulting news reports.

A favourite candidate for the identity of The Loch Ness Monster is the Plesiosaurus, a creature which was a contemporary of the dinosaurs. The story writers have compared this reptile with the stars of Steven Speilberg's film and have found similarities. To them dinosaurs and Nessie are one and the same. This assumption is very wrong and highly misleading to the general public.

Plesiosaurs were more closely related to lizards and crocodiles than dinosaurs and it is for this very reason that the identity of the Loch Ness Monster must lie in a different direction. Presented below are the arguments to support my lack of belief in the living fossil hypothesis which is still popular at Loch Ness.

The Question of Respiration.

At Loch Ness the chances of witnessing a surfacing of one of the monsters are very low. Only a lucky few have such an honour. This tends to suggest that the monsters cannot be dependent on breathing surface air. Evidence from the use of Sonar seems to bear this out.

In his book *The Monsters of Loch Ness*, Professor Roy Mackal compared the diving profiles of a Weddell Seal (*Leptonychotes weddelli*) and a Sonar contact obtained from the Loch.

The profile of the air breathing seal is very characteristic. It makes a deep dive from the surface and returns to it all in the space of 10 minutes whereas the contact is first detected at the depth of 200 feet but only for two and a half minutes, whereupon it dives so deeply that it is lost from the sonar coverage only to be picked up again five minutes later, again at the depth of 200 feet the whole episode having lasted the same amount of time as the seals.

Professor Mackal considers this behaviour to be totally foreign to any of the Loch's known fish species, and I agree wholeheartedly. The creature that was responsible for the contact could not have possessed a closed swim bladder because such rapid changes in depth are impossible with such a device.

The creature must have an ability to extract oxygen from the surrounding water presumably either through the skin or by the use of gills. This would seem to rule out a Plesiosaur as the creature responsible for the contact. Plesiosaurs were definitely air breathers and like all sea creatures of this ilk they would be dependant on air - the main weakness of such animals.

The Behaviour of Plesiosaurs.

Whilst holidaying in Norwich during the summer of 1989 I visited the local museum to view the various events on show. To my great surprise, I discovered a painting which depicted two Plesiosaurs fighting, some fossil bones from a Plesiosaurs paddle and a few small paragraphs which commented on the uncanny resemblance between the Plesiosaur and the sightings from Loch Ness, but it was the painting that drew my attention rather than the other two exhibits. If this painting was a faithful rendition of typical Plesiosaur behaviour (and I have no reason to believe that it isn't), and if the Loch Ness creatures are indeed Plesiosaurs then why has noone reported such distinctive activity at Loch Ness?

One of the following two statements are usually given:

(1) They are shy and wary of man and his ways.
(2) Being Plesiosaurs, they have two nostrils set high on the head, so that when they require more air they only have to expose ths part of their body in order to do so.

Such explanations have some validity, but we are talking about real live Plesiosaurs here. You would expect such creatures to indulge in the same activities that other animals do constantly, hunting for food, patroling for territory, and especially mating (for the main purpose of an animals existance is the succesful passing on of its genes to the next generation) This urge to procreate is so strong that it is still performed even when outside influences begin to interfere.

Would 'real' Plesiosaurs perform their courtships underwater (like in Sir Peter Scott's painting 'Courtship at Loch Ness'), or would they perform them on the surface of the lake or even on dry land?

I cannot see that it would be possible for any male Plesiosaur in Loch Ness to succesfully woo a female underwater. The low level of visibility underwater has been stated in every book or magazine article ever written about the Loch and its monster. How could a male show off before its intended partner if it could not see further than ten feet in the gloomy water? Visibility in the Mesozoic oceans where the ancestral plesiosaurs lived was probably so much better. A predatory hunter like the Plesiosaur would not be able to afford a colourful skin with which to attract a mate under such conditions because this would only make them highly conspicuous to their prey.

It would appear therefore that the only possible answer is that the creatures must have conducted their courtship rituals at the surface. They could then have retained their normal colour scheme used in hunting, but when was the last report that you heard from Scotland

of two large humped monsters carrying out a courtship routine on the surface of the Loch oblivious to whoever was watching? When seen at the surface the creatures are usually alone in the rare event of there being more than one creature visible there is seldom any friction between them to indicate any kind of mating behaviour.

Lack of Land Sightings

In the early days of the Loch Ness saga there were many instances of the monsters being seen ashore, but from then until the present day the number of lands sightings has dwindled away to nothing. If the creatures who had been responsible for the earlier reports had indeed been Plesiosaurs such a reluctance to come ashore would be very puzzling, and would perhaps even be a trend that could lead to their long overdue extinction.

Paelentologists commonly believe that Plesiosaurs were egg laying creatures. When the time was due for laying they would swim to some isolated island or estuary, clamber ashore, excavate a pit into which would be placed the precious eggs, and then return to the sea. Some of the people who support the case for living Plesiosaurs in Loch Ness argue that some Plesiosaurs might have given birth to living young, neatly explaining why nobody has seen a Plesiosaur weighing several tons digging up the Loch's rocky shoreline.

Of the two methods of reproduction, the case for Plesiosaurs being Egg Layers is the stronger for several reasons.

The sea has always been a place of great danger for younganmals. The seas of the Mesozoic were no exception. In them lived such mighty hunters as the Ichthyosaurs, the ancestors of todays sharks and several other branches of the Plesiosaur family. It would not appear to be advantageous to Plesiosaurs to introduce living young to such an uncertain world. It doesn't take much imagination to realise that such defenceless creatures wouldn't last very long. A far better optoin would be to retain their young in eggs and to deposit them in relative safety on land well away from marine predators. This may well eliminate one source of predation but it now presents another. The way to counter this secondary threat is illustrated by present day Crocodiles and Turtles. They either construct a nest (in the case of crocodiles), or excavate a hole which is filled in after the eggs have been laid (in the case of turtles). It would seem likely that Plesiosaurs did something of the kind.

Now another question arises. Did Plesiosaurs simply abandon their eggs after laying them like turtles, or did they stand guard over them like crocodiles? I thnk it likely that they could have made use of either strategy depending on the type of land where the eggs were laid. If the eggs were laid on a small island, for example, the possibility of indigenous predators would be low . Under these circumstances the eggs would be abandoned. If, however the creature had chosen to lay its eggs on the shores of a large continent they would require protection as such a land mass would be teeming with predators!

Applied to Loch Ness, this would mean that at certain times of the year Plesiosaurs should be easily visible either laying their eggs on the shore or patrolling a section of the Loch on a regular basis. Clearly this isn't the case!

The Neck of the Plesiosaur.

In restorations of Plesiosaur skeletons the most striking feature is the long, graceful neck. During the history of the phenomena of Loch Ness sightings of such long necks have been made on numerous occasions. There appears to be a correlation here. No other Marine or Freshwater animal known to science as being alive today has a neck of comparable length so the case for living Plesiosaurs in Loch Ness would appear to be extremely strong on this point..Or is it?

Ever since the first Plesiosaur skeletons were discovered Paelentologists have argued about how flexible the necks of these creatures must have been, and what their purpose was. Certainly they were efficient enough to catch fish with, but was this their only use? I think not. All the other parts of the Plesiosaur had more than one use so why not the neck as well? It has been theorised that the neck was of such a length because the Plesiosaur developed it as a kind of periscope to scan above the waves at the surface for prey, but there could be yet another use for such a long neck, and one which would also be directly tailored to the pursuit of prey.

Again referring to Professor Mackal's book *The Monsters of Loch Ness*, we come across a reference to the stomach contents of a fossil Plesiosaur. Not only containing the normal prey items of a fish and a cephalopod it also contained the remains of a Pterodactyl inferring that it must have been snatched out of the air by the scavenging Plesiosaur.

This then is the additional advantage of a long neck for what was a primarily sea based creature- the ability to catch airborne prey, but here again we see the paradox of the Loch Ness evidence. In all the thousands of sightings, not one describes Nessie plucking a bird from the air in mid flight.

Conclusion.

So what is the true identity of the mysterious denizens of The Loch? I don't know . We have some information on various parts of their anatomy, but no idea of what a complete monster looks like. Some results give us the impression that they don't require air to breathe, but for reasons unknown they are still occasionally seen at the surface, but of one thing I'm sure. Loch Ness doesn't harbour any near lizards (the literal English Translation of Plesiosaur), but that somewhere in the depths lurk creatures whose body form can easily be mistaken for one.

It Ain't Nessiecerally so..

If we know anything at all about the way that monster hunters minds work then we expect a hail of controversy to result from the above article. We are not taking sides but will present all sides of the discussion until the matter is finally resolved. We would, however like to receive feedback about this article from the pro-plesiosaur lobby of Loch Ness Investigators and indeed anyone else with views on the subject. At the recent Fortean Times conference we met veteran Nesswatcher Rip Hepple, the editor of Nessletter. We suggest that anyone interested in the Loch Ness phenomenon contact him at 7 Huntshield Ford, St John's Chapel, Bishop Auckland, Co Durham, DL13 1RQ

If you go down to the woods today.....

the Bear facts from Jan Williams.

The ancient forest of Wychwood, straddling the border of Oxfordshire and Gloucestershire, was once a favoured hunting ground of kings. In the nineteenth century it was a wild and lawless place, the haunt of highwaymen, Black Dogs, and the dreaded Snow Foresters - strange spirits whose howls and screams could be heard echoing through winter nights, and which were known to attack snowbound travellers.

Remnants of this ancient woodland still exist along the valley of the Evenlode. Despite its proximity to the busy modern city of Oxford and the tourist traps of the Cotswolds, Wychwood remains a secret forest, a refuge for fox, badger and deer, and a memory of Old England.

Residents of Charlbury, within the forest bounds, have taken a lighthearted view of reports of a bear roaming the woods. The village baker sold *"Buns to feed the Bear"*, the butcher displayed *"Bear Steaks"* in his window, and local publicans played host to bear-suited regulars.

Charlbury's previous claim to cryptozoological fame lay with 'Skippy', an escapee wallaby which bounded around the village for a few months in 1985. Wallabies are becoming commonplace in England, but the wolf which killed 14 sheep in 1935 was more of a rarity. An escapee from Oxford Zoo at Kidlington, it was tracked down by a photographer from the Oxford Mail. Face to face with the wolf, he decided that discretion was the better part of valour and shot it with gun rather than camera.

Whilst many villagers are sceptical regarding the bear, Mr Waring, landlord of 'The Bull' at Charlbury, is keeping an open-mind. He has tracked bears in Canada, and believes a bear could easily survive in the area. *"It is the right sort of terrain, and there is plenty of food in the woods."* And he has found large and unusual prints in the woods, though sadly these were too distorted for a definite identification.

The main witness is John Blackwell, who runs a mixed farm at Dean and keeps a variety of livestock. In September 1992, Mr Blackwell saw an unusual animal near his 21-acre wood. Remembering 'Skippy', his first thought was of a wallaby *"with its tail chopped off"*, but closer sightings on the following two nights convinced him that it was a bear.

The animal was the size of an Old English Sheepdog, with small pointed ears, *"massive great hocks"*, and no tail. Its thick fur was a dark rusty-brown, with lighter sandy-brown patches on belly and flanks. The ears were held down, and it walked on all fours with a pronounced *"waddling"* motion.

The 'bear' was not seen again for several months, but there were indications that something strange was living in the woods. Huge prints were found on the land, the farm dogs barked continually in the area of a thickly overgrown bank, and two fish ponds on the farm were visited by some large animal which left a trail of smashed and flattened rushes. On one occasion cows on the farm were so badly frightened that they refused to eat for five days.

In late May 1993, Mr Blackwell heard a strange hooting noise from the wood. He walked towards the sound, thinking at first that it was a cockerel crowing, but as he got nearer it changed to a continuous howl. Two fallow deer were grazing on the woodland edge. As they moved off, the bear-like animal came out of the trees, following them at a run. It left huge prints, which Mrs Blackwell measured against her size 9 wellingtons. The prints were larger and showed long claws. On the following day the animal appeared again. It was lying in long grass and put its head up as the farmer approached. Mr Blackwell estimated that it was a third larger than in the previous September. The farmer says none of his livestock have been attacked and the animal seems curious rather than aggresive towards people. He felt it should be left alone, and only came forward when other reports appeared in the press.

In January of this year, bus driver Greg Gilbert and passenger Sarah Cooper saw a reddish-brown animal walk across the Charlbury road. In contrast to Mr Blackwell's sightings, the creature walked upright, on its hind legs. Another witness, James Graham-Cloete of Chadlington, stated he had seen it standing by the roadside. A spokesman for the nearby Cotswold Wildlife Park was dismissive. He suggested witnesses were seeing a badger. But John Blackwell is a traditional farmer with an interest in wildlife, who sits up at night and watches badgers. A bear in Oxfordshire may seem unlikely, but is it any more likely that a man who has been watching badgers for twenty years should suddenly mistake one for an exotic animal?

Press reports of unusual animals often encourage other witnesses to come forward, and it seems the 'bear' is not the only strange creature roaming Wychwood. Earlier this year, Mrs Nicky Sherbrook, of Taston near Dean, was surprised to find one of her sheep killed and half-eaten. She said it had been "ripped to shreds". Shortly afterwards, Mrs Sherbrook's 17-year-old son, Harry, was walking with a friend in a field bordering onto woodland when they disturbed a fox-sized animal. It was a light silvery colour, with a black stripe down the spine, a flat cat-like head, and a big bushy tail. It ran very quickly down the field and into the woods, passing a third boy who dashed up to ask the others what it was. All three teenagers are used to foxes, and were quite certain it was not one.

It looks as though Oxfordshire's 'secret forest' is harbouring cryptic creatures - or was that a Snow Forester howling in the woods?

*   *   *   *

Additional Refs:

Oxford Mail 27/1/94, 28/1/94, 3/2/94
Daily Mail 23/2/94, 25/2/94

Is this *"Animal"* Behaviour?

by 'Paterfamilias'

When the children were young we kept bantams, *'Bunter'* a cockerel had a number of assorted *'wives'* over whom he fussed, behaving more like an elderly father with a family of young girls than a devoted and hard working *'husband'*.

I didn't take too much notice of the bantams - they were, in fact a bit of a nuisance because they scratched about in the garden where they shouldn't have scratched and generally made a nuisance of themselves, but one morning when the boys were at school, I happened to be passing by the shed in which the bantams roosted and in which there were some old, full-sized nest boxes, when I became aware of a strange hissing noise. Having lived and worked for some years in the West African *'bush'*, my first thought was of snakes, but thankfully snakes that make that sort of noise are rare in the west of England, and I tiptoed to the door of the shed and peered in. There I saw a remarkable sight.

'Bunter' with his wings outstretched, was gently driving one of his *'wives'* into one of the nest boxes. She didn't want to go, not one little bit, she didn't but *'Bunter'* was very firm, and he pushed and nudged her, all the time, making a curious, un-birdlike noise. Eventually, she entered and he stood outside, as it were, on guard, until she settled down on her nest. The following morning she had laid an egg - her first and I couldn't help wondering how *'Bunter'* knew that she was about to deliver.

After this episode I took a greater interest in the activities of the bantam family. *'Bunter'* was clearly very much in charge and he took his duties very seriously and I enjoyed watching him scratching in the vegetable garden, uncovering worms, not for himself but for his *'wives'* who stood back and let him do all the work.

Then one evening I witnessed a scene which I shall never forget. I normally went around the garden towards dusk, shutting up the greenhouse and turning the lock on the shed door, but on this particular evening, I cannot remember why, I was late and it was almost dark. As I approached the shed, again I heard another strange noise, not a bit like the hissing which had accompanied the nest box incident. This time it was more like a cat's purr, only louder. I switched on my hand lantern and there, on the perch, was *'Bunter'*, with both his wings outstretched and four of his *'wives'* cuddling up close to him, two on each side, literally under his wings   as he *'sang'* his song to them and they settled down for the night.

I have always disliked anthropomorphism and people who treat their pets as if they were humans make me feel slightly bilious, but there was no doubt that *'Bunter'* the little bantam cockerel, was exhibiting what we somewhat arrogantly call *'human'* characteristics- and then I wondered. Did *'Bunter'* say to his wives:

"My dears, isn't it extraordinary how some humans behave just like Bantams?"

Alpine Enigma

by Roger Hutchings

My earliest encounter with the subject known as cryptozoology took place sixty years ago in Paris. In 1934 I was an expatriate teenager washing dishes in the resteraunt kitchen at *Le Dome* in the *Boulevard Montparnasse*. During the afternoon b reak between lunch and dinner service I often used to visit the nearby Natural History Museum, outside which a vociferous old gentleman was wont to parade bearing a sandwich board proclaiming that THERE ARE BIPED LIZARDS IN THE ALPS!

In conversation with him I learnt that despite a mass of witnessed evidence presented to the authorities over many years his claim had been persistently dismissed, and his demonstration was in protest at the official denial of the facts as known to him. His name was **Maurice Masse**, born and bred in the Alps of Provence where he asserted that biped lizards were commonplace, as they were throughout the Alpine region spreading through Switzerland and southern Bavaria and into Austria.

He corrected my initial presumption that the creatures moved upright on hind legs by explaining that they possessed only forelegs, despite which they moved swiftly when observed, to vanish from sight into rocky retreats in the mountain heights where they dwelt. He also told me that where he came from, in the sparsely inhabited countryside of Upper Provence, they were taken for granted and that all his neighbours could affirm their reality, as accepted by his and their forebears for generations past. He added that other forelegged species found in Central America, at a comparable latitude, were scientifically accepted, and in his opinion they confirmed yet another significant link with the lost continent of Atlantis.

My abiding curiosity about unrecognised creatures learnt nothing further about these Alpine lizards until reading Bernard Heuvelmans' *"On the Track of Unknown Animals"* (originally published in French in 1955 and in English in 1958). This described a *"stumpy lizard at least two to three feet long"* living in The Alps and frequently encountered but never captured to be classified scientifically. Recorded observers agreed that it was more or less cylindrical in shape with a wide mouth and large, round eyes. Those who had seen it at close quarters asserted that it had short forelegs but no hind legs at all. Heuvelmans devoted over four pages to the subject with reports and drawings from nineteenth century sources and a photograph said to have been taken in Switzerland in 1934.

In the German speaking Alps the creature is called various names including, notably *Bergstutzen*, *Stollenwurm* and *Tatzelwurm*. In the French Alps of Provence where I resided between 1964 and 1968, it was known to my neighbours as *'Le Gros'* (the big one), although some older folk said that their parents or grandparents used the patois name *"Arasas"*. Everyone loudly claimed to have seen it at least once, and those whose activities took them to the more solitary areas- shepherds, herb and truffle gatherers-referred to it with casual familiarity. They said that the creature could often be observed basking in sunlight close to holes or clefts in the rocks, into which it would vanish with lightning speed if disturbed. Those who had viewed it briefly at close quarters described it in terms which closely echoed those quoted by Heuvelmans. I should add that none of my witnesses' reports were the outcome of leading questions, and that certainly none of them were aware of the existence of Heuvelmans' book.

Readers who collect examples of Fortean "coincidence" may be interested to learn that amongst the Provencal witnesses was a lavender grower who found a "flying saucer" parked on his land in 1965. Two little beings with pointed chins, slit mouths and eyes that curved round the sides of their heads emerged and imobilised him by pointing a pencil-shaped instrument at him before retreating into their vehicle and ascending into the sky. His name was Maurice Masse, and in common with his namesake outside the Museum in Paris his story was dismissed by the scientific authorities. Of particular significance is the fact that before this experience he was entirely unaware of the worldwide UFO and extraterrestial phenomena. (For further details: Flying Saucer Review 14:7).

A   Hard Day's Night Parrot
by Alison Downes.

A month long expedition to Cooper's Creek in   N.E   Australia in December '93 was, unfortunately unsuccesful in locating the elusive Night Parrot *(Geopsittacus occidentalis)* . The ,main reason for this failure is believed to be the heavy rains over the last two years in that region giving many more waterholes for birds to drink at, and therefore vastly expanding the range available to them. Many people believe this bird will once again be found as a living species. Reliable but unconfirmed sightings have been turning up at regular intervals during the 20th Century, including the sighting of four specimens at Coopers Creek in 1979 and at a Dam near Alice Springs (date unknown). Remains of birds have also been found after having been killed and eaten by feral cats and nomadic aborigines. A more exciting discovery was made in 1990 when Walter Bowles, an Australian Ornithologist, found a recently killed Night Parrot which had been hit by a car, near Mr Isa in Queensland. This was no doubt unfortunate for the bird but at least it proved that the species was still in existance.

The Night Parrot is a short dumpy bird, very shy in its habits, and mostly ground dwelling. To make matters even harder in tracing it is that although some sources have described it as 'flightless' it has been reported that it can actually fly for extensive distances especially at night. It is also known to spend most of the day in rocky caves or in self made tunnells in the tussocks of grasses. At dusk it comes out to feed on grasses and seeds. For people wishing to see what it looks like may I refer them to the excellent Zoological Museum at Tring , where they have a mounted specimen of an adult male which lived for a very short time in captivity at London Zoological Gardens in 1867.

REFERENCES.

1. Cage and Aviary Birds: October 1993.
2. Cage and Aviary Birds: June 18th 1994.
3. SHUKER   Dr Karl P.N: The Lost Ark (1993)
4. RUTGERS   AND   NORRIS   (Ed):   Encyclopaedia of Aviculture Vol 12. (1972)

Green Lizards in Devon and Dorset?

Herptological anomalies from **Jonathan Downes.**

An 1877 resume of the Reptiles of Devonshire includes the European Green Lizard *(Lacerta viridis)* a species not recognised as a member of the British Herptofauna (except in The Channel Islands), although it is a common species in fossil and sub fossil deposits. It is generally thought to hgave died out during the last Ice Age and notr to be hardy enough to withstand the rigours of a British Winter. The 1877 record is particularly interesting, (and I quote it in full)   (1)

""I include this species on the authority of two Gentlemen, namely J.E.C.Walkeley Esq, Ide and W.R.Crabbe Esq of East Wonford. Mr Walkley informs me that he has known this animal to have been taken in the county; and the latter gentleman saw two specimens near the memorial erected to the memory of the late Mr Fish at Sidmouth in June 1869. Whether thesespecimens had escaped from confinement I have no means of knowing but the warm, dry locality in which they were seen on the edge of the cliff may secure them from molestation. A specimen was also seen at Bickleigh Vale.

Mr John Wolley in Zoologist p 2707 wrote 'seven or eight years ago a school fellow of mine at Eton, a natiive of Guernsea assured me that he had seen lizards in Devonshire precisely similar to those of his own land".
It is hard to dismniss all of these records as either a misidentified specimen of one of the native species or an escapee.

Over the county border in Dorset reports of this species are even more widespread. The correspondence in the Proceedings of the Dorset Natural History and Antiquarian Field Club over the three years 1928-30 is not only interesting but it provides valuable insights into the importance of hearsay and local oral traditions (which are after all the basis for all folklore) and the study and indeed the mythologisation process, of all unknown animals. The definitive reference is from 1928 (2):

"Two letters from Mr R.B.Charlton raised an interesting question as to the ocurrence of the large Green Lizard (lacerta viridis) in Dorset. He tells me that he has received many from the country where though not native they are well established and fairly numerous. The species has a length of about fifteen inches whereas the two native species are about seven and five and a half inches respectively...I have never seen these large lizards from Dorset except on one occasion when on lifting a very large stone at Ringstead in about 1908, in search of Beetles, a very large greenish lizard was beneath. The lizard is said to have occured near Wareham..."

The same article notes that a famous 18th Century naturalist recorded Green Lizards of an unknown species, but which he presumed were *L Viridis* from Surrey, but I have been unable to confirm this.

The following year four further records were noted (3):

"Mr W.R.G.Bond reported having seen one probably about 1902, crossing the road not far from Kingbarrow near the Holme Toll Bar on the Wareham - Tyneham Road. Mr L.G.Pike writes to Mr Bond that he knows nothing of the large species as occuring although the two smaller kinds frequent his garden and. he has heard it said that there are larger ones on the heath. Taken in conjunction with Daniel's report in the early sixties of 'three or four' specimens half a mile south of Wareham and the Ringstead specimen Mr Bond's record may be significant."

In 1930 (4) the debunking process was begun with the whole episode being dismissed as sightings of aberrant Sand Lizards (*Lacerta agilis*) of the green form. The difference in size between the seven inch Sand Lizards and the fifteen inch Green Lizards being completely ignored as is the local oral tradition recounted in both the previous reports. This local tradition is probably the most valuable piece of evidence in the whole affair, because as I have found colouration morphs of the European *Lacertidae* vary widely and can make positive identification difficult. For example; at the end of the 1970s I obtained a freshly killed lizard which turned out to be almost certainly a very unusually marked Common Lizard. In the best traditions of Fortean discovery, however the corpse disappeared under extremely unusual circumstances before I was able to make a firm identification...my parents cat ate it!

It is the geographical area in which all of these sightings, both in Dorset and in Devon have occurred which makes the accidental occurrence of *L viridis* within a relatively small area, seem noi at all unlikely. The animals could well have originated from specimens which came into the country from France and disembarked surreptitiously at Weymouth which has historically had a widespread cross channell traffic. The species is widespread on The Channel Islands as well and it would seem even more likely that lizards from Jersey and Guernsey could have been accidentally imported in cargos of vegetables as traffic from these islands, being part of the United Kingdom are not subjectedto such stringent administrative controls as those from mainland Europe.

REFERENCES

1. Transactions of the Devonshire Association Vol 9 pp 241
2. Proceedings of the Dorset Natural History and Antiquarian Field Club 1928 pp 74
3. Proceedings of the Dorset Natural History and Antiquarian Field Club 1929 pp 123
4. Proceedings of the Dorset Natural History and Antiquarian Field Club 1930 pp 113

NESS THAN ZERO
by Petrovic

With all the controversy over the alleged debunking of the 'Surgeons Photo' by people who claim that even if the photo IS a fake, a monster could not have been fabricated out of plastic wood and a tin submarine- at least not in the early 1930s, one e of the sillier but ultimately oddly disturbing coincidences of the case has been ignored. Two of the main protagonists, Weatherall and Spurling have the names of characters in 'Time Enough for Love' and other novels by Robert Heinlein. Lets face it, the whole scam feels like something Lazarus Long wouldhave thought up! Maybe 'World as Myth' isn't such a stupid idea after all?

NERVOUS TWITCH

Our regular peek through Fortean Binoculars at the areas of Ornithology where even seasoned Twitchers sometimes fear to tread!

I'll name that fowl in...

A small yellow, orange and green bird discovered in the Choco area of Columbia hit the media recently, when an offer to allow someone to name the species for the sum of £75,000 or was made. The bird was discovered in 1991 by an expedition from Anglia University lead by Paul Saloman. He has made the offer in order to raise money to preserve the rain forest where the bird lives. All cheques should be made payable to 'Birdlife International'. *(Birdkeeper June 1994 ; Wolverhampton Expreess and Star 23.4.94)*

Wild Goose Chases.

A man called William Lishman has been trying to train his sixteen geese. He set up an experiment to see whether captive bred birds could be taught to migrate. He managed to lead them to Virginia using an aeroplane last autumn, but they have since disappeared. If they don't turn up soon he has said that he will go out and look for them. *(BBC Newsround Teletext 6.4.94)* Another odd avian experiment has proved that the Ostrich (a highly exciteable bird at the best of times) is calmed down by music..especially that of Andrew Lloyd Webber? I hope they don't play them the theme from 'Cats'! *(BBC1 Countryfile 27.4.94)*

Its in the papers..its got to be true!

Many wild birds including Magpies, Rooks and various finches have albino mutations,. An interesting Victorian display of these can be found in Taunton County Museum, which also contains some deliberate fakes. Some aviculturalists specialise in breeding mutations of British Birds and funnily enough a photograph of one such captive bred, and close ringed albino Blackbird was used by The Daily Mail to illustrate their feature article on mutations, as *'spotted in the wild'*. Journalists eh? (Cage and Aviary Birds 11.6.94)

Row over British List Revisions

Twitchers have been shaken up recently by a controversial decision from the British Ornithology Records Committee to omit several species from the UK List. They claim that The Asian Brown Flycatcher, The Mugimaki Flycatcher and Pallas' Rose Finch (which have only been seen once in the British Isles) are escapees from captivity whilst the Twitching Fraternity is adamant that they are true vagrants. The BOU has also deleted three American Sub Species of bird from the British list because it now seems certain that the recorder, legendary naturalist Richard Meinertzhargen was lying when he claimed to have shot them in The Hebrides. Meinertzhargens Warbler from Morocco has also been disproved and much of the fine work that Meinertzhagen did has now been tainted. Thanks to David Bromwich at the Taunton Local History Library for the clippings. *(Daily Mail 30.5.94 ; The Times 7.5.94 ; Daily Mail 6.5.94)*

DUCK!!!

A Muscovy Duck has apparently been terrorising the Bedfordshire village of Toddington attacking villagers and even ripping off the trousers of one elderly man. Local residents are trying to get it sent to a bird sanctuary but not suprisingly noone wants to catch it! *(BBC Teletext Newsround 23.6.94)* More avian aggression was reported from Michigan, USA when a flock of turkeys caused traffic chaos and the State Troopers had to be called in. The turkeys became veryt agitated and started *"Clucking and gobbling in an intimidating manner"*. The troopers had to use pepper spray to disperse them. *(ITV Teletext news 17.4.94)*

WHAT CAN YOU SAY ABOUT CURLEWS?

A pair of Eskimo Curlews *(Numenius borealis)* thought to have been practically extinct since the 19th Century have been sighted at the traditional wintering area in Argentina. Two eggs were discovered last year in Canada, and there were four reliable reports of the species in 1987. The birds, once commn were killed in large numbers by hunters as they migrated, *(BBC Newsround Teletext 3.5.94 ; Channel 4 Teletext Green News 3.5.94 ; Illustrated Encyclopaedia of Birds)*

THE FABULOUS FURRY FREAK FOWL.

A racing pigeon fancier was in court recently accused of growing Cannabis . He claimed that he grew the hemp seed purely for his pigeons, and said that they had won more races since he had been giving them tea made from the leaves. I would have thought that birds raised on such a diet would be more likely to coo incoherently for a while, eat ridiculous amounts of corn and then go to sleep in the corner of their loft! *(Cage and Aviary Birds 28.5.94)*

...IN A PEAR TREE

Gamekeeper Granger Jordan was fined £250 for breach of the 1981 Wildlife and Countryside Act when he released 92 Chukar Partridges on an estate in Norfolk. There is a very real danger that the native British species may disappear as a result of hybridisation with this European species. *(C4 Teletext Green News 22.4.94)*

POLLY WANTS A CRACKER ALREADY

Many pet birds can 'talk' but few can dance! One bird who can is Ronnie a parrot given to the son of an Israeli Military Advisor by Idi Amin in 1961. The son spent many hours teaching the bird to dance to Jewish tunes, but when he died in the 1973 Middle East War the bird was passed on to Bird Sanctuary owner Mr Eytan Porat. Seven months ago, however the bird was stolen, Mr Parrot (whoops Porat!) visited Tel Aviv Bird Market regularly looking for Ronnie. Eventually he spotted the bird and called the Police. They weren't too impressed by his claim until Ronnie danced and kissed Mr Porat proving his identity, *(Cage and Aviary Birds 16.4.94)*

The A-Z of Cryptozoology

Part two of Jan Williams' exhaustive trek through the Cryptozoological alphabet

BADIGUI: Large amphibious dinosaur-like creature, reported from lakes and rivers of the Central African Republic. Said to keep its body submerged and stretch the long neck to browse upon lakeside vegetation. The neck is smooth-skinned, lighter ventrally than dorsally and terminates in a flat head.

BAGENZA; Large ape, or ape-man, reported from Zaire.

BAI-XIONG; White bear of Shennongjia Province, China, which may be albinistic morph, or sub-species of the Brown Bear (Ursus arctos), or possibly a separate species. Several are held in Chinese zoos.

BAKANGA; Mystery cat of Central African Republic, with red-brown coat bearing leopard-like spots. Said to bark like a dog.

BAN-MANUSH; Yeti-like ape-man of Bangladesh.

BARMOUTH MONSTER; Creature seen on Llanaber Beach, North Wales, in 1975. Described as "like a dinosaur", ten feet in length, with a long tail and neck and huge green eyes. The feet were like huge saucers, each with three claws.

BATUTUT; Small Bornean ape-man resembling the Orang pendek of Sumatra.

BEAST OF LE GEVAUDAN; Carnivore which terrorised Languedoc, France, from 1764 to 1767. Held responsible for deaths of up to 100 people. Initial reports concerned a donkey-sized beast, with a long tail, reddish hair and a piglike snout, but wolves and werewolves were implicated over the years. In June 1767 a strange creature eas shot and was dissected by a court surgeon. It was 5 feet, 7.5 inches long, 32 inches high, and had 40 teeth. No clear description exists, and the beast was never identified.

BRENTFORD GRIFFIN; Winged dog-like creature reportedly seen flying over Brentford, West London, in 1984 and 1985.

BIGFOOT: Giant ape-man of North America. Reports date back to the early 19th century, with sightings in most mainland states and concentrations in the Pacific North-West and Florida. Bigfoot ranges from 6 to 11 feet in height, with very broad shoulders and chest, an ape-like head, and legs, feet and hands resembling those of a human. It is covered in hair, generally reddish-brown, occasionally black, white, beige or silver. Characteristics include a revolting smell, eyes which glow ed, yellow or green, and unearthly screams. Material evidence consists of footprints measuring from 12 to 22 inches in length and having 2 - 6 toes (most commonly 5). Film taken by Roger patterson and Bob Gimlin in 1967 remains controversial. Some Bigfoot reports are associated with UFO sightings and paranormal phenomena.

HELP

(The Coleopterous visual pun is dropped this issue due to lack of space)

Each issue we try to answer readers' questions on any subject of Fortean Zoological interest. Alberto Lopez Acha from Spain asked for information about the Atlas Bear that we mentioned briefly in the last issue. Many thanks to Dr Karl Shuker for help in my research for this article (shucks, he <u>was</u> the research for this article)

THE ONLY BEAR IN AFRICA?

The Brown Bear *(Ursos arctos)* is an ancient and widely distributed species that once ranged across much of the Northern Hemisphere. Like The Wolf or The Tiger, it is one of the most easily recognised animal archetypes in human culture, and like the aforementioned species, its status is' becoming so precarious in certain parts of its range, that certain subspecies and regional races of U arctos are of more interest to the Cryptozoologist than to his more conventional cousin who has already consigned them to extinction.

The High Atlas mountains of Morocco are areas of great Cryptozoological interest. If The Barbary Lion *(Panthera leo leo)* still exists in the wild it will be here, there are a few surviving Barbary Leopards *(P.pardus panthera)* there are persistant reports of 'ape men' (although they usually turn out to be the children of mentally deficient Tuareg tribesmen) and until fairly recently it was the last stronghold of the only species of bear to live in Africa in historic times. (The semi mythical 'Nandi Bear' of East Africa is most probably nothing of the sort. Two of the most popular suggested identities for this classic cryptid are a surviving Chalicothere or a giant Hyena).

Although the *'Libyan Bear'* was well known to the ancients (100 were taken to Rome in 61 BC by Domitius Ahenobarbus) the animal was only described after the type specimen was obtained by a Mr Crowther in 1841. Even then it was an extremely rare animal, a remnant from the days when North Africa was a land of forests, and it is generally thought that the animal died out within about fifty years of its recognition by science.

It was described as being slightly smaller but a little more robust than the North American Black Bear, with a short broad face, and short claws and with shaggy brownish black or black hair, although the under parts are an orangy-rufous colour. It was originally described as *Ursus crowtheri* or *Crowthers Bear* but long after it was deemed to have been wiped out Scientists revised their taxonomic ideas and demoted it to subspecific status under the name *Ursos arctos crowtherii.*

As far as mainstream zoology goes, there the matter rests, but up to the present day there have been rumours and vague reports of sightings. Heuvelmans noted in *'On the Track of Unknown Animals'* that the species may still survive in Spanish Morocco, and there have been various tangental folkloric references from such diverse sources as 'The Master Musicians of Joujhouka' and farmers of Marijuana plantations in the most remote parts of the mountains which suggest that, once again mainstream science has been over enthusiastic in consigning this creature to extinction. JD.

 **MYSTERY LIZARDS IN KENT**

Suzanne Stebbings from Kent writes with a herptological query. *"I keep the European Green Lizards Lacerta Viridis and Lacerta Tulineata. One large female laid some eggs in late summer and I sent them to Chris Davis of the British Herptological Society. Two of the eggs hatched, and Chris was amazed that the young lizards were not Lacerta viridis, but resembled the Canary Island Gallotia stellina. There was no mistake with the eggs, and the lizards did not hybridise with my Gallotia stellina as they are kept seperately. Gallotia tend to be aggressive towards green lizards, and are unlikely to hybridize anyway.*

Two months after hatching the lizards remain unidentified. They were suffering with rickets when hatched, but have made good progress on vitamin and mineral supplements.

Can anyone suggest an explanation?"

POLECAT PROJECT IN SCOTLAND

Dr Andrew Kitchener from the National Museums of Scotland writes after reading the article on Martens in issue one:

"At the National Museums of Scotland and in collaboration with Dr Johnny Birks of the Vincent Wildlife Trust we are currently investigating the specific identity of polecat like animals in the West Midlands. In particular we are trying to establish whether these are polecats originating in Wales, which are recolonising their former range since persecution levels have dropped and rabbit numbers have recovered, or feral polecat ferrets, or even introgressive hybrids between ferrets and recolonising polecats. This involves the study of pelage, skeletal characters and DNA.

We have also been investigating various unofficial reintroductions of captive bred polecats into various parts of Britain. At first we thought that this was confined to Cumbria and parts of Scotland, but new information indicates that these may have occurred elsewhere in southern England. Therefore it is more likely that records of polecats in England outside the West Midlands refer to unofficial introductions rather than the survival of relict populations.

Your readers could assist our project considerably by sending us carcasses of dead polecat - like (and even Marten - like) animals with uncrushed skulls that they find. We would be happy to refund postage but would point out that this research is fairly long term, because of the low rate of acquisition of specimens. Large sample sizes are required for statistically significant results. Anybody who can assist our project should freeze any carcasses they find and call me on 031-225-7534 before sending them on."

We would ask anyone finding Marten carcasses in the South of England or any Mustelid carcasses in the West Country to contact us first. We will pass all material on to Dr Kitchener but we would like to examine the carcasses first.

HELP

Mr D Walker from Enfield is interested in the 'big bird' phenomena so prevalent during the mid to late 1970s but he wonders if there have been any more recent sightings? Thanks to Mr Walker and to everyone else who has sent press cuttings. Please keep on sending them in. We are trying to build a definitive archive which will soon be available to subscribers through The Internet. We are also collecting specimens for a planned museum of Fortean Zoology but we need your help. Donations of money, time, specimens or equipment are always gratefully recieved. The Centre for Fortean Zoology is still a very young organisation and we need representatives across the country. If you feel brave enough to help and want to know what it entails please write or phone. We also want information on the following:

* Fortean Zoological Pub Signs. We know of , The Lambton Worm, several dragons, a wyvern or two, and three Black Dogs but we need a Yeti's Arms to complete our collection.

* Comics with a Zoo-Fortean theme. We know about *Alpha Flight* featuring Sasquatch and the R> Crumb *Bigfoot* series but there must be more.

* We will pay for Living specimens of any of the larger aquatic salamanders or any species of soft shelled turtle. Books, articles and press cuttings on the natural history of Hong Kong.

* lists of preserved Martens in British Museums and information on the Sutherland Polecat.

* Our Lancashire representative is collecting data on strange fish in UK waters.

* We want all sorts of specimens including a preserved 4 legged chicken and a halved gynandromorph butterfly.If you have anything that you think may interest us please get in touch.

PLACES TO GO AND PEOPLE TO SEE

During our travels around the country over the Summer we have visited a number of places of interest to the enquiring Fortean and should you be in the area at any time we strongly urge you to go and visit them.

TORQUAY AQUARIUM. As well as a well presented and interesting collection of fish and marine life, there is a fascinating display of press cuttings and photographs on a range of marine mysteries including Sea Serpents and Giant Squid. There is also an extremely large Leathery Turtle (dead) which was washed up on a West Country beach several years ago.

PLYMOUTH AQUARIUM This features a display of sightings of Cetacea and stranded Turtles as well as a preserved two headed dogfish.

PARADISE PARK, HAYLE, CORNWALL. One of the best bird gardens we have visited it includes a colony of a recently rediscovered species of macaw as well as several other species extinct, (or nearly so) in the wild.

POTTER'S MUSEUM OF CURIOSITY, BOLVENTOR, CORNWALL. This is possibly the most amazing treasure trove of forteana that I have ever been priveliged to examine. Founded in the last century this collection of wonderful things is an object lesson to us all of what a museum should be and in these dull and tedious days at the end of the millenium so seldom is. There will be an article on the museum in a future issue and we are preparing a book on this priceless and irreplaceable collection!

BOOKS.

Keltic Animal Lore and Shamanism by Kaledon Naddair (Keltia Publications)

This budget priced (£2.99 each) two volume work is an eclectic and fascinating work of scholarship from the pen of a man who deserves a far wider public profile than that which he actually achieves. Cross referencing from subjects as diverse as Ogham script, Celtic mysticism, Herbalism and even conventional zoology he paints a picture of a complex and beautiful world which is now almost lost to us. I was initially a little phased by the inclusion of some of his poetry along side descriptions of ancient Celtic animals and men, but he is a good poet and his poetry complements his prose in what is a demanding but ultimately fulfilling journey through the animal lore of ancient Scotland. I cannot reccomend this book too highly. Contact Keltia Publications at PO Box 307, Edinburgh, Scotland EH9 1XA

The Book of The Toad by Robert Degraaf (Lutterworth Press)

A beautifully produced collection of folklore, history, poetry and prose which explores man's attitude towards the toad, a gentle and beautiful creature who like so many others has been treated so cruelly across history. This is a fascinating sourcebook for all herpeto-fortean investigators but if I have a criticism, it is that it is too glossy and like a McDonalds Hamburger it promises more than it delivers and leaves the consumer ultimately unfulfilled.

MAGAZINES.

We welcome an exchange of publications with other magazines within our sphere of interest (and as anyone who has ever seen The Editorial bookshelf will vouch, that is pretty wide).

HOAX, 64 Beechgrove, Aberhonduu, Powys, Cymru, UK, LD3 9ET This magazine is wonderful. It gives an anarchic and funny insight into both the hoaxes of its title and the genesis of much contemporary folklore and the issue we were given recently even includes an article on Cryptozoological hoaxes.

NEXUS, PO Box 177, Kempton IL, 60946-0177 USA A beautifully produced round up of alternative science, and forteana. It borders on new age philosophy but does so without getting twee and annoying like so many of its peers. A good, sturdy magazine.

THE SKEPTIC, PO Box 475, Manchester M60 2TH. I like this magazine but then I would. Any magazine which good naturedly debunks the soggier end of forteana and playfully ridicules new age thinking is OK by me!

ANIMALS, FREEPOST, SIDUP, KENT. This is the official magazine of the British Zoos supporters Club and it arrived quite unsolicited on my doormat the other morning. The most recent issue includes a fascinating article on Asiatic and Barbary Lions and Przewalski's Horse. Probably the best magazine of its kind that I have seen.

TOUCHSTONE, Surrey Earth Mysteries Group, 25 Albert Rd, Addlestone, Surrey. An excellent little magazine covering Earth Mysteries, UFOs etc. Well worth a look.

TEMS NEWS, 115 Hollybush Lane, Hampton, Middlesex. A wonderful collection of forteana from veteran UFO investigator Lionel Beer. It is as good as you might expect it to be.

FROM OUR FILES..

In the news pages of this issue is an account of a horrific attack on a baby by an Urban Fox, We have searched through our files for a number of other nasty pieces of foxlore.

There are a number of accounts of quasi vampiric attacks on domestic animals from all over the world but in Devon there was a spate of such attacks on sheep during the winter of 1951/2 when a large number of animals were found on Ugborough Beacon with twin punctures to the neck and a large amount of blood missing. For reasons that can only be described as the flimsiest pieces of circumstantial evidence these killings were blamed on foxes. *(trans Devonshire Assoc Vol 88 p251)*. Another interesting story comes from Devon folklorist Theo Brown who wrote in *Tales of A Dartmoor Village* about a man who disappeared on Dartmoor one winter and whose bones and skull were eventually found by a foxes hole on the side of Longaford Tor. Ever since then ghostly foxes are reputed to bark and show themselves on The Tor in the week before Christmas.

As is his wont Petrovic has contributed this excerpt from a tome called *Confessions of a Pop Performer* (published in 1975)

. *"Mr Muckredge shakes his head. 'I can't do that. We've already got the old age pensioner who was bitten by a fox'. Mr M leans forward challengingly. 'At the top of a block of high rise flats! She heard something at the door, opened it, and the fox ran in and bit her!'*

'It must have been a dog', I say. 'You wouldn't get a fox up there. I mean it wasn't being chased by a pack of hounds was it?'

Mr M's face clouds over for a second. 'I didn't check that. No, I don't think it could have been. Otherwise people would have seen them. Especially if they'd had the horses and the pink jackets. People notice things like that on The Clem Attlee estate.'"

The final word must come from the entirely mythical Lazarus Long who noted *"when the fox bites...SMILE"*.

.......AND IN THE END

The biggest problem that any of us have in producing this magazine is that there is simply TOO much information and too much happenning for us to cover it all. As we were going to press we recieved reports of a giant worm in Eastbourne, a Sea Serpent in The South China Sea and the capture of the first living specimen of The Vu Quang Ox. , as well as a host of big cat reports and a number of out of place birds. The next issue of Animals and Men will be pubvlished in October but having found that the actual contents of Issue Two bore no resemblance to what we 'said' would be in it, so we make no claims whatsoever for what will be in it, but we promise you that it will be a corker!

ISSN 1354-06

Issue III
October 1994

Issue III October 1994

Issue three – that difficult third issue – was actually nothing of the kind. It was the first issue entirely put together from submissions. The cover, which featured a picture of an anomalous giant worm found in a pleasure gardens in Eastbourne caused quite a lot of queries, because the printers inadvertently left the caption off. Hapless readers were therefore presented with a picture of a geezer with a dodgy haircut and an even dodgier grin leering at what appeared to be a piece of giant pasta. This was probably the precursor to some of the more enigmatic bits and bobs which have appeared in the magazine intermittently ever since.

We were indebted with this issue to Colonel John Blashford-Snell for permission to reprint an excerpt from his rare and out of print book *Mysteries* which dealt with his investigations into the Artrellia – the fabled giant monitor lizard of New Guinea. The issue also featured the second (and to date last) contribution from my father who seemed overjoyed that his eldest son was writing about something other than sex, drugs and rock and roll and was quite happy not only to encourage him in this endeavour but to ignore his frequent liaisons with folk like "Doc" Shiels as he did so. (I think I should point out here that my liver has probably sustained more damage because of my cryptozoological relationship with the good Doctor than it ever did on the road with various musical ensembles.)

Animals & Men

The Journal of The Centre for Fortean Zoology

ISSUE THREE   £1.50

Animals & Men

This issue of Animals & Men was put together by the following band of Cryptozoological malcontents:

Jonathan Downes: Editor and computer moans.
Jan Williams: Newsfile and Catfish theories.
Alison Downes: Ornithological Administratrix.
Lisa Peach: Typing Tea and Ferrets.
Jane Bradley: Cartoons.
John Jacques; Sole Representation.
Graham Inglis: Video.
Michael Williams age 7: Additional artwork.
Dave Symons: Software jockey

Contributors this issue:

John Blashford-Snell, Stephen Shipp, Roger Hutchings, 'A retired Colonial Officer', Nick Morgan, Martien Mannetje.

Regional Representatives

LANCASHIRE; Stuart Leadbetter.
ROVING SCOTLAND AT WILL; Jane Bradley.
SUSSEX: Sally Parsons.
CUMBRIA AND LAKELANDS: Brian Goodwin.
HOME COUNTIES Phillip Kibberd.
EIRE Co Clare Richard Muirhead.
SPAIN: Alberto Lopez Acha.
FRANCE: Francois de Saare.

Advertising Rates by arrangement.
Please contact:

The Centre for Fortean Zoology
15 Holne Court
Exwick, Exeter.
Devon EX4 2NA

0392 424811

Special thanks this issue to:

Bernard Heuvelmans, Janet Bord, Craig Harris, Dr Karl P.N.Shuker.Congratulations to Richard and Sian.

SUBSCRIPTION RATES

'Animals and Men' appears four times a year in October, January, April and July. A four issue subscription costs:

£.600 UK/Eire
£ 7.00 EEC
£7.50 Europe non EEC
£9.00 OZ NZ USA Canada (Surface Mail)
£12.00 OZ NZ USA Canada (Air Mail)
£10.00 Rest of World (surface mail)
£12.00 Rest of World (air Mail)

Cheques in Sterling or IMO or Eurocheque payable to A&J Downes.

CONTENTS

The picture on the front cover was taken by Terry Connolly and is reprinted with the kind permission of The Eastbourne Gazette.

Animals and Men is compiled and typeset by Jonathan Downes on an Amiga A500 using Penpal 3.1 and Pagesetter 2 Software, decaffienated coffee, and a small kitten called Pixel. Thou art God.

THE GREAT DAYS OF ZOOLOGY ARE NOT DONE

Dear Friends,

Probably the best thing about running a magazine such as this is the great variety of people with whom you deal. One of the most interesting people that I have come into contact with in the past three months is Ray Nelke. Ray is a man with a mission. Some people collect stamps, some people collect records, some people collect butterflies, in my time I have collected all three. Ray Nelke has a collection too..but Ray collects unusual data. He has an exhaustive collection of unusual information on a bewildering range of subjects which span the widest ranges of Fortean interest and many other fields besides.

The really unusual thing about Ray is the fact that he is prepared to share his collection with anyone who is interested, and he is prepared to do it for nothing! We contacted Ray on the off chance, without really knowing anything about him, and he sent us (by return of post), an enormous bundle of photocopies on an unbelievably wide range of subjects. The material ranged from scholarly though esoteric knowlege to complete nonsense, and after a couple of hours leafing through the material he sent and listening to his sampler tape I was hooked.

We will continue to work with Ray's organisation COUD-I and we shall send him any material of interest to him whether or not it is within our particular sphere of interest. Could you please send us any clippings of a broadly Fortean nature, or better still contact Ray direct at: COUD-I, 2312 Shields Avenue, St Louis, MO 63136 USA

If you do contact him direct please tell him that we sent you. We hope that you like issue three. It has more pages, more illustrations and more information than ever before. We have over twice as many regional representatives and double the number of subscribers that we had three months ago, and we are determined to get even bigger and better. Thank you for all your help and goodwill,

Best wishes,
Jonathan Downes, (Editor)

NEWSFILE

Compiled and Edited by *Jan Williams* with the aid of her intrepid band
of Newsfile Correspondents and the odd (sometimes VERY odd)
interjection from The Editor.

'ONE TWO THREE WHAT ARE WE SEARCHING FOR?

As more news comes from Vietnam, cryptozoology begins to feel like waiting for a bus - nothing turns up
for ages, then 6 new large mammal species are discovered within a couple of years. Vietnamese biologist
Nguyen Ngoc Chinh found the skull of an animal known to local hunters as the *Quang khem*, in the *Pu Mat*
jungle 50 miles north of Vu Quang. The *Quang khem*, or slow-running deer, has two short antlers
resembling the horns on a Viking helmet. Dr John Mackinnon has collected other skulls of the species -
including some from boxes of unsorted bones at Hanoi's Institute of Ecology and Biological Resources.

Mackinnon also has antlers from two further species. The first is known to locals as the *'Mangden'* or black
deer, and the second as *Linh duong* or holy goat.
(Time 3.7.94; Independent on Sunday 3.7.94; Wild About Animals Sept '94)

NEW 'ROO IN IRIAN JAYA

Several years ago Tim Flannery of the Australian Museum in Sydney received a photograph of a hunter
holding a baby tree kangaroo. Flannery, an expert on the fauna of Melanesia, was puzzled by the animal,
which didn't seem to be a standard tree kangaroo. In May of this year he led an expedition to the remote
Mauke mountain range in central Irian Jaya, the Indonesian province on the island of New Guinea, and
found a primitive black and white tree kangaroo, known to the Moni tribe as *'bondegezou'* or 'man of the
forest'. The kangaroo has very long black fur over most of the back and head, a white front, two white
blazes across the black muzzle and a white star in the middle of the forehead. Adult males can measure 4
feet from nose to tail tip, and weigh up to 33 lbs. The tail, about 20 inches long, is the shortest of any
kangaroo, relative to body size. The creature is very primitive in its body type and behaviour, according to
Flannery. Although it appears to be adapted for life in the trees, it spends most of its time on the ground,
and descends from trees tail first, unlike other tree kangaroo species. The 'bondegezou' is regarded as
sacred by the Moni people. It seems unafraid of humans, and greets them by standing on its hind legs and
whistling.

News of this discovery must bring renewed hope to Ned Terry, who believes Thylacines may still exist in
the high country wilderness of Irian Jaya. Terry showed photographs of Thylacines to local hunters who
named the animal as *'Dobsegna'* and described its behaviour, paw prints and eating habits. They fear the
animal and associate it with evil spirits. Fossil evidence suggests that Thylacines were once common on
New Guinea, and the island to search for positive evidence. Could Irian Jaya be another Vu Quang?
(Minneapolis Star & Tribune 26.7.94; Westfalenpost 22.7.94;

BORNEAN BAY CAT REDISCOVERED

The last confirmed sighting of the Bay Cat, or Bornean Red Cat, *(Profelis badia)* was in 1928. The species was known from only 6 incomplete specimens, of which five were collected prior to 1900. Nothing is known of the Bay Cat's biology, and little about its behaviour, and for 65 years there were only occasional unconfirmed sightings to suggest that the species continued to survive.

In November 1992 an adult female Bay Cat was captured by trappers on the Sarawak-Indonesian border, and kept in captivity for several months. It was eventually taken to the Sarawak Museum but was dying when it arrived.

This specimen bears a striking resemblance to a miniature Temminck's Cat *(Profelis temmincki)*. It is hoped that genetic analysis of blood and tissue samples will help to clarify confusion as to the Bay Cat's taxonomic status.

(Oryx, vol 28, no 1, January 1994)

WILL THE REAL SCOTTISH WILDCAT PLEASE STAND UP?

A study by Scottish Natural Heritage , now at draft report stage, has reached the surprising conclusion that it is impossible to differentiate between Scottish Wildcats *(Felis silvestris grampia)* and domestic cats on the basis of markings, skull size or even genetic testing. The research was carried out at the request of the Scottish Office, following a court case in 1990 in which a gamekeeper was accused of killing three Scottish Wildcats, protected under the 1981 Wildlife and Countryside Act. The case had to be dropped because no expert witness could verify that the animals were in fact Wildcats.

The Scottish Wildcat was defined in 1907 by the British Museum; the chosen type specimen being an animal killed at Drumnadrochit in 1904. From this point the species 'evolved' by unnatural selection - gamekeepers supplying Wildcats to museums and zoos were paid only for the ones which conformed to the type specimen. The SNH research found that the marking theories of the Natural History Museum did not stand up to rigorous examination: a tabby, striped coat, and bushy tail with six distinct bands are just as likely to be found on a domestic tabby, or a feral cat.

Genetic testing established distinct groups of larger cats in various parts of the Highlands. While most of the animals in these groups resemble the traditional wildcat, some have widely variable markings, including large patches of white or black. David Balharry of SNH states 'There is a type of cat that the environment is selecting in some areas . . . Whether that population is a remnant of the original Scottish Wildcat, I don't know.' The team have applied for funding for further research, including comparing the DNA from bones of ancient cats from the Inchnadamph Caves with that of modern cats. Research to date leaves the true Scottish Wildcat (if it still exists) with no legal protection, and a lot of museums displaying animals which may well be feral domestic cats.
(The Scotsman 15/8/94)

JUST TAKING THE ALLIGATOR FOR A SWIM ...

Joerg Zars became the least popular resident of Neuss, near Cologne, Germany on 11th July when he took his pet alligator Sammy for a swim in the lake. Four-foot long Sammy slipped his lead and swam away. Two thousand tourists were evacuated from the leisure park lake as police marksman equipped with searchlights and sonar scanners hunted for the alligator. Sammy was eventually captured alive five days later by a reptile expert, and transferred to Cologne Zoo, whilst Zars faced a #65,000 bill for the search and the park's lost takings.

On 18th July, as Sammy pondered on what might have been, Minnesota Public Radio broadcast a report of an alligator on the loose east of Bemidji, MN. A DNR spokeman confirmed that numerous reports of the creature had been received from a swampy area with many lakes, but they had little hope of catching it.

(Daily Mail 13.7.94, 14.7.94, 16.7.94, MPR 18.7.94)

LOST . . .

Fifty snakes, many belonging to rare species, were stolen from The Serpentarium at Walsall, West Midlands on 18th July. They were part of a world-famous collection built up by reptile expert Dave Leicester, who died in May.

(Daily Mail 19.7.94)

Lecter, a three foot long monitor lizard, escaped from owner Mansoor Masood's home in Violet Bank Road, Sheffield in July. Masood described his pet (named after Hannibal the Cannibal) as a cross between a pit bull terrier and a cat, and warned that it could eat a small dog and might even savage a child.

(Daily Mail 29.7.94)

. . .AND FOUND

Customs officers raided a terraced house at Canton, Cardiff, and seized 100 exotic reptiles, including a poison arrow frog, royal python, rainbow boa constrictor and a cayman.

(Daily Mail 4.8.94)

A two-headed grass snake was found in a dung heap in Winchelsea by Les Paine, who named the creature 'Four Eyes' and gave it to a mini-zoo in Seaford. There will be more details and hopefully a photograph in the next issue.

(Daily Mail 17.9.94)

CREEPY CRAWLIES...

A three and a half inch long black red and cream caterpillar found by nine year old Gemma Thorpe in her grandfather's garden at St Leonard's, East Sussex, was identified by Colin Pratt of Hastings Museum as a Spurge Hawk Moth, last seen in England in 1949.

(Daily Mail 31.8.94)

SACRED BUFFALO

A white buffalo calf born at Janesville, Wisconsin, has been hailed by American Indians as a sacred beast, harbinger of astonishing and historic events for all Native Americans. Legend states that the white buffalo will unify the nations of the four colours, the black, red, yellow and white. Representatives of Indian tribes visited David Heider's farm to hold ceremonies, and leave offerings to ensure the health and safety of the calf, named Miracle. The cow calf has brown eyes, showing that she is not a true albino, and may become just another brown buffalo when she sheds her coat in the spring.

(Daily Telegraph 3.9.94, Daily Mail 3.9.94)

ARCTIC FOX

An animal resembling an Arctic Fox has been reported scavenging from a waste bin in a layby at Sprowston Hill on the A1151 near Norwich, Norfolk. It was seen on two or three occasions in May and June by motorists who described it as white, with shorter legs than a normal fox.

THE BEAST OF CHISWICK

A strange animal appeared in the London suburb of Chiswick in June. Residents reported a 'scrawny-looking' creature with the body of a dog, a pointed face like a kangaroo, and long thin tail. It had fur the colour of a grey squirrel, and, according to some residents, white spots. Surprisingly, the press failed, for once, to identify it as a 'puma'.

Regular night-time sightings continued through July and August, covering an area of three square miles, with the animal accused of disembowelling pigeons and tearing open sacks of rubbish.
(London Evening Standard 9.8.94)

A NORFOLK SNARLEYOW

Amid a wave of mystery cat fever in Norfolk, another odd creature appeared and stayed around long enough to have its photo taken. RAF historian Raymond Trew noticed the jet-black animal prowling across the sugar-beet field behind his house on the outskirts of Watton at 7am on 3rd July. Raymond had never seen anything like it, and he grabbed his camera and took five consecutive photographs.

The animal was larger and longer-bodied than a big dog, had a snub nose, and a bushy-ended tail which was longer than its body. The line of the stomach was about 6 inches above the sugar beet - then about 9 inches high. As Raymond watched, a hare started up in the field, and the black animal chased it. It 'loped, bounced, pounded along but with no real speed' and eventually disappeared on the other side of the 100 acre field, still in pursuit of the hare.

Picture;   Raymond Trew Copyright 1994

Raymond phoned the local police who contacted the Eastern Daily Press. He gave the unprocessed film to the newspaper, who printed one of the photos under the headline 'Puma Caught on the Prowl'.

One of Raymond's neighbours had been puzzling over three unusual prints he had found in a freshly dug patch of earth. They were almost round, and reminded him of domestic cat prints, but were much larger. The soil was soft and sandy, and it was only possible to discern a large central pad, a gap, then a groove about three quarters of an inch wide. Another neighbour had noticed dirty marks on top of the four foot high gate into her garden, and large dark-coloured droppings in the middle of the lawn.

Seen through a magnifying glass, the creature photographed does not appear to be a big cat, nor does it look much like a dog or a pony - two other suggested identities. Raymond himself is certain it was neither of these, because of the way it moved. Folklorists will note that the sighting was close to the Peddars Way - long reputed as a haunt of *Black Shuck*, the huge black ghost hound of Norfolk. So what is this creature? Answers on a postcard, please . . .!

(Eastern Daily Press 27.6.94, Thetford & Watton Times 30.6.94)

MYSTERY CATS

Cornwall

Bob Crooks was driving between Lamanva and Mabe when a large cat crossed the road in front of him. It was three feet from nose to tail, very slender, with a long tail which curled up at the tip. From 40 yards away it looked completely black, but as Mr Crooks got closer he could see patches of dark brown.

(Western Morning News 27.7.94)

Kent

Dave Riches of the *Many Hoots Owl Rescue Centre* at Studdal, near Deal, and P C Ian Woodland are closely monitoring reports of leopard-, puma-, and lynx-like cats in East Kent. Reports date back to 1970, but have become more numerous in recent months. Dave has seen a black leopard-like cat on several occasions, and describes it as four feet long, 18 inches to 2 feet tall with a 2 & a half to 3 foot tail.

Prints, territorial markings and faeces have been found, and leopard-like sawing calls heard. But those of you thinking this is a straighforward case of an escapee leopard really should know better! The black cat has orange/amber eyes, and Dave and other witnesses have seen the cat in company with a cub which is light grey with darker 'ink blot' markings.

As far as I can ascertain, neither is normal for a black leopard, 'though there have been other reports of black mystery cats with orange eyes. Anyone with information on these anomalies in leopards, please write in! *(East Kent Mercury 25.8.94, 1.9.94, 28.9.94, Dover Express 15.9.94)*

Hampshire

Armed police searched the New Forest around Lymington on June 6th for a 'black panther' said to have attacked a collie and broken its leg.

Basingstoke police hunted a lioness following eight sightings around the villages of Bramley and Tunworth between 16th and 20th September. Witness Peter Giles saw the animal 100 yards away in a ploughed field, and pointed it out to a gamekeeper who observed it through binoculars. The animal is described as seven feet long and three feet high, and light brown in colour. Prints found compared in size to those of a Siberian Tiger. The search, involving a police spotter plane, thermal imaging equipment, and six marksmen, was called off on 23rd September. *(Daily Mail 20.9.94, 21.9.94, Radio 5 News 21/22/23.9.94)*

Oxfordshire

Malcolm Warner of Fencott looked out of his window at 7am, and saw a large jet black cat in a tree at the end of the garden. He was surprised by the brilliance of its yellow eyes, which were very obvious despite the distance of 50 yards. He walked down the garden towards the tree, and took a photograph from about twenty-five yards as the cat began to climb down. Realising how large it was (longer than a labrador), he retreated to the house and the cat walked away into a field of long grass behind the house.

Malcolm had the film developed about a week later, and gave the negative to police when his neighbour 15 year old Lewis Watson had a similar encounter. Lewis was cutting a neighbour's lawn with a motor mower when the cat came out of a hedge about 6 feet away. It stopped and stared at him, then walked back into the hedge. The cat was bigger than Lewis' pet labrador, with jet black, medium length, velvety fur. Further reports were received from Mercott and Stonesfield. *(Daily Mail 22.7.94)*

Norfolk

A brief summary of multiple sightings throughout the summer months:

June 24th: Armed police hunt for puma-like cat seen at Costessey.
June 28th: Groundsman at Thetford Grammar School reported a dog-sized black cat near the school playing fields.
July 4th: Big cat seen at Brome, where a calf had been found injured a week before.
July 19th: Labrador-sized black cat reported at Mattishall near Dereham.
July 25th: Dark cat-like animal, size of an alsatian dog, crossed road at Talconeston in one bound. Carrying rabbit or hare in mouth. And big cat *'slightly smaller than a Rottweiler'* reported at Ashill near Watton.
August 8th: Long-tailed cat-like animal crossed road 30 yards ahead of *Animals and Men* reader Frank Durham on B1108 at Scoulton, near Watton. Described as height of a whippet but longer-bodied, black with vertical grey streaks on sides of body, and white round jowls running down into neck.
September 4th: Large black cat crossed A1088 near Thetford
in front of motorist. (*Eastern Daily Press 15.7.94, 21.7.94, 23.7.94, 25.7.94, 27.7.94*)

Nottinghamshire

A *'black panther'* was reported in Sherwood Forest by Kath Eggleshaw, who was out walking with her five year old daughter.(*Western Morning News 20.7.94*)

Humberside

Police closed off three square miles of moorland around the village of Rudston Parva, near Bridlington, on 17th August, following a report of a lioness. Mrs Sue Hutchinson saw the animal walk past the hedge at the end of her garden, and watched it through binoculars for ten minutes. She described it as three feet high with a long tail, and was certain it was a lioness. Tourists were advised to avoid the area, and local people to stay indoors, whilst armed police, an RAF helicopter, and vets from the local zoo, 4searched the area. (*Radio 5 News 17.8.94, Daily Mail 18.8.94*)

Co. Durham

Droppings found near a sheep carcase at Whorlton were analysed by Dr Hans Kruuk, who pronounced them to be leopard or puma. (*Daily Mirror 30.8.94*)

Tayside

Warnings were posted at Crombie Country Park, near Dundee, folowing a sighting of a collie-sized black cat-like animal, with a small head and long tail, on 11th May. Investigations revealed earlier sightings, at

Tannadice near Newbigging, where David Drummond had seen a very large cat like animal near Downie Den in November and again in January.*(The Courier & Advertiser 13/14/18.5.94)*

THREE LEGGED FROGS IN CHINA

Workers in China uncovered a bizarre freak of nature. Work stopped when the builder constructing a school in a village near Beijing, found more than three hundred three legged frogs living in a pit. The cause of the deformity is not known. *(ITV Teletext p. 324 Sept 18th 1994).*

A CRYPTO SAFARI TO NEW ZEALAND

Rex Gilroy, described as *'Australias biggest butterfly collector'* is going to New Zealand in search of the 'Bush Moa' and the legendary New Zealand Man Beast, known to the Maoris as *'Moehau'..."Despite scientific scepticism"*..he said, *"I prefer to keep an open mind. Lacck of evidence does not always imply lack of existance"*. We wish him every success. A selection of recent Man Beast sightings will be found FROM OUR FILES on the inside back page. *Wellington NZ Evening Post 22.1.94 Via COUD-i*

PUMA KILLS JOGGER

We are very loth to print this story for fear that it will add creedence to the lobby whose opinion is that Alien Big Cats are a real danger to human beings but unlike some organisations we could mention we are not in the business of allowing our hidden agenda to stand in the way of the free dissemination of information! Barbara Schoener, a young mother of two was jogging along a popular nature trail near Sacramento California, when she was apparently killed by a lone Mountain Lion. Her body which was mutilated and partially eaten was found covered by leaves soon afterwards. Several weeks later a female Puma whose dentition matched the teeth marks on the corpse was shot by Park Rangers who were afraid that this atypical behaviour could have been caused by rabies. The tests proved inconclusive but the female puma turned out to have been a nursing mother and when the cub was taken to Sacramento Zoo, in a delicious twist of irony over twice as much money was pledged by wellwishers for the purpose of looking after the cub than was pledged as a result of a similar appeal formoney to aid the orphaned children of the dead jogger. Weird huh? *St Louis Post Despatch 30.4.94, 2.5.94, 23.5.94 all Via COUDi*

"WHERE DO WE GO FROM HERE IS IT DOWN TO THE LAKE I FEAR? DA DA DA DA..."

A lake monster known to the locals as 'Nahuelito' was seen by more than 20 people on Lake Nahuel Huapi in Argentina. Jessica Cambell, who lives in Bariloche says *"It was about 10 metres long and had several humps and was a grey-green colour"*. Her friend Paula Jakab said: *"When it came up, it made a lot of waves and what really made an impression on me was the way it breathed.It made a really loud sound that was like a snorting or a lowing"*. Photographs have been taken of the beast which some locals believe is a surviving dinosaur. *Northern Advocate (New Zealand) 5.1.94 Via COUD i*

Newsfile Correspondents: Alan Beattie, Phil Bennett, Alan Brennan, Pat Buckle, Frank Durham, John Goldsmith, Mhairi Hendrie, Dianne Jones, Angel Morant Forres, Steven Shipp, Dr Karl Shuker, Wolfgang Schmidt, Heather Thurgar, Raymond Trew, John Jacques, Jane Bradley, Sally Parsons, B Williams, R A J Williams.

THE BLACK DOGS OF DARTMOOR.

by Stephen Shipp.

Dartmoor is an area of mysterious raw beauty- one of the last remaining regions of natural wilderness left in England. Step onto Dartmoor soil and one steps onto a land rich in history, legend and mystery. It is here that people have lived and worked for over 3000 years, and scattered between the great granite tors that are such a dominating feature in this National Park, one can find much evidence of earliest inhabitation. The stone huts and enclosures mark the places where these people lived; while stone circles, stone rows, cairns and kists stand testament to their worship and burial practises.

With such a long history and the fact that Dartmoor remains a remote and sparcely populated area-legends and tales of the strange and paranormal have seeded themselves in the fertile imaginations of the local people and grown through centuries as they have been passed down from one generation to the next, and can still chill the bones of the modern 20th century visitor.

There are probably more stories of spectral black dogs and other unearthly hounds in this country than any other animal, and they allegedly haunt many of the lanes, roads, gates and bridges of Devon, with their appearence surviving in place-names, inn signs and lane names. They are always associated with evil, as though they were the hounds of hell descending upon the peaceful Devon countryside. Dartmoor is no exception to the rest of the country.

The Wish, wist or whisht hounds (also known as the Yeth or Heath Hounds) are certainly the most infamous beasts to roam the Dartmoor wilderness and are probably the inspiration for Sir Arthur Conan-Doyle's classic Sherlock Holmes story *The Hound of the Baskervilles*. These spectral black dogs with red eyes lead by the Devil (otherwise known as *'Dewer'*) who rides an eight legged headless black horse, are said to hunt at night for the souls of unbaptised babies.

Wistman's wood (sx 612 773) , half a mile north of two bridges, is an ancient wood of stunted Oaks growing between large granite boulders, and it gives an idea of what Dartmoor would have looked in prehistoric times. These woods are claimed to be one of the most haunted places on Dartmoor, and also the home to the Wish Hounds. It is from here, at midnight, that the feared Wish Hunt is said to emerge in full cry and sweep across the moors in search of their prey. Even when the hounds cannot be seen, their hellish baying and barking, along with Dewer's hunting horn can be heard threw. Anyone unfortunate enough to see this spectre is doomed to die within the year, or even be chased to their death by it.

One story has it that on a wintery night the prints of a naked human foot and a cloven hoof were found in the snow near Dewerstone Rock (sx 538 639), where the the hunt has a habit of leading any curious follower over the precipitous crag there, whilst they vanish to the sounds of hollow laughter, baying and peals of thunder. Another tells of baying and peals of thunder. Another tells of a drunken farmer returning home from his local inn and meeting the Wish Hunt in full cry. He called out to Dewer asking him if they had caught anything that night. In reply, Dewer threw him a sack which the farmer took believing it was the nights kill. But when he arrived home, he and his wife openned the sack to find that it contained the dead body of their own child!

Hound Tor (sx 743 790), one of the massive granite tors on Dartmoor, has also been linked to this ghostly pack of dogs; it is claimed to be the pack turned to stone, whilst the nearby Bowerman's Nose (sx 742 734), a natural rock formation that has all the appearences of a human head wearing a hat, was the mighty hunter Bowerman. Both were petrified by local witches after they had had their coven disturbed by the Hunt whilst it was in pursuit of its quarry.

The next strange case involves Lady Mary Howard of Fitzford House in Tavistock (sx 48 74) who was said to have married four times, with at least two of her husbands meeting a premature death from her poisoning them. She is also supposed to have murdered two of her children, and these alleged crimes, she has been condemned every midnight to leave the gateway of Fitzford House in a coach built from the bones of her two murdered husbands. This phantom coach is pulled by headless black horses and a headless coachman, with a huge black dog running in front of it. The dog, which is only meant to have one gleaming eye, is said to be Lady Howard herself! This entourage heads to the Norman Castle of Okehampton, where the dog has to pluck a single blade of grass and then return to Fitzford House. It is only when all the grass has been removed will her spirit be free.

Another wierd tale of a person being transmuted into a dog after death and given an endless task of Weaver Knowles of the little hamlet of Deanscombe (sx 722 643). The day after this skilled weaver was put into his grave, his family heard noises coming from his upstairs weaving room and looking round the door were shocked to see the old man still working at his loom, obviously refusing to accept he was dead!. They sent for the vicar who told the ghost to come downstairs; this is no place for thee. Thou art in thy grave. Eventually Knowles relented and, as soon as he had descended the stairs, the vicar threw a handful of church consecrated soil into his face. The ghost instantly changed into a black dog and obediently followed the clergyman outside to a large pool near Dean Burn, where the vicar gave him a nutshell with a hole in it. He then told the phantom hound "when thou shalt have emptied the pool with this shell, thou may'st sleep". The place these days is called Hound pool or Houndpond, and it said that at noon and at midnight the poor animal can be seen working hard trying to empty the pool.

A black dog may be encountered on the road between Princetown and Plymouth, where a local legend states he was the pet of a murdered traveller. This phantom hound is believed to travel along the road searching in vain for his dead owner and had been met on atleast one occasion. In the last century, a visitor to the moors, was walking along the road during winter time when he was joined by the animal. Having a liking for dogs he tried to pat its head only to find his hand passed right threw it, and he was suddenly hit by a flash of lightening which rendered him unconscious. He did'nt wake up until the following day!.

A further legend surrounding a large black pig also involves a black dog! A local man returning from the Hexworthy to Pondworthy (sx 701 738) came across a large orest inn at Hexworthy to Pondworthy (sx 701 738) came across a large black dog which was wondering about. He caught the animal, tied his scarf around its neck and led it home. Here the dog was locked in the stable for the night, but the following morning when the man came to inspect his captive he found instead a large black pig with his scarf around its neck!.

Recent cases of black dog sightings are rare though the following report from the 1950's is worth a mention. It occured along a narrow lane leading to Okehampton where a woman was taking her daughter for a donkey ride. Suddenly, a very large black dog jumped in front from out of a hedge and stood glaring at them before vanishing. The donkey then refused to take another step forward and a longer route home had to be found. The woman knew the lane very well and has never seen the dog before or since this strange encounter.

Finaly, and by way of a contrast (quite literally!), there is a white spectral hound which is claimed to still haunt Cator Comon (sx 673 778) near Widecombe. It was seen by one woman in the 1960's when she was walking along the edge of a plantation near Cator Gate. In full daylight she saw, coming towards her, a very large cream-coloured dog with a long coat and long ears. As it came close, she put out her hand to stroke it, whereupon it simply vanished.

The map references given are for Ordnance Survey Landranger 191, 201 and 202 (1;500000.

REFERENCES

Barber s. & c. DARK AND DASTARDLY ON THE MOOR Obelisk
Publication 1988.
Bord J. & C. ALIEN ANIMALS Paul Elek ltd 1980.
Brown T. DEVON GHOSTS Jarrold 1982.
Coxhead J.R.W. LEGENDS OF DEVON Western press 1954.
Farquharson-coe A. DEVON'S GHOSTS James Pike ltd 1975
(revised)
Pegg J. AFTER DARK ON DARTMOOR John Pegg Publishing 1984.
St.Leger-Gordon R. THE WITCHCRAFT AND FOLKLORE OF DARTMOOR Robert Hale 1965.

The search for Artrellia-the Papuan giant lizard

by John Blashford-Snell

(The material in this article has been abstracted and condensed by with kind permission from the author from a chapter in his book 'Mysteries-Encounters with the unexplained')

Mysterious animals were very far from my mind as the Cessna winged past the billowing cumulus boiling up over the vast Sepik Swamp in Papua New Guinea. The endless dark green mat of vegetation, bisected only by the huge meandering river, crept slowly past my window. Watching the brown water I saw only the occasional dugout being paddled by jet black, near naked warriors. A few brightly coloured birds flitted around in the tangled growth at the edge of the waterway, but for the most part this enormous morass seemed totally lifeless. 'In Africa or South America', I said turning to the Papuan officer sitting beside me, 'this area would be teeming with wildlife-does anything large live in these swamps?'

'The biggest mosquitoes in the world's down there', he said with a broad grin, 'then there's the Puk-Puk - that's crocodile, and pigs. 'We talked about elephants and African big game which my friend had never seen, then he said slowly, 'local men say there's something called Artrellia-a sort of giant crocodile that climbs trees'.

'Have you ever met anyone who claims to have seen it?' I asked. 'No-but there are men at Green River whol might tell you about it' said the officer, adding, 'But I'm not sure if these people just see them in their dreams'.

It was early afternoon when we landed at the new concrete runway at the little border settlement of Green River. The heavy humid wall of heat hit us as we stepped out and in seconds perspiration was oozing from every pore. The Defence Force Engineers Camp was a short way from the airfield and as we bumped along the dusty corrugated road in a battered Land Rover I turned to the tanned Australian Sergeant-Major who'd come to meet us, and said casually:

'Ever heard of an animal called Artrellia?'
He shook his head, 'Nope, what is it Colonel? I told him of my conversation in the plane. 'Well - my guess is that they're talking about a salt water croc that gets stuck up a mangrove tree when the tide goes out', he smiled and then said, 'but there'll by an old chief at the 'Mu-Mu' tonight. According to the boys he was quite a hunter in his day, Maybe he could tell you something-you speak Pidgin?' As I didn't a young Papuan Lieutenant wearing a live marsupial like a Davy Crockett hat would give a hand.

The aroma of cooking pork wafted up from the fires as we sat beneath the thatched roof of the mess hut sipping our 'tubes of Fosters'. It was late when the old warrior arrived-he'd put on all his finery for the occasion and seemed delighted that someone was interested in his exploits-but all he knew about Artrellia was based on one sighting thirty years before and that wasn't a particularly close encounter. However of one thing he was certain-it was no 'Puk-Puk'. So I tried to draw what he described-it wasn't easy, but eventually he seemed satisfied with something which looked vaguely like a dinosaur with a long tail.

'He says it walks upright, climbs trees and breathes fire', I told my hosts. *'Sounds like a bloody dragon'* laughed the Sergeant Major, *'better send for St George'*. I pushed the sketch in my diary and forgot all about the Artrellia.

It was three years later and the Papua New Guinea phase of Operation Drake was in full swing. Working late one evening I found myself marooned in my office at our headquarters at Lae, by a fearsome tropical storm. Lightning crackled and thunder crashed overhead, shaking the wooden chalet uncertainly and beyond the mosquito netting the rain fell in rods, whipping the surface of the nearby pool into a frenzy.

'No point in getting soaked going for the car', I thought, so I poured a large shot of J and B into the green plastic mug and pulled over a large illustrated book on New Guinea wildlife that was sitting in my 'In' tray. Attached to it was a note from Alan Bibby, our resident producer: *'See p.278-what do you think?'* it said.

So I leaned back in the old canvas chair, took a welcome wig of the Scotch and flipped open the volume. The last paragraphs of the page leapt at me,...'...*dinosaur like....a legendary giant lizard....said to exist in Western Papua...*'

Oblivious to the raging storm I read on. It appeared that many years ago a young Papuan Warrior staggered breathlessly home to his village in a state of shock after a lone hunting trip and blurted out an amazing story. It was said his grandchildren still recall it vividly and they will repeat it word for word, to anyone who penetrates far enough up the Binatori River to reach their isolated but idyllic village of Giringarede.

It seems that their grandfather was feeling rather weary after hours on the trail and went to sit down and rest on a fallen tree trunk only for the 'tree' to rear up under him and reveal itself as a dragon! It stood over ten feet tall on its hind legs and had wicked looking jaws like a crocodile. The old man did not wait to see if it breathed fire at him-he ran for his life and never once looked back to see if the monster was pursuing him.

It all sounded a bit far fetched but instantly I recalled the meeting with the old chap at Green River. The book mentioned stories very similar to those described in travellers' tales that have been coming out of PNG since the end of the last century-and many of them have come from very reputable sources During the Second World War Allied and Japanese Patrols operating deep in the most remote parts of the jungle reported catching glimpses of what was most often described as a *'tree climbing crocodile'*.

Some scientists and wildlife experts came to the conclusion that what people might have seen was a giant lizard of the type first officially identified in 1978 as Salvador's Monitor-a close relation of the famed Komodo Dragon of Indonesia. A number of very large specimens of this reptile have been caught in PNG over the years. One, seven foot in length was trapped near the mouth of The Fly river in 1936 by a scientific expedition whilst a trader named John Senior-who ran a general store on the Kikori River-has a skin nailed to his wall which, in life, must have measured a good ten feet. On this evidence, there seemed every reason to suppose that somewhere in the most inaccessible recesses of the jungle there might lurk some outsize freaks-the equivalent of those 'grandfather' pike and other big fish that anglers sometimes hook from deep, dark pools.

Miss Somere Jogo the PNG Government liaison officer lived in a village in the Western Province so Colonel Blashford-Snell asked her about the mysterious Dragon...

Her smile disappeared, her eyes widened and dropping her voice she leant forward and said with meaning, 'I know it exists-many of my people have seen it. They say it climbs trees, walks upright-especially at night-kills men, makes a whistling sound, and breathes fire'.

I gulped the last of my whisky. This girl was deadly serious. 'Have you ever seen one?' I questioned.
'No, but they are to be found in the bush and swamps near my home. The people are very afraid of them. An old man was killed by a female a few years ago.'
'What do you call it?' I asked. 'Artrellia-or in English, Dragon', was the instant reply. The last flickers of lightning were on the Eastern horizon as I walked to my car deep in thought. What a challenge.

The next day a couple of phone calls to Government scientists confirmed the general belief that there was something worth going after -and that the authorities would welcome an investigation. So Dorian Huber, a Swiss Young Explorer, accompanied by Somere went off on a recconnaissance and ten days later came back with photographs of a seven foot lizard and reports of others even bigger. These were not Artrellia, but nevertheless I decided to mount a search for what would undoubtedly be the longest lizard in the world.

After a not uneventful three day voyage, we came into Daru, the provincial capital at midday, and whilst the good ship Andewa refuelled, I rushed off to find Somere and to meet her uncle Mr Tatty Olewale OBE, Premier of the Western Province. We found him at home having lunch and reading from a gigantic leather bound Bible, whilst his pet parakeet hopped about on his shoulders. The Premier rose to greet us with the words, 'Colonel it is the Lord who has brought you to us'. I was inclined to agree. In no time Mr Olewale summoned his brother, the head postman, who was able to tell us a great deal about Artrellia. He confirmed that an elderly man had died in the Daru hospital after being attacked by one which appeared to be a female protecting her nest. The Premier wished us well and presented everyone with a small gift before sending us off with his niece, Somere, and a wizened old pilot as river guide.

Next day we anchored off Masingara and marched the half mile inland to Somere's well ordered home village of traditional stilt supported bamboo huts. There, I was ushered by her brother, Seyu, towards a hundred year old woman, who was the most senior citizen and who was said to know more than anyone about the Artrellia having seen several in her lifetime.

The white haired old lady confirmed many of the things that we had already heard: that these creatures grew to over fifteen feet in length; that they often stood on their hind legs and so gave the appearance of dragons, or to our mind mini dinosaurs; also that they were extremely fierce.

This last point brought much nodding from the village hunters, who made it quite obvious that they treated even the smaller six or seven footers-which they said were quite common-with the greatest respect. This came as no surprise since we had already been told of an incident in another village where a captured Artrellia had smashed its way out of a stout cage and killed a large dog, before escaping back into the forest. Now we learned that the creature's method of hunting was to lie in wait in the trees before dropping onto its victims and tearing them to shreds with its powerful claws. Apart from that, it posessed a very infectious bite as a result of feeding on carrion and this could bring death within a matter of hours. There were plenty of stories of men who had been attacked and killed by the Artrellia.

During the next few days we split into four patrols and combed the surrounding jungle; everyone we met understood immediately when we explained what we were looking for and claimed that they themselves had seen such creatures. The nearest we got to a sighting was when the local dogs which accompanied one patrol put up something that crashed off heavily through the undergrowth without showing itself.

'It's said to move at night-so we'd better try a spot of night hunting', I said to the slightly dispirited patrols so at dusk three of us set out, armed to the teeth, and carrying an Army image intensifier which enhances existing light to such an extent that even that of a few stars will enable a soldier to shoot accurately at a hundred yards using the device as a rifle sight.

After an exciting and eventful night when the patrolmanaged to spot several interesting denizens of the Papuan forest but after several false alarms singularly failed to spot anything even slightly resembling a monstrous lizard Colonel Blashford-Snell in his own words 'decided that there must be easier ways of solving this mystery'.

On the Sunday before Christmas, he went to Matins in the little village church and after the service he paused to talk to the vicar.

'Do you believe in Artrellia?' I asked. He'd been educated in Australia and I reckoned he would be a sensible vicar.'I know he exists-I sometimes wish he didn't, 'cos my people think him's a devil, like an evil spirit, 'but him just an animal-bad animal sometime'.'Well if we caught one would it convince your flock that it was no evil spirit?' I asked.'Sure', he nodded his head.'Then how on earth can we do that?''Oh you fellows won't catch him-you makes too much noise tramping around the bush-you needs good hunters', he stated firmly and added as an afterthought,'My choir boys is plenty good hunters'.

'How much to hire your choir?' I asked.'I needs a new church roof', smiled the little priest looking wistfully at the tattered thatch. 'How much will that cost?' I asked.

'Ten dollars' was his quick reply. However he suggested that I offer the reward to the village council that evening and in that way I'd get all the hunters helping. Ten dollars (or Kina) would be a months wage. 'But don't tell 'dem fellows about the reward 'til 7 o'clock', he cautioned, 'cos I want to leave at 5 -oh yes, and can you let me have some shotgun shells?'

Sure enough the mere mention of money was followed by a mass exodus into the jungle of every able bodied man in the village, armed with everything from bows and arrows to an antique blunderbuss.It was as we steamed back down the Pahotori after a trip upriver which produced no actual sightings but plenty of confirmation   that   what   we   were   looking   for   did   indeed   exist,

We received a radio message from the base reporting that the vicar had managed to shoot a big lizard deep in the forest and was on his way back to Masingara with it. We returned to the village at full speed and by the time we arrived, a large crowd had already gathered around a strange creature which was lying at their feet roped to a bamboo pole. *'It's alive'* muttered Mike as Ian bent to examine the reptile. Chris Sainsbury's cameras were already clicking as I handed the ten kina bill to the vicar who assured me that this was Artrellia. Its dark green skin was flecked with yellow spots and its square head housed a set of needle like teeth. The eyes twitched malevolently as it tried to squeeze itself out of the vines binding it to the pole, but the most impressive part of its anatomy were the claws-at the end of its short thick legs were enormous, black scimitars, out of proportion to the rest of its body. The tail was long and thin and twice the length of the body. I noticed that the village dogs kept well away from the dying beast with its terrible talons. The mouth and tongue gave a red/yellow effect-*'fire'* said the priest and I saw how the legend had been started by the tongue flickering in sunlight. Ian pushed in the syringe and Artrellia passed quietly into death. As soon as it was safe to handle measurements were taken.

It was no dragon, but, it was still a pretty fearsome creature at just over six feet from head to tail. Once Ian had performed his post mortem he was able to confirm that it was only a youngster which left plenty of room for speculation about what size an overgrown adult might reach. A patrol that had been keeping vigil beside a remote water hole, which we had been told was a haunt of the creatures, came back with reports that they had seen several sizeable specimens coming down to drink, but had been unable to get near enough to photograph them in the dark. We did catch a glimpse of one monster with a head like a horse peering at the photographers over a fallen log. Ian made several sightings of impressive adult lizards of lengths up to twelve feet, and from our specimen we know that Artrellia was indeed Salvador's Monitor-but no-one had dreamed of the size to which these killers can grow. But the question now is how big DO they grow?

OROBOROUS IS ALIVE AND WELL AND LIVING IN EASTBOURNE

We are indebted to our Sussex Representative Sally Parsons for this fascinating story and for the accompanying photograph which was so 'odd' that we had to put it on our front cover. The photograph originally appeared in the Eastbourne on May 25th this year accompanying a story headlined: YEUK! KEN GRIPS MONSTER WORM! about a *'seven foot wriggler'* found on a flower bed at Manor Gardens in the town. According to Bruce Porterthe contracts manager at Sercoserve (presumably the private firm contracted to clean municipal areas in the town) *"I was told by my staff who came face to face with it that it appeared to be very similar to an earthworm although there was a suggestion that it was a parasitic worm"*.

Sally interviewed Bruce Porter by 'phone on the 30th June. He confirmed the details given in the 'Gazette' article. The worm was found dead on a flower bed by a member of the public raising the question of whether the animal came out of the ground at this point or whether it was carried there by some other agency. Regretfully I have to dismiss Sally's suggestion of a secret society called 'Worm Dumpers Anonomous', and can only say that Ken Hughes (see front cover) who was on the spot and examined the carcass confirms that it was one single worm and not a deliberate fabrication of small ones joined together or a similar hoax. From his experience in the gardening trade he says that it appeared to be an ordinary earthworm. Although the creature was of local interest as a 'freak' it was not a record holder (the British record Earthworm was 13 feet in length and the world record is held by a South American 33 footer)' after being photographed this 20th century descendant of 'Oroborous the Midgard Serpent' was consigned ignominiously to the rubbish skip!

MYSTERY CATS - WHERE DO WE GO FROM HERE?

by Jan Williams

The biggest mystery relating to mystery cats is why, more than thirty years after the *'Surrey Puma'*, they remain a mystery. Why, in a country which is home to some of the greatest zoological institutions in the world, it seems impossible to explain a minor item in the annals of cryptozoology.

For a variety of reasons, mystery cat reports produce extreme reactions in a way that other immigrant species, like wallabies or muntjac, fail to do. At times the whole thing feels more like an evangelical crusade than an attempt to understand a fascinating aspect of natural history.

A few years ago, enquiries to orthodox zoologists regarding 'mystery cats' were generally met with the kind of wary reserve the British tend to use for someone who gets on the bus wearing striped pyjamas and a bucket over their head. One would be kindly informed that the General Public were incapable of recognizing animals such as foxes, deer, dogs, and so on, and frequently became firmly convinced that next door's moggy was, in fact, a full grown lion. There was little point in anyone with a proper job investigating such reports - it wasn't as if there was any real evidence.

Such attitudes die hard, and, although dented by recent video evidence, still prevail amongst the very people whose expertise is needed to understand the nature of the various Beasts. Many will now accept the existence of a few escapee animals, but will not countenance eye-witness reports suggesting that large cats exist, and are breeding, throughout Britain.

Norfolk Cats.

Acceptable physical evidence, in the form of spoor, hair samples, remains of prey, dens, and the carcasses of the cats themselves, has proved remarkably hard to find. There are three main problems; firstly, the elusive nature of cat species; secondly, knowing what to look for; and thirdly, having sufficient time and enthusiasm to keep searching.

The efforts of Heather, Louise and Jane Thurgar over the past twelve months have produced at least some definite evidence of large cats in the vicinity of Aslacton in South Norfolk. The county has a long history of cat reports, although it has never attained the notoriety of Bodmin or Exmoor. Heather, local representative for *Farmwatch*, an organisation set up to monitor attacks on livestock, became involved when she was called out to see a dead calf, which did not seem to have been killed by dogs or foxes.

Very briefly, the evidence is as follows:

1.   Faeces found near to the carcass of a day-old calf at Forncett St Peter, and containing calf hair. The sample was sent to Michael Lawrence, joint author of 'The Country Life Guide to Animals of Britain and Europe' (Newnes Books, 1984), and 'Mammals of Britain' (Blandford 1967), who stated that it did not conform to that of any British carnivore, and corresponded in size and appearance to that of a puma.

2.   Casts of prints taken from a field at a point where a large puma-like cat had been seen crossing the road. Measuring 7cm wide by 9cm long, and sunk deeply into clay, the prints clearly show 3 lobes at the rear of the heel pad. Large claws are evident on both prints, and retractile claw sheaths can be seen on two toes.

Prints are frequently dismissed as 'dog' purely because they show claw marks. This is not an acceptable diagnostic technique, as can be seen from the following extracts from 'A Mountain Lion Field Guide' (H.G. Shaw, 1979; Special Report No. 9; Arizona Fish and Game Dept, Phoenix, Arizona)

'Size and shape of the heel pad is the best characteristic to use in distinguishing (mountain) lion tracks from those of large dogs... Most diagnostic are the three distinct lobes in the rear of the heel... Some dogs can travel on hard ground without showing distinct claw marks, while a lion moving fast will often show claws.'

The Norfolk prints were shown to Michael Lawrence who confirmed they were those of a large cat, probably a puma. More large prints were found in snow at Caistor St Edmund and confirmed as cat prints by John Goldsmith of Norwich Castle Museum.

3.   A den located in the side of a dry ditch, measuring 4 feet 6 inches in length, 2 feet in height, and 2 feet 6 inches in depth. Well concealed behind an ivy-hung fallen tree, the den showed none of the signs normally associated with fox or badger. Scratchmarks and broken and chewed branches were found on a tree directly behind the den, and several large holes had been dug into the earth by an animal powerful enough to rip through tree roots. A trail of large and small prints, showing the definitive three lobes on the heel pad, was found a few yards from the den site, suggestive of an adult and cub.

4. Hair samples taken from a barbed wire fence (Sample A) and from the den (Sample B) were sent to Dr Andrew Kitchener of the Royal Scottish Museum and Dr Lars Thomas in Denmark, who had kindly agreed to attempt analysis.

Dr Kitchener commented:

'I don't think your samples are similar to either puma or leopard (or cats in general)'.

Dr Thomas agreed with this.

He considered Sample A to be from a cow or horse, and B possibly a canid. This was obviously disappointing, although the connection between the hair samples and large cats was tenous. Electron microscope photographs of the samples, together with those of puma and leopard, are reproduced here (with thanks to Dr Kitchener) and, if anyone has the facilities and interest to take this further, sample hairs are available!

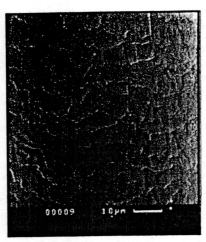

Electron Microscope Photograph of
Sample A.

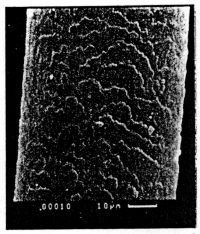

Electron Microscope Photograph of
Sample B.

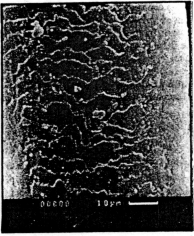

Electron Microscope Photograph of
Hair Sample from Leopard
(*Panthera pardus*).

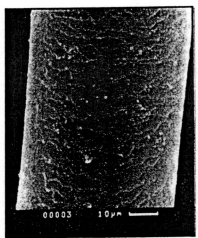

Electron Microscope Photograph
of Hair Sample from Puma (*Felis
concolor*).

5. Remains of prey. The calf found dead at Forncett St Peter in August 1993 had been totally eviscerated some 50 to 60 lbs of meat having been eaten. The left ear had been pulled out by the roots, and the tongue eaten. It was a very clean kill, with little trace of blood left in the field. Another calf had been found dead about three quarters of a mile away, the previous week. One ear had been pulled out and the tongue eaten, but there were no other injuries. This was one of twins, born during the night, and it was assumed it had been born dead. The killing of the second calf may have been triggered by scavenging on the first.

A sheep found dead a few miles away, and attributed to 'the puma' was a messier kill, and probably the work of stray dogs which were known to have attacked sheep on a nearby farm. No other attacks on livestock were reported in the area, despite frequent sightings of large cats over a twelve month period, but the rabbit population decreased noticeably!

The figure of 300 lbs of meat per week is often quoted as the requirement for an adult puma, and leads sceptics to suggest that a feral puma would cause very obvious devastation to livestock. This figure is a ridiculous over-estimate, a point well-made by zoo-keeper Alan Pringle of the Welsh Mountain Zoo in a letter to *Fortean Times* (No. 74). He pointed out that zoo pumas are adequately fed on 10-20 lbs of meat (on the bone) per day, and a wild one could survive on one roe-deer a week, or a diet of small mammals and birds. Reports of large cats, along with those of more normal British predators, have increased dramatically across the whole country in the last couple of years, closely following the recovery of the rabbit population.

6.   Eye witness evidence comprises sightings of at least three different cats. The first, sandy-brown in colour, is larger than a labrador dog, with a noticeably longer body and tail, and a small cat-like head. It is capable of running extremely fast and leaping over 8 foot hedges, and has been seen jumping out of a tree. The second animal is slightly smaller, heavily muscled, and jet black in colour. The two were seen together on one occasion.

A third, smaller cat, was seen very close to the den site. This was brown, with darker spotted markings, and may have been a cub. Recent reports of a plain brown coated cat, smaller than the one referred to above, could possibly be this same animal, now a young adult. These three cats have been seen within a small area of less than twenty square miles. Elsewhere in the county, there have been numerous reports of large cats - some puma or leopard-like, others bearing unusual markings or thick woolly coats, and difficult to identify with any known species.

To the north of Norwich, a dog-sized cat-like animal was found dead in a country lane, by a motorist who described it as having a pale sandy coat with darker markings like 'cartoon seagulls', and with the texture of short lambswool. Unfortunately, it was several days before he mentioned it to anyone with an interest in the subject, and the carcass had, by then, disappeared. The lane runs alongside an area of woodland where a very large black cat (larger and more powerful than a Rottweiler dog according to reports) has been seen many times over a five year period.

Variations on a Theme.

The variations in size, build, colour and markings described by witnesses, are perhaps the most confusing, and

The most intriguing aspect of mystery cat reports. Unfortunately, they also push the subject beyond the limits of belief for many people. A few escapee pumas, or even leopards, in the country are one thing - cats which don't conform to any known species are something else altogether. In an article in SCAN News 18 months ago, I suggested Asian Jungle Cats could be responsible for many reports - an idea which, in the light of new evidence, I have reluctantly abandoned as regards the country as a whole, though it remains relevant in the North Midlands and parts of Hampshire and Surrey.

Hybridization between species is a possibility which is frequently dismissed out of hand. Technically, leopards are 'Big Cats' (genus Panthera) and pumas 'Small Cats' (genus Felis) and therefore should not interbreed. However, prior to 1940, a number of German Zoos did succeed in producing leopard/puma hybrids. Armand Denis refers to one reared at Carl Hagenbeck's Tierpark in 'Cats of the World' (Constable, 1964: 'It was apparently the survivor of three sets of twins lborne by a leopardess to a male puma. It had male characteristics, a long tail, and was intermediate in coat colour and pattern between its parents - having pale
leopard-like spots on a puma ground - but it was only half their size'

A photograph of this animal (for which I am indebted to Dr Karl Shuker) shows it to be strongly muscled, and very broad-chested, with a small head, thus conforming to many eye-witness descriptions of the 'Beast of Exmoor', amongst others.

Time of change.

In the course of the last year, the status of British Mystery Cats has suddenly altered. Things are getting serious. On 30th August, a conference was held in Bodmin to discuss the alleged activities of the 'Beast of Bodmin Moor'. Organised by North Cornwall MP Paul Tyler, it was attended by Mike Highman, regional director of the Ministry of Agriculture, Fisheries and Food, and representatives from the Department of the Environment, National Farmers' Union, Country Landowners Association and Police. Whilst the evidence presented was deemed inconclusive, it was agreed that MAFF would investigate further and present a report to Angela Browning, Junior Agriculture Minister, who would decide on further action.

On 6th September, the Eastern Daily Press in Norfolk ran an article headlined 'It's OK To Shoot Killer Lions, Farmers Are Told', based on a (perfectly correct) statement from a MAFF spokesman to the effect that the cats are not protected by law. Similar articles appeared in the West Country and the Midlands, whilst reports of large cats in Kent caused a run on rifles and shotguns in the biggest gun-shop in the area, as would-be Big Game Hunters sought their moment of fame. Animal welfare groups and farming organisations expressed their concern at the danger posed by amateurs taking pot-shots at large, and as yet unidentified, predators; not to mention other inhabitants of the British countryside like livestock, children and courting couples.

Four police hunts have taken place during the last few months, with armed marksmen backed by helicopters and fixed wing aircraft. I doubt if Jim Corbett would have endorsed these methods, though they should be of comfort to those among us who would prefer the animals to survive; and are perhaps safer than the method suggested earlier this year by a gentleman who shall remain nameless, which involved army helicopters equipped with heat-seeking missiles.

Where Do We Go From Here?

In the transformation of British Mystery Cats from mass hallucination to Public Enemy Number One there seems to be a step missing - that boring bit involving things like evidence, investigation, analysis, identification, truth, and so on. There are theories in abundance, but none are, as yet, proven. Before we bring the full might of modern weaponry into play against these animals, might it not be a good idea to use some of our more civilised skills to find out what they are, and how much danger they actually pose?

The evidence detailed in this article has been collected by a small group of people, and analysed by others whose time and expertise has been freely given. There are many people in Britain who are in a position to contribute to the investigation - naturalists, zoo-keepers, natural historians and zoologists in museums and universities. If they would treat the subject objectively, consider the facts not the fallacies, and make use of the techniques and equipment available, I have no doubt that this particular mystery could soon be resolved.

Whilst the Bodmin Conference has increased the level of serious interest in the subject, concern has been expressed regarding the choice of MAFF to lead future investigations. The legal situation is confusing, but it would appear that exotic escapees are the responsibility of the Home Office, whereas MAFF take responsibility for established (breeding) populations of exotic animals, and the Department of the Environment may be involved if the cats are a native species. Given the probability of claims from farmers for damage to livestock if the existence of these large cats is proven, and the build up of evidence showing that they are indeed breeding in the wild, MAFF's objectivity is certain to be questioned.

When government departments become involved in 'mystery' areas, conspiracy theories begin. Rumours of suppression of information, destruction of evidence, and secret plans to deploy army divisions to beat through woodland shooting any large cats they may happen across, are already rife. The relationship between rumour and reality is a tenuous one, but the atmosphere of mistrust created prevents people from volunteering information, and is not conducive to an objective investigation.

British mystery cats are no longer a joke. The subject concerns us all, and deserves a properly conducted scientific investigation by an independent study group, with funding and resources supplied by central government. Decisions regarding responsibility, and any action to be taken, should not be made until the necessary information is available. Zoology, like charity, ought to begin at home.

Editorial Comment: Both Jan Williams and I would welcome responses to this article submitted for publication on our letters page. We would not only like responses to the evidence enclosed above and to the various theories included within the article but we particularly want to discover the views of the 'Animals and Men' readership as to what should be done next by both private researchers and most importantly by The Government and Official Agencies who have now become involved in, whatever your viewpoint, is undoubtedly the most exciting event in British Natural History for several centuries.

LETTERS

> this issue, by popular demand, we are instigating what we hope will become a
> forum for debate, discussion and good natured arguement. The editor reserves
> the right to edit letters for publication on grounds of space. Opinions expressed
> are not necessarily those of the editor or of The Centre for Fortean Zoology.

Dear Editor

I wonder if you or any of your contributors would care to comment on a phenomenon which we had the priviledge to see some years agowhen serving in West Africa. My wife and I had been on tour in bush and had just returned to our bungalow in station when we found that the gardener or nightwatchman (known in Nigeria as the watchman) had left a filthy pile of old potato sacks on the back verandah . Our house servant was a very sophisticated townie from Lagos a bit of a wide boy who dispised all the locals with whom we had dealings *"Dey be bush men to much!"* he would say implying that he and his fellow townsmen were vastly superior to Northern Nigerian peasants.

Ignatius, for that was his name helped me move the sacks murmuring to himself about the stupid bushmen who had left such a mess when from under the sorid pile ran a large black scorpion. I went to crush it with my boot but Ignatius pushed me aside and said *"No touch him Master"* and to our astonishment picked up the scorpion placed it on the pink palm of his hand and carried it gently towards the compound hedge. We could see the insect stinging his palm, over and over again but he took no notice and talked gently to it as he walked slowly away from the bungalow towards the surroundig bush. My wife and I whatched in amaizement and, when he reached the hedge, he gently placed the insect on the ground and it scuttled away into the bush. We expressed our astonishment but Ignatius, for a moment , no longer a Lagos 'wide-boy', but very much a wise tribal 'elder', was not prepared to discuss the incodent except to explain that his people (presumably his sub-tribe), had some kind of pact with scorpions- he added, we should never kill scorpion while he was in our employ. We had heard of strange relationships of this kind but never thought to witness such an extraordinary spectacle.

Can anyone explain it?

yours sincerely

Retired Colonial officer.

People who lived and worked in the former Colonies were in a unique position to collect otherwise unobtainable data. As the colonial era ended for the most part thirty years ago, if such fascinating anecdotal evidence such as this must be collected while there is still time. Our latest project is to make a collection of such stories from Ex Colonial Service Officers. If you feel that you can help us in this very important project please contact us at the Editorial Address

" NOT A LOT OF PEOPLE KNOW THAT... BUT RABBITS DO."

Domestic rabbits almost invariably make their nests and keep their young in the back left-hand corner of their hutches. This is taken for granted by rabbit fanciers and confirmed by my own long experience not only in Britain but also in France. South of the equator, however, I have observed that it is the back right-hand corner that is chosen, again with almost invariable frequency. Is this due to the same mechanism that alters the direction in which the bath water flows downthe plug hole in Southern hemisphere? Or is it an effect of Dr.Rupert Sheldrake's "morphic resonance"?. ROGER HUTCHINGS

"THAT'S ANOTHER FINE NESS YOU'VE GOT ME INTO"

predictably enough Stuart Leadbetter's article in the last issue excited a lot of comment...

I would describe myself as an ever -hopeful sceptic when it comes to reports of the Loch Ness monster so I reluctantly agree with Stuart Leadbetter's views about the Plesiosaur.However, an even stronger case against a surviving dinosaur is simply the fact that Loch Ness was under miles of ice only 10,000 years ago.Much as it disopoints me this fact alone I think points to a non-cryptozoological explanation for the Loch Ness creature (and therefor by implication for most 'northern' lake monsters). I'm not even sure we have a creature whose 'body form can be easily mistaken for (a plesiosaur)'as Stuart puts it. This assumption is apparently based on many eyewitness accounts (although certainly not the 'thousands' referred to)but as a keen birder I've got to say how poor the observation skills of most people are.

The only truly consistant reports from Loch Ness refer to the 'upturned boat' shape which gives rise to rather more mundane explanations than a long snakelike neck.I personally think that the reports of the head and neck (which are less numerous than those of 'humps') are probably cases of mistaken identity undoubtedly influenced by the famouse, but now apparently discredited, Surgeon's Photograph.The other arguement against a 'monster' is the lack of hard evidence from earlier periods namely with the one exception of a newspaper report referring to a 'giant fish' in the loch I'm not aware of any reports whose publication predates the 1930's monster flap.

Why, for instance, did General Wade's men not report anything unusual during their road- building period at the loch? Why weren't there a spate of sightings at the hight of the Victorian fascination with the Highlands and for that matter if there was such a strong local tradition of a monster why didn't the Victorian entrepreneurs exploit it?.As I've said before I hope I'm proved wrong on this issue but unless anyone can put up a convincing altrnative case I remainsceptical of anything more than a wayward sturgeon being responsible for the phenomenen.

Yours sincerely,

Nick Morgan

Dear Mr Downes,

Let me first congratulate you with your fine journal. I think that the contents of the issues so far is very good. I have been studying the Loch Ness matter for 15 years now and as you asked for opinions on the article by Stuart Leadbetter I thought of writing some lines about it. I think the article is very clear and makes it very obvious that a plesiosaur is not a likely candidate for a Nessie. It is however not the first time that the plesiosaur-theory was critisized in this way so the article was not that revolutionary. What I would like to point out is that Nessie may not be a Plesiosaur but eyewitness accounts give the impression that it has Plesiosauric features, especially in shape.

This is what probably constructed a Plesiosaur-theory which should be pointing to a plesiosaur-shaped animal and not a actual Plesiosaur (for the obvious reasons mentioned in the article). I would also like to make a comment on the statement that *"In all the thousands of sightings, not one describes Nessie plucking a bird from the air in midflight"*. Let me start by saying it is very dangerous to be so certain about this as I wonder if Mr.Leadbetter actually read all these thousands of sightings. Personally I still wonder if there are thousands of sightings. In the 15 years that I am working on the subject, I have been able to contact "only" 1300 (a slowly growing number has some books still have to be worked on) sightings from some 150 books, 700 newspaper clippings, some videos and some tapes. I am sure that that's not all of them but I never heard of someone actualy having/showing a larger collection. Another point that I would like to make is that there is a sighting, if my recollection is right, where a Nessie was in Inchnacardoch bay but I would have to check all my material to be certain and that takes quite a lot of time and I dont think it realy that important.
Keep up the good work.
yours faithfully,

Martien Mannetje, The Netherlands.

More letters on the subject of Loch Ness, both for and against the theories propounded by Stuart Leadbetter will be found in the letters page of the next issue.

In brief..

We received several letters about the mysterious creatures of Lake Niu Gini in Papua New Guinea as mentioned last issue. These letters were not submitted for publication so we shall not quote them verbatim. Mike Grayson of London drew our attention to *Heuvelmans' 'Annotated Checklist of Apparently Unknown Animals' (1986)*, which mentions 'Migo' a giant crocodile described by W.T Neill in 1956. Mike suggested that although as pointed out by Karl Shuker during his talk at Unconvention 1994, the vertical undulations of the spine observed in 'Migau', suggest a mammalian. identity (Roy Mackal suggests a Zeuglodon), in his opinion *"the rather uncertain food supply of the fish free lake...would better maintain the metabolism of a cold blooded reptile"*. Dr Heuvelmans wrote to us including a copy of the original 1956 reference, and suggested that as the vertical spinal undulations made a mammalian identity certain, a possible identity was his own 'many humped' beast described in *'In the wake...'*. Me? I'm staying out of it until I see the video

THE A-Z OF CRYPTOZOOLOGY

Part Three by Jan Williams

BOOAA; Huge hyena-like beast of West Africa, whose name comes from its screaming cry.

BOOBRIE; Legendary giant water bird of Argyllshire lochs, Scotland.

BRUCKEE; Plantigrade water monster, said to live in Lough Shandagan, Ireland.

BUNYIP; A 'catch all' term for various Australian mystery beasts and 'Bogey Men'. Where as in Cryptozoology it is usually used to describe various large aquatic and semi aquatic denizens of marshes and lakes all over the continent, (the two most familiar are a long necked 'Nessie' type creaturew and another large animal which is most probably either a freshwater seal or less convincingly a large freshwater Sirenian), the term 'Bunyip' in popular parlance in Australia and New Zealand is used to describe any unknown 'bogey man' figure only generally believed in by children and unsophisticated adults.

A Childrens Television programme called 'Bunyip' which was screened in the late 1980s featured the adventures of a sub ET type creature with mildly entertaining psi powers stranded on earth (actually a mddle class Melbourne housing Estate populated by 'cute kids') after its flying saucer had broken down.

BURU; Aquatic animal which once lived in the valley of the Apa Tanis in the eastern Himalayas, and may still exist in the Rilo Valley. Thick-bodied, with a long and powerful tail and extended flat-tipped snout, the Buru reached a length of up to 13.5 feet. They had long forked tongues, four stumpy limbs, and a fish-like skin with 3 bony plates on the head and rows of spines along the back and sides.

In winter, the Burus disappeared into the mud at the bottom of the swamp and in summer sometimes crawled onto the banks to bask in the sun. They occasionally gave a loud bellowing call, which may be the origin of the name.

NERVOUS TWITCH

more tales of the wild, the wonderful and the downright wierd from the world of Ornithology.

POLLY WANTS A WEE DRAM SQUAWK!!!

I recently received an amusing story from our roving Scottish reporter, of a somewhat unusual advertising campaign, in 19th century Edinburgh. It seems a firm called Pattison and co.(Whisky blenders and brokers) decided to promote their product using parrots! They acquired several hundred African Grey parrots and spent many hours teaching them to say *"Drink Pattisons Whisky"*. The birds were then handed around to the pubs and bars in the area to pass on their message. Things went a little awry, however,when many of them escaped, and took to the rooftops of Edinburgh, still frantically urging people, years later, to *"Drink Pattisons Whisky! "* Beats T.V commercials any day!
(Edinburgh Evening News 8.6.94.)

SCOTTISH GUINEA FOWL

Guinea Fowl are reputed to be roaming the wilds of Angus, in Scotland, after game dealers brought them in to diversify their trade. Some birds escaped and are believed to have bred in the wild. Guinea Fowl originate from the grasslands of Africa, but have long been domesticated. In the wild they live in very large flocks, and although mostly ground dwelling, roost in trees. They can be recognised by the bright scarlet patch on their heads. *(14.5.94)*

QUACK!!!

A pair of Merganser ducks living on the Exe Estuary, in Devon, have bred this year and produced a family. These ducks are hardly ever seen south of Yorkshire in the U.K. Also seen recently on The Exe was a large Black Swan. Australian. Black Swans have been kepy for many years in Dawlish, some fifteen miles away but the bird seen several times over the summer appeared to have a white beak rather tham the red one more usually associated with the Australian species. One of the witnesses was in fact the Editor of this magazine who vouches for the fact that in other respects the bird seemed identical to the Dawlish birds. Here it should perhaps be noted that the British Black Swan itself is a mythical heraldic beast with slightly unpleasant undertones. The swan in any case is the embodiement of lies and falsehood because although its feathers are snowy white its skin and flesh are black, the allegorical meaning of an all black swan is therefore more than a little disturbing!
(Exeter Express and Echo 14.10.94)

SOME FOLK ARE SOOOO GULLIBLE!

A young man was travelling along the road on his motorbike, in Tuscany, recently when he was unexpectedly attacked. However, it was not by muggers or thieves as you might think, but by seagulls! A flock of approximately 100 of them flew up from the ground and assaulted him violently, knocking him off his bike. They then continued to peck at him as he lay on the road. One bird died in the scuffle, and the young man was taken to hospital where he was treated for cuts and bruises. *(Daily Telegraph 28.6.94)*

A WHITER SHADE OF PALE..

A very rare albino cormorant was seen and photographed in the Forth Estuary during July this year. Many species of birds have albino mutations occasionally, but this is extremely rare in cormarants. (about 1 in 50,000). This bird has been seen regularly on the rocks known as the Haystacks, off Inchcolm, and has been seen flying in with nesting material. Twitchers are hoping that it will breed. If it does, its offspring are likely to be a mixture of albino, mottled and normal black coloured. An albino puffin has also been recorded in the same area in the past. *(Edinburgh evening News 15.7.94)*

BLOWING IN THE WIND..

In the Isles of Scilly a Yellow Browed Bunting, blown off course from Asia, caused quite a stir. This species has only been seen in Britain 3 times before. Another rare visitor, the Red Flanked Bluetail, was also seen this week, in Norfolk. *(BBC.Ceefax Newsround 20.10.94)*

TO WIT TO WOO

Controversy is raging at the moment in the owl keeping world. The Baytree Owl Centre, at Weston, near Spalding, has managed to breed a South American Burrowing Owl with a Little Owl. This has angered some bird keepers, and also the World Owl Trust, who consider this to be irresponsible, and liable to endanger the species by dilution. However, this was not a deliberate breeding attempt. It was the birds who took the initiative. The two species were housed together in a large aviary at the centre, and for some reason a male Burrowing Owl ejected his own female, and took a female Little Owl as his mate. To everyones surprise she nested underground, contrary to the Little Owls usual habit of nesting in holes in trees, and successfully reared a youngster. Nobody is quite sure why this happened. Maybe it was love at first flight! *(Cage and Aviary Birds 3.9.94, 15.10.94.)*

I would just like to mention the 10th Anniversary Psychic Questing Conference on the 5th and 6th November, at Conway hall in London. With speakers such as Doc Shiels, and many interesting and diverse lectures, for only 10.00 a day it represents very good value. Go along and give them your support. We'll certainly be there! (PROBABLY IN THE BAR...ED)

HELP

This is the part of the magazine where we attempt to answer your queries, help with your research work and appeal for assistance with our various projects...............

It is always nice to be able to givesome Answers for a change, and this issue due to the kind services of Sally Parsons and Karl Shuker I am able to give some information asked in our first issue six months ago by our good friend and Spanish Representative, ALBERTO LOPEZ ACHA. He asked about the animal that then, was the most exciting discovery in mammalology for fifty years. As can be seen from our news pages this issue and elsewhere mammalologists especially in Vietnam are suffering from the most acute forms of Ennui suffered by anyone since Darwin, (one can just imagine him sitting in his cabin on The Beagle yawning *'Oh Lord not ANOTHER new species!'*) but by anyone's standards the Vu Quang Ox *(Pseudoryx nghetinhensis)* is a remarkable discovery.

Vu Quang is an almost forgotten area, a tiny strip which runs along the border between the old North Vietnam and Laos. It has only been inhabited for about sixty years. The first inhabitants were Vietnames refugees running away from the French who, although the area was nominally a French colony, never colonised or even explored the place. The Americans didn't bother to bomb it and didn't even spray the ancient trees with napalm or Agent Orange, and perhaps therefore it is not that suprising that this ancient and remote area still harbours some secret residents.

The first thing that anyone in the west heard about the animal which is known to the Vietnamese natives as 'son duong' or 'mountain goat', was in the summer and autumn of 1992 when Dr John MacKinnon, the Senior Conservation Officer of the WWF was pictured in Time Magazine and in The WWF News brandishing two impressive pairs of bovine horns at a press conference to announce that a recent expedition that he had lead to Vu Quang had discovered a new species of fish, a new species of box turtle, a new subspecies of sunbird, and most excitingly evidence of what they believed was going to turn out to be a new species of mammal. At this stage noone was sure what this creature would turn out to be. The expedition had not actually seen one but had obtained their specimens from the local hunters who, as is always the way, were perfectly familiar with the beast.

A year later Dr MacKinnon and a Vietnamese scientist with the marvellous name of Vu Van Dung obtained the first complete carcass and, as BBC Wildlife announced in July 1993 the "mystery Vietnamese horns gained head and legs", and so the taxonomy of this suprisingly large cryptid was at last no longer a matter for speculation.

The story was still not over however because at that time noone had managed to photograph or capture one. In July this year, however a young female looking distressingly cute and Disneyesque was captured and photographed. I believe, but have no references that soon after a young male was also captured and that the two animals were moved to a place of safety where their keepers hope that they will breed as prolifically as other bovids, but this, for the moment at least remains to be seen.

HELP

IF MUSIC BE THE FOOD OF CRYPTOZOOLOGY...

Much to his great glee, (and to the chagrin of all the other bibliophiles in the Crypto world who have heard about it), Dr Karl Shuker recently managed to buy a copy of the sheet music for the semi legendary "Ogopogo: The funny Foxtrot" as featured in practically every book ever written about lake monsters. Interestingly enough it proves that the snatch of lyric quoted in most of these books about the legendary beast having 'a little bitty tail', is completely wrong and the lyric actually says 'I want to put a little bit of salt on his tail'. This provoked a question from both Dr S and the Editor. about other pieces of cryptozoological music. There's 'Puff the Magic Dragon' of course. Karl vaguely remembers a B side of a single on 'Manticore Records' (seems appropriate) called 'Bigfoot' and the Editor has similarly vague memories of a Canadian heavy rock band called 'Sasquatch', and of course there was a folk group called 'The Yetties' but does anyone know any more? It is reasonably well known that the Father of Cryptozoology himself was once a Jazz musician, and the legendary 'Doc' Shiels has been known both to sing and tinkle the ivories from time to time. I will ignore Karl's wonderfully bizarre suggestion that we team them up to record a selection of songs about unknown creatures under the name 'The Crypto Concerto', and will move on to the next subject only pausing to answer one last musical query from Tim from Brighton who asked about the name of the magazine. The answer, sir,is track four side two of an LP called 'Dirk wears White Sox' by 'Adam and the Ants', and previous to that an art exhibition in about 1930 by (I think) an Italian Futurist Painter.

CRABS, WARTHOGS AND MAMMOTHS!

Sally Parsons who has cropped up more than once this issue, is after bits of warthog or thylacine for her own collection but also wants to get in touch with anyone who has kept any species of land or freshwater hermit crab as a pet apart from Coenabita clypeatus. She is also interested in recent research about the possible survival of mammoth species in what used to be Soviet Central Asia.

MY SISTER IN LAW AND OTHER ANIMALS

My sister in law, Sian who has the dreadfully antisocial fixation with livestock which has infected most of my family wants any information on a very small armadillo, probably called 'The Fairy Armadillo'. She has searched everywhere for information and this is the last court of appeal!

HOW YOU CAN HELP THE CENTRE FOR FORTEAN ZOOLOGY

We are still looking for exhibits for our museum. This summer we have narrowly missed being able to buy the pub sign from the legendary 'Black Dog' at Uplyme from Palmer's Brewery, and several other items of interest have eluded us, although our collection of cuttings, books and general odds and sods has got bigger and bigger. Please keep on sending them in. If you want to be a regional representative please contact us. We have a fact sheet for people who are interested. We are always interested in purchasing live specimens of the larger aquatic turtles and salamanders as well as any books, cuttings, video or museum material on the wildlife of Hong Kong. If you have any of 'Doc' Shiels's other books apart from 'Monstrum' please let us know (even Doc doesn't have some of them).. Generally, to misquote the words at the base of the Statue of Liberty. Send us your clippings..send us your tat and we shall make great use of it.

BOOK REVIEWS

DEAREST PET:On Bestiality by Midas Dekkers (Verso)

This is one of those unfortunate pieces of work when a (presumably) well known author attempts to use asalacious or shocking format in order to sell a relatively innocuous book dealing with a far less outrageous subject. In this case the real subject-the breakdown of barriers between man and beast, which covers such undoubtedly fortean subjects as feral children, Kaspar Hauser syndrome and circus 'freaks' is dressed up as socially aware pornography in order to line the pockets of a rather dull dutchman who peers out from the back of the dustjacket like a chimeric cross between a vacuum cleaner salesman and a Butlins Redcoat. The book is too revolting to be erotic, too analytical to be pornographic, too lighthearted to be studious and too dull to be entertaining. It is very difficult to see what the point is. All the way through one is expecting a punchline of some sort but it never arrives. The print quality is mediocre and the design, whilst mildly pleasant is extremely unimaginative. I would sincerely encourage everyone to leave this rather nasty publication well alone. If you must buy it wait six months because it will be remaindered everywhere for about 99p, which is really all that it is worth.

YOU'LL NEVER BELIEVE IT by Mark Sloan, Roger Manley and Michelle Van Parys (Virgin)

This is a well compiled collection of photographs from the collection of Robert Ripley, the quasi fortean (with a small F) whose syndicated newspaper column 'Believe it or Not', not only set many an earnest young fortean on his way but also spawned a minor industry. Unfortunately from the point of view of this magazine there is very little of relevance inside it and although photographs of contortionists, strongmen and young women with ridiculous tattoos are very entertaining, I am very glad that I didn't actually pay for my copy.

PERIODICALS

We welcome an exchange of periodicals with magazines of mutual interest

BIGFOOT RECORD, Bill Green, c/o The Bigfoot Centre, 21 Benham St, Apartment F, Bristol, CT06010 USA This free news service for bigfoot buffs is bi-monthly and has a refreshingly informal style

DRAGON CHRONICLE, The dragon trust, PO Box 3369, London SW6 6JN. A fascinating collection of all things draconian which appears three times a year

NEXUS 55 Queens Rd, E Grinstead, W Sussex RH19 1BG Intelligent look at the fringes of science. Well put together.

NESSLETTER Rip Hepple, 7 Huntshieldford, St Johns Chapel, Bishop Auckland Co Durham DL13 1RQ. Rip Hepple is a genuine original. This magazine has been appearing regularly for many years and cannot be reccomended highly enough.

CREATURE RESEARCH JOURNAL, Paul Johnson, 721 Old Greensberg Pike, N Versailles, PA15137 USA. An intelligent look at the interface between Cryptozoology and UFO research.

TRACK RECORD, Bigfoot Research Project, PO Box 126, Mt Hood, Oregon 97041USA. Excellent for anyone with even the most passing interest in North American Manimals.

DELVE, Gene Duplantier, 17 Shetland St, Willowdale, Ontario, Canada M2M 1X5. Intriguing and eccentric collection of forteana and general oddness.

BIPEDIA, Francois de Saare, CERBI, BP65, 06202, NICE, CEDEX 3, FRANCE. A magazinbe about Initial Bipedalism, scholarly and concise.

TEMS NEWS, 115 Hollybush Lane, Hampton, Middlesex, TW12 2QY. An engaging collection of quasi fortean odds and ends from veteran UFO buff Lionel Beer, who also runs Spacelink books and is compiling a Crypto booklist.

TOUCHSTONE and PEGASUS, Jimmy Goddard, 25 Albert Rd, Addlestone, Surrey two neat UFO/Fortean mags. Well produced and collated.

THE CRYPTO CHRONICLE, 50Green Lane, Worcester. General Crypto Mag with a bigfoot bias.

ANIMALS, Freepost Sidcup, Kent. The magazine of the British Zoos Supporters Club. Highly reccomended.

FROM OUR FILES

This issue we take a trawl through the files of the Western Bigfoot Society for some recent BHM sightings.

1. Raynold Furrell was hiking in late August 1994 in the Mt Washington wilderness area in Oregon. He parked on Hy242 near the Dee Wright Observatory in McKenzie Pass and hiked north on the Cascade Crest Trail about 20 miles (T14SR8E), and was off the lightly forested trail when he and his companions noticed a particularly foul smell. He said it might have been a bear but wasn't sure and called the WBS. A wildlife expert says bears are known to roll in offal the same as a dog will roll on something dead to cover its scent.

2. On 19.9.94 Tex Occanaa was camped at Hilsome-Sanyo camp near Baldwin Mountain NE of San Bernadino Ca when a Bigfoot was sighted between 20.30 and 21.00 hours. The creature was glimpsed in the camp ground lights and ran away in a loping fashion after seeing Tex. The 7 foot creature turned and grinned/grimaced at Tex displaying fangs. It had long arms proportional to its body, brown shaggy hair and a bad smell putrid or sulphurous. There was howling in the woods. Tex notified a park ranger.

3. An unnamed naturalist/geologist was hiking at 10.30 AMbetween Polallie Camp and Surveyors Ridge east of Mt Hood, Oregon, The trail was dusty and a light rain overnight had settled and smoothed the dust. Animal and game tracks were common and there were no other human tracks. He studied them and came across a single barefoot human print in the trail as if it had crossed near a big tree. Later he heard noises of something large in the undergrowth and felt he was being watched. On his way back he noticed a heavy sweet sour odour. The print was 14" x 5.5", the big toe was 2.5" long.

Issue IV
January 1995

Issue IV January 1995

This was the issue which was the precursor to our first great coup. We were the first people in the west to get hold of a copy of the infamous Migo video which purported to show a lake monster swimming in Lake Dakataua on the island of New Britain in the Bismarck Archipelago. As events turned out it actually showed a pair of copulating crocodiles, but we were the first people to print that as well so I guess we can be forgiven.

I have to admit that I was highly impressed by my initial sightings of the video, and I defended it for some time until Darren Naish pointed out some tell tale signs about the morphology of the creature. This issue also included a fascinating piece by Dr Karl Shuker, a hero of mine who, I am happy to say has since become a friend. Indeed at the time I felt that I was somewhat of a fraud – that my cryptozoological reputation was really because I was a mate of both Karl Shuker and Doc Shiels rather than because of any intrinsically valuable work I had done off my own bat.

I'm glad to say that I think I have rectified this over the years......

Animals & Men

The Journal of the Centre for Fortean Zoology

Issue Four

January 1995

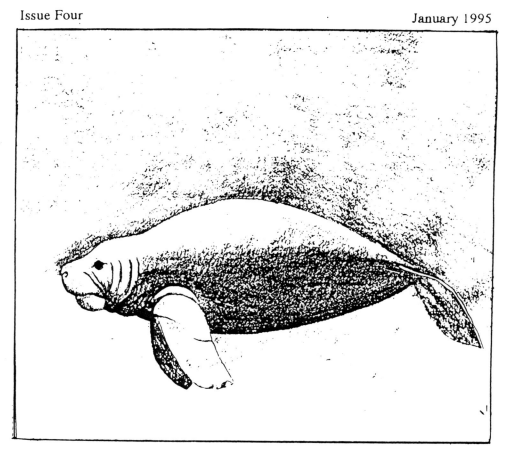

Mystery Manatees of St. Helena,
The Thylacine; The cryptid most likely to..
Lake Monsters of New Britain

CONTENTS AND CREDITS

This issue of Animals & Men was put together by the following band of Animals and Men:

Jonathan Downes: Editor and Fall Guy.
Jan Williams: Newsfile and Catfish.
Alison Downes: Ornithological Administratrix.
Lisa Peach: Cover Art.
Jane Bradley: Cartoons.
John Jacques: Sole Representation.
Graham Inglis: Video.
Dave Symons: Software jockey
Nigel Smith: "SHUT UP NIGEL!"

Contributors this issue:

Alan Pringle, Dr Karl P.N.Shuker,
Dr Lars Thomas, Paul Nathan, G.M.Stocker,
R.A.Carter, Stephen Nice

Regional Representatives

LANCASHIRE: Stuart Leadbetter.
SUSSEX: Sally Parsons.
CUMBRIA AND LAKELANDS: Brian Goodwin.
HOME COUNTIES: Phillip Kibberd.
EIRE Co Clare: Richard Muirhead.
SPAIN: Alberto Lopez Acha.
FRANCE: Francois de Saare.
MEXICO: Dr R.A Palmeros.

Advertising Rates by arrangement.

The Centre for Fortean Zoology
15 Holne Court
Exwick, Exeter.
Devon EX4 2NA

0392 424811
Special thanks this issue to:

Bernard Heuvelmans, Janet Bord, Tony 'Doc'
Shiels (Buy the record), Dr Karl P.N.Shuker.

SUBSCRIPTION RATES

'Animals and Men' appears four times a year in October, January, April and July. A four issue subscription costs:

£.600 UK/Eire
£ 7.00 EEC
£7.50 Europe non EEC
£9.00 OZ NZ USA Canada (Surface Mail)
£12.00 OZ NZ USA Canada (Air Mail)
£10.00 Rest of World (surface mail)
£12.00 Rest of World (Air Mail)

Cheques in Sterling or IMO or Eurocheque payable to A&J Downes.

CONTENTS

Animals and Men is compiled and typeset by Jonathan Downes on an Amiga A500 using Penpal 3.1 and Pagesetter 2 and I want a PC486 Someone please..

if you want to know more about the monster then you really must buy the record..
'what do you mean right mind?'

THE GREAT DAYS OF ZOOLOGY ARE NOT DONE

Dear Readers,

This has been a momentous year for us at the Centre for Fortean Zoology, and as I write this the year is only thirteen days old. Yesterday the government announced that they are holding an official enquiry into the British Mystery Cats. We would love to take the responsibility for this after Jan's article in the last issue but unfortunately we think that it is highly unlikely that it has anything to do with us at all..but we can still daydream!

The investigation is being chaired by Junior Agriculture Minister Angela Browning M.P and as I write this Alison is downstairs on the telephone with Ms Browning's Private Secretary, so although we may not have been in at the start of this affair it looks likely that we are just about to enter the fray.

Recently I did a radio phone in show on the subject of mystery beasts on the newly set up Gemini A.M Radio Station. It was hosted by a delightfully eccentric Australian D.J called Steve Browning (no relation), and it was actually quite a success. Hopefully we might repeat the experiment sometime.

In conjunction with the Devon County Council Adult Education Department I am presenting a series of three saturday morning 'Summer School' lectures on Cryptozoology in Exeter over the summer, and assuming that these are a success I shall be teaching a ten week course entitled 'Men, Myths and Monsters in the Modern World' during the autumn. More details of my ventures into the sacred groves of academe in the next issue.

Finally. We are not the easiest people to get hold of especially during the summer months, so for all of you who have tried, but failed to telephone us we now have a 24 hour 'sightings hotline', for people who see anything odd within the world of animals, or people who have specimens for us (and we still want a skull from one of those large grey 'hill foxes'), or if you just want to leave a message for us telephone: 0881 106094 and leave a message. We will get back to you within a couple of days.

See you next time,
Best wishes,

EDITOR

NEWSFILE

EDITED BY JAN WILLIAMS
With the odd interjection from The Editor

HOLY GOAT PHOTOGRAPHED

We return yet again to Vietnam, current hotbed of cryptozoological discovery, with news of the capture of a *Linh duong* or *holy goat*, previously known only from antlers *(see issue 3)*. Sadly, the animal died in captivity, but photographs are exciting interest, and its remains may yield further information. *(BBC Ceefax 4.1.95)*

WILD MAN EXPEDITION

China's National Academy of Science are planning an expedition in search of Wildmen in March of this year. The plan follows a sighting by 10 engineers and senior railway administrators of a 'Wild Man family' on a little used road in the Shennongjia Mountains on 9th September 1993. *(Daily Mail 26.12.94)*

MULTIPLYING MUNTJACS

Farmers and Forestry Commission rangers are expressing concern at the rapid increase in numbers of Muntjac deer in Britain. The deer were first introduced by the Duke of Bedford in the late 19th century. Current estimates suggest the population has increased to around 200,000, and muntjac are moving into densely populated areas like Birmingham, Coventry, Derby, Wolverhampton, and Central London. They are accused of causing thousands of pounds worth of damage to trees and crops and decimating woodland wildflowers. *(Sunday Times 20.11.94)*

SUPER DADDY LONGLEGS

A large and hungry strain of leatherjacket - larva of the Crane Fly - is devouring cereal crops in the Scottish Highlands. The life cycle differs from that of the normal crane fly, causing the leatherjackets to appear at the same time as the young wheat shoots on which they feed. Research is in progress at the Scottish Agricultural College, Aberdeen, where entomologist Geoff Armstrong says the new type seems to correspond to the increase in popularity of Oil Seed Rape.(Daily Mail 14.11.94)

NO HOPPER

A wandering wallaby died after being hit by a car on a road near Teignmouth, Devon in August. *(Sunday Mirror 21.8.94)*

IN THE PINK

Stratford Butterfly Farm, Warwickshire, are breeding Cabbage White Butterflies in various shades of pink. Manager John Calvert said the colour appeared to be a natural mutation. The caterpillars are a normal green-yellow colour, but the chrysalis is a deep reddish-pink instead of greenish-white.*(Independent on Sunday 30.10.94)*

MYSTERY CATS

Hertfordshire

Snow Leopards are rare in their normal high mountain territory in Central Asia. and even less common in commuter villages beside the A1 motorway, so the one which loped through Welwyn on 29th November caused some surprise to villagers.

Armed police were called out to track down 16-month-old Tara, who had forced her way out of a cage at a private reserve. Tara lived up to the species' reputation for being easily captured. She took refuge in a tree in nearby woodland and was shot with a tranquilliser dart before being netted and returned to the reserve.*(Daily Mail 30.11.94, BBC Teletext 29.11.94)*

Kent

A photograph of a large cat in a ploughed field near Ashley, taken by investigator Dave Riches. was printed in the East Kent Mercury on 24th November. The photo shows an adult black cat with large ears and a long tail. and is one of several taken by Dave, some of which show the adult cat with a smaller grey cub. *(East Kent Mercury 24.11.94, 27.11.94)*

Staffordshire

A huge black cat, 5 feet long and 3 feet high, was seen by a driver at Stretton near Wolverhampton in early December. Stretton lies a couple of miles to the north of Gifford's Cross, which marks the spot where Sir John Gifford of Chillington Hall killed an escapee panther in the 16th Century.*(? Wolverhampton Express & Star 7.12.94)*

Norfolk

A 'very muscular' black cat, the size of a Labrador dog. was seen 4on two separate occasions walking through fields in South Norfolk. The fields contained cows. calves. horses, and foals, and witnesses stated the livestock seemed totally unconcerned by the animal.

Something attacked an aviary in the same area. and took two pheasants and a pigeon. Mesh netting was torn out of the ground, and the lower part ripped to shreds. A piece of the netting supplied to me shows what appear to be paired fang marks. with a gap measuring 4 inches between the two teeth.

Cornwall

Reports of livestock attacks continue on Bodmin Moor. where farmer John Goodenough has now erected signs saying *'Danger: Big Wild Cats - Keep Off'*. Further south in the county, landlady Jane Wilson and 3 guests at The Old Quay Inn, Devoran, near Truro, reported a large black cat loping rapidly across fields near dense woodland in August. In the same month a large grey cat like animal was seen by three witnesses at Pendeen, near St Just. Dr Arnold Derrington and his wife Helen described the animal as 'fluffy', with short legs, a light coloured chest, long tail, and ears 'almost as big as hare ears'. It ran away in leaps and bounds. *(Daily Mail 31.12.94, West Briton 1.9.94, Cornishman 18.8.94)*

JUMPING JELLYFISH

Strange. inexplicable blobs of a jelly like substance have fallen from the sky during a rain shower in Oakville, Washington State, USA. One suggestion is that these are the remains of a school of jellyfish which have 'blown literally sky high'. After the first blob shower three people who had come into contact with the mystery substance complained of bouts of nausea and dizzyness, (one was so ill that she was hospitalized), and a small kitten that came into contact with the material from the second fall died nine days later after a struggle with severe intestinal problems. This news item is included. not only because of the suggestion that these mystery objects were jellyfish, (creature falls are well within our sphere of interest), but because we are also collecting data on the possible causes of the mass and usually inexplicable animal deaths which happen intermittently across the world, and what could kill a kitten in the Pacific North West today....*Seattle Post Intelligencer* via COUDi 18.8.94

BAAL IN SILENCE DINES ON VULTURE SOUP

In scenes reminiscent both of the Hitchcock movie *'The Birds'* and more disturbingly of the events in nearby West Virginia during 1967 recounted by John Keel in *'The Mothman Prophecies'*.Stafford County, Virginia is haunted by a plague of *'Black Vultures'* which have begun to prey on household pets and domestic livestock to an alarming degree. The usual *'concerned citizens'* are muttering about children being carried off by these impressively unpleasant raptors, but as far as we are aware no-one has been abducted..YET! This is a little surprising as the species referred to in the report, which is presumably *Coragyps atratus* only reaches a length of 58-9 cm, while the only other species usually found in the vicinity *Cathartes aura* is only marginally different. It is hard to imagine that people in the area would get so hysterical over such reasonably sized creatures and one is tempted to wonder whether the *'big birds'* that used to be such a familiar feature of the cryptofauna of the area during the fifties, sixties and seventies have made some kind of a comeback? *The Columbus Despatch 20.2.1994 via COUDi*

By the way, for no reason at all the first person to tell the editor who wrote the above snatch of lyric, and from which play it was taken will get an unspecified prize.

HERE KITTY KITTY (1)

When a 65lb Western Cougar wandered into Delores Slappy's back yard in suburban Miami she corralled it like any other pet, grabbing its collar, putting a leash on her and shoving her unceremoniously into a dog pen. The newspaper report goes on to say that these animals are fairly common pets in Florida, but that they require licenses and cages. What the report does not say is that Florida is one of the last bastions of the Eastern Cougar, where about a dozen live in The Everglades, which (British Mystery Cat buffs will be thrilled to know) is one of the only two places within the range of Felis concolor where BLACK pumas have been reported. If escapee pets are a regular occurrence then this, possibly the rarest cat subspecies in North America could be doomed because of genetic dilution if not for more conventional reasons. *St Louis Post Dispatch 20.7.94 Via COUDi*

REST IN PEACE

The two captive specimens of the Vu Quang Ox (which our Eastbourne rep insists on referring to as 'the Voo Moo') have died in apparently unconnected illnesses effectively putting paid to the idea of a captive breeding programme..for the moment at least. *St Louis Post Despatch via COUD' 10.10.94*

HERE KITTY KITTY (2)

The best headline we have received lately is from the St Louis Post Despatch (which as regular readers will notice is rapidly becoming essential reading for those in search of strange Cougar stories. Again it comes to us via those awfully nice people at COUDi, and it reads: WOMAN SLAYS PUMA WITH BREAD KNIFE IN BRAWL; COLLIE, 2 CAMPERS INJURED. It is self explanatory so we won't bother to print the story itself.

THE BEAR NECESSITIES

A 760lb (334kg) giant black bear struck and killed by a tractor-trailer in North Ontario may well be the biggest specimen of its species ever taken in North America. *The Toronto Star 16.9.93*

SPIDERMAN STRIKES AGAIN.

I love stupid and pointless stories. Clayton County police arrested a man found lying on the pavement behind a shopping centre at 'high noon' with a five gallon bucket of large spiders beside him. When he finally spoke to police officers he refused to tell the police who he was or why he had the spiders with him so he was arrested and charged with loitering and obstructing an officer. *The Atlanta Journal 4.9.94 Via COUDi.* Even this isn't't as stupid as the story in the same issue of the same newspaper of the woman dressed as a chicken who threw a pie at C&W singer Kenny Rogers in protest against him setting up a chain of roast chicken restaurants. If it had been in protest against him making awful records it would have made far more sense. By the way it is the Editor who put in this an someof the other sillier inclusions in this Newsfile so don't blame Mrs W honest!!

LOOK AT THAT 'S' CAR GO!!!

Tiny snails not seen for 140 years have been found in a Devon river. The smooth Rams Horn Snail was first spotted in the River Leat 1850 by a Miss Bolton, and has now been rediscovered by her namesake David Bolton from the Albert Memorial Museum in Exeter. *C3 Teletext Westcountry News 13.10.94*

WHALE MEAT AGAIN

A Pod consisting of two large killer whales and twelve smaller ones followed the body of one of their number who had died at sea, and swam too near the land whereupon it seems that eight of them were washed ashore on Uist, the most northerly of the Shetland Islands. Seven of them were saved by islanders who physically pushed them back out to sea. The same day, twelve Sperm Whales were beached during a force eight gale on the Orkney Island of Sandaybut because of their enormous bulk there was nothing that the islanders could do to save them. *The Times 8.12.94 Teletext Greennews C4 8.12.94.*

YOU DIRTY STINKING RAT

Port Health inspectors from Weymouth to Lerwick are reporting that Russian Trawlers are infested with Black rats, prompting fears that this species may become common in Britain again for the first time in hundreds of years since its place in the ecosystem was taken over by the Brown Rat. In the same report the BBC stated that 4% of properties in London, 8% in North Wales and 16% in Eastern England were now infected. *Greennews C4 Teletext Nov 16th 1994.*

THE MONSTER MASHED

Various newspapers reported that after a strong gale near Murmansk in the Russian Arctic. a mysterious corpse was washed ashore on or about the 26th October 1994. The corpse was described as a Russian 'Nessie',, and was about twelve metres long, one and a half metres wide and covered with 'feathers' or fur. It was this last point that gave away its identity, because whereas, as most cryptofolk now know the decomposing remains of one of the large Selachians, (usually a Basking Shark), can be distorted by wave action into the familiar form of a 'nessieform' long necked sea creature, decomposing whale blubber, in salt water and especially in near zero temperatures has a disconcerting habit of turning into feathery wisps, and despitethe interest shown by the Institute of Marine Biology in Murmansk, who announced that they were sending a team to investigate the corpse most of us at Crypto Mansions assumed that it would turn out to be a dead whale, probably a Sperm Whale...and you know what?   We were right! *Westfalenpost Oct 26th 1994 and October 28th 1994.*

TWO HEADS ARE BETTER THAN ONE

In the last issue we promised that we would print more details and a photograph of the two headed grass snake that was recently found in Sussex. Unfortunately the grass snake now has a press agent who wants to charge twenty quid for each photo and presumably even more for an interview with the people who own it. This is beyond our meagre budget and is somewhat against my principles (didn't even pay when I interviewed Led Zeppelin-Ed) and therefore we have regretfully had to pass. However as a sort of a consolatio prize we can tell you that a number of newspapers including the German publication Die Welt (6.10.94) reported the existance of a healthy five month old terrapin (either a painted turtle or a Red Eared) with two heads. This unusual beast is residing somewhere in Taiwan.

Newsfile Correspondents: Phil Bennett, Frank Durham, Lorna Lloyd, Diane Jones, Steven Shipp, Heather Thurgar, B Williams, RAJ Williams, COUDi,   Wolfgang Schmidt, Sally Parsons, Jane Bradley

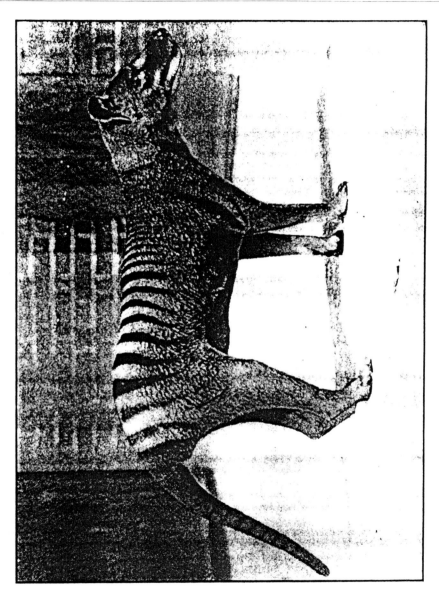

Picture Copyright Fortean Picture Library

The Thylacine
The liveliest extinct animal around!
by Alan Pringle

Imagine the scene. In 1982. a Tasmanian wildlife officer. Hans Naarding. is surveying birds in a remote part of North-West Tasmania. At two o'clock one morning he awakes from a fitful sleep in his vehicle. As always on such occasions, he switches on his spotlight in order to scan the surrounding area for any passing, nocturnal wildlife. What he sees is something that most of us can only dream about, for there, caught in the beam, is a fully grown Thylacine. For three spellbound minutes Naarding has a clear view of an animal declared 'probably extinct', in 1936! This exciting encounter is by no means unique and is only one of a growing number of sightings being made in Tasmania, and, more controversially, on mainland Australia and even in New Guinea.

The Thylacine. Tasmanian Wolf or Tasmanian Tiger (Thylacinus cynocephalus) is the largest known marsupial carnivore. Superficially dog like enough to explain the popular name, its most striking characteristic is the series of 15-20 dark brown. vertical stripes ranging down its back to the long. inflexible tail. Hence the name 'Tiger'. Other equally unusual names include 'Zebra Wolf', 'Wolf Opposum', 'Opposum Hyena', and 'Dog Faced Dasyurus'. A tireless pursuer of small mammal prey, Thylacines measure up to 160 cm in length, including a 50 cm. They are unique amongst marsupials in that the male has a rudimentary pouch, and they are also famous for their enormous gape, the largest of any mammal. They are known from fossil records to have existed on mainland australia over 3000 years ago and in Tasmania until the arrival of European settlers in the early 1800's. Persecuted as a sheep killer, they were systematically exterminated until the last wild one was shot in 1930. A captive specimen lived on at the now defunct Beaumaris Zoo in Hobart until September 7th 1936. About ninety Thylacines were held by Zoos between 1850 and 1936, but there are no records of any captive breeding.

Since 1936 there have been many expeditions to various parts of Tasmania in an attempt to determine whether or not the species survives. Using snares, live traps, automatic cameras and hours of patient observation in some of the world's most inhospitable terrain, these admirable groups of naturalists and trackers obtained no hard evidence although many tracks were found and hair and faecal samples collected.

Sightings have been steadily increasing, however, over the years, and many of us still believe that the animal is not lost. Because of the island's vast tracts of rugged mountains, temperate rain forests and steep river valleys very few people are ever IN the position to see one. The anglers, hikers and bushmen who do are usually. however the sort of experienced people who know what they are seeing. More often though, thylacines are fleetingly glimpsed in the headlights of vehicles traversing the island's lonely roads.

This happened in 1990 to two fishermen who were driving home through the Cradle Mountains in the north of the island. In the same year an adult with cub was seen not far from the same spot. One of the most recent sightings, in July 1993, involving an alleged Thylacine crossing a road witnessed by two motorists. This sighting. however. occurred in Western Australia, where the species is supposed to have died out thirty centuries ago! There have been some colour photographs taken in Western Australia although scientists are divided on their authenticity and the motives of the photographer.

The latest piece of the Thylacine jigsaw involves New Guinea. Like Australia, the Thylacine is known there only from fossil evidence. but recently one researcher has \received reports of Thylacine like animals known to the highland people of Irian-Jaya. The upland country there is similar to parts of Tasmania, but much less explored, and would provide ideal conditions for Thylacines. The people there seem to know the animal well and are NOT confusing it with wild or feral dogs.

With over a thousand sightings of this enigmatic animal SINCE its official demise in 1936, surely it will not be long until irrefutable proof, i.e good, clear, film is obtained. A dead animal would, no doubt satisfy the scientific community but with a species obviously as rare as this, they need to be left alive. as the population. although recovering, is still very valuable indeed.

Besides. the animal still has official protection in Tasmania because of a law passed in 1936 - ironically the same year that the last known Thylacine died!

•••••••••••••••••

Anyone wishing to correspond with the author or who can
offer ANY material on the Thylacine can do so c/o The Welsh
Mountain Zoo, Colwyn Bay, Clwyd.

REFERENCES

GUILER E: 'The Tasmanian Tiger in Pictures'.
MOELLER H: 'Bentelwolfe in Zoologischen Garten und Museen'.
SMITH S: 'The Tasmanian Tiger - 1980'.

Picture; Copyright The Fortean Picture Library

The Saga of the St. Helena Sirenians

By

Dr Karl P.N.Shuker

(This article was originally printed as part of a larger
piece on 'Mystery Ungulates' which originally appeared in
Strange Magazine. It is reprinted with the kind permission
of the author).

Those highly modified aquatic ungulates, the Sirenians are already well known to Cryptozoologists by virtue of the extensively documented (yet incompletely verified) claim that they are responsible for many of the Mermaid sightings reported from around the world. Other Sirenian claims upon the cryptozoologists attention involve the largest of all modern day species, the supposedly extinct Steller's Sea Cow (Hydromalis gigas), still survives, [1] , the exposure of the New Guinea ri as the Dugong (Dugong dugon), [2] ,the one time disputed existence of the Dugong in Chinese waters ,[3]. and the likelihood that an unidentified beast reported from various West African lakes, and another such creature from eastern South America's Lake Titicaca may comprise unknown species of sirenian. [4]. In addition there is the case presented here, not previously documented within cryptozoological literature.

There are three known species of modern day manatee. The Amazon Manatee (Trichechus inunguis), inhabits the estuaries of the Orinoco and The Amazon; the Caribbean Manatee (T.manatus) is distributed from the coasts of Virginia in the southeastern United States to the West Indies and the northern coasts of Brazil; and the African Manatee (T.senagalensis) frequents the coasts and rivers of West Africa from Senegal to Angola. At one time, however there were also persistent reports of putative manatees around the coasts of St Helena, a small island in the south Atlantic, almost equidistant from South America and Africa.

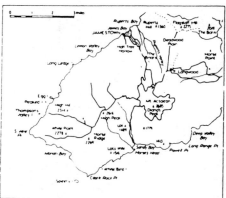

The Island of St. Helena.   JD

In view of the fact that there is a region on the southwestern coast of St Helena that is actually named Manatee Bay (sometimes spelled 'Manati'). one could be forgiven for assuming that there was never any uncertainty about these creatures identity, but in reality this entire matter has still to be resolved satisfactorily, remaining to this day one of the most vexing issues ever raised in relation to Sirenian systematics, as evinced by the following selection of reports and opinions.

As documented in an account by F.C.Frazer. [5] ,in 1655 Cornish traveller Peter Mundy journeyed to India on the *Aleppo Merchant*, and during his return voyage the following year on the same vessel he paid a brief visit to St.Helena. While walking along the beach near Chappell Valley he saw a strange creature lying ashore,

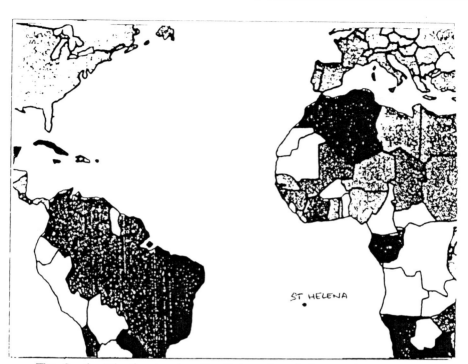

The South Atlantic showing St. Helena in relation to the manatee populations in West Africa, South America and The West Indies.

apparently severely injured. Mundy went nearer to examine it:

'However when I touched it, (it) raised its forepart, gaping on mee (sic) with his wide and terrible jawes (sic). It had the collour (sic) (yellowish) and terrible countenance of a lion, with four greatt (sic) teeth, besides smalle (sic), long, bigge (sic) smelling hairs or mustaches'

The creature attempted to make its way back to the sea but Mundy dispatched it with stones. It was evidently very large:

'..in length about ten foote (sic) and five foote (sic) about the middle. Some say it was a seale (sic), others notte (sic). I terme (sic) itt (sic) a scalionesse (sic), being a femail (sic)..'

In his journal Mundy included a sketch of this animal (reproduced in Fraser's account) which leaves no doubt that it was indeed a pinniped of some type. As uncovered by St Helena resident G.C.Kitching [6], the public records of Jamestown, (the islands capital) contain many allusions to alleged manatees or sea-cows (including what appears to be the first usage of the name 'Manatee Bay', which occurs on January 27th 1679). For example, one such record, for August 28th 1682, listed the capture of 'several sea cows', and on March 20th

1690, another record noted the following incident:

'Tuesday. Goodwin and Coales brought up for killing a sea cow and not paying the companies royalty. They desire pardon, and say the Sea Cow was very small; the oyls (sic) would not amount to above four or five gallons.'

On May 11th 1691, a record mentioned that a Sea Cow had appeared on shore at Windward, just a month before traveller William Dampier visited St Helena. Dampier became most intrigued by the alleged existence of manatees around the island's coasts:

'I was also informed that they get Manatee or Sea Cows here, which seems very strange to me. Therefore enquiring more strictly into the matter, I found the Santa Helena Manatee to be, by their shapes, and manner of lying ashore on the Rocks those creatures called Sea-lyons; for the Manatee never come ashore. Neither are they found near any rocky shores, as this island is, there being no feeding for them in such places. Besides, in this land there is no river for them to drink at, tho' there is a small brook runs into the Sea, out of the Valley by the Fort'.

Back to the records: On August 29th 1716, they reported that 400 pounds of Ambergris were found in Manatee Bay, and on September 11th 1739, ' A Sea Cow (was) killed upon Old Woman's valley beach, as it was lying asleep by Warrall and Greentree'.

John Barnes's 'A Tour through the island of St.Helena' (1817), contains a detailed account of these supposed sirenians as described by reliable observer and St Helena resident Lieut. Thomas Leech, who identified them as Sea Lions. [8]. Yet, in complete contrast, another equally reliable observer, Dr Walter Henry, just as confidently described them as manatees, stating:

'We had sea-cows at St Helena, the Trichechus Dugong, but they were not common. When shooting near Buttermilk Point with another officer one calm evening, we stumbled on one lying on a low rock close to the water's edge, and a hideous ugly brute it was, shaped like a young calf with bright green eyes as big as saucers. We only caught a glimpse of it for a few seconds, for as soon as it noticed us, it jumped into the sea, in the most awkward and sprawling manner' [9].

It will be noticed that Dr Henry couched his reference to these creatures' existence around St Helena in the past tense. This is because the last recorded appearance of such animals here took place in 1810 when one came ashore at Stone Top Valley beach, where it was shot by a Mr Burnham. It measured 7 ft. in length, and 10 gallons of oil were obtained from it. Another of these creatures was also reported in 1810, this time from Manatee Bay. [10].

Since then St.Helena's purported manatee appears to have been extinct, and as is so often the case it was only then that science began to take an interest in it. After reading an account of this creature in J.C.Mellis's 'St Helena: A Physical, Historical, and Topographical Description of the Island' (1875), in which Melliss claimed that it belonged either to the African or to the Caribbean species of manatee [11] on June 20th 1899, zoologist Dr Richard Lydekker published a short review of the subject [12] which included a number of the accounts given here. Although stating categorically that he did not wish to express a definite opinion concerning whether or not the animal could definitely be some form of sirenian, he nevertheless ventured to speculate that if this were indeed its identity then it probably comprised a distinct species, (perhaps even belonging to a separate genus), as he felt unable to believe that it belonged to either of the species nominated by Melliss. [13].

In 1933, the entire matter was the subject of an extensive examination by Dr Theodore Mortensen of Copenhagen's Zoological Museum. [14] After careful consideration of the varied and often conflicting reports that he had succeeded in gathering, Mortenson came out in support of the views of Mundy and Leech, that the St Helena manatee was in reality a Sea Lion. [15] He even identified its species - the Cape Sea Lion (*Arctocephalus antarcticus*) [16], and believed the matter to be closed, reviving it briefly on March 17th 1934 in *Nature*, [17] merely to include mention of Dampier's account, which he had not seen when preparing his detailed paper. Certain other records-given here but again not seen by Mortensen-were presented by way of reply to his Nature note in Kitching's own Nature report, published on July 4th 1936, [18] but Kitching did not express any opinion regarding the creature's identity.

By way of contrast, as outlined within his report of Mundy's sighting, in 1935 F.C.Fraser had leaned very heavily in favour of one specific identity-once again involving a pinniped, but not a sea lion this time. On the contrary raser nominated a true (i.e., earless) seal-a young male Southern Elephant Seal (Mirounga leonina) [19]. As its scientific name suggests, it does bear a fancied resemblance to a lion-like beast, and hence is more reminiscent of a sea lion (albeit one of massive proportions), than are most true seals; but notwithstanding this, it bears rather less resemblance to the creature depicted in Mundy's illustration.

Since the 1930s, the St Helena manatee-or sea lion, or elephant seal-seems to have been forgotten, like so many other 'inconvenient' animals, but could it really have been a sirenian? The reports on file are not sufficient in hemselves to provide an unequivocal answer-all they can do is offer up certain important clues. For example, as manatees measure up to 15 ft. long the St Helena beasts were evidently long enough and their description as calf shaped by Henry also confirms with that identity. Conversely, the saucer shaped eyes of Henry's beast contrast markedly with the small, relatively insignificant ones of the generally myopic manatees. Large eyes are characteristic of pinnipeds, as are the fearsome jaws and teeth of Mundy's animal. The same can also be said of the latter's moustaches-but as manatees have a bristly top lip too, this feature is less discriminatory.

If the St.Helena beasts were sirenians, their presence around this island indicates that they may truly have constituted a species in their own right-for as Lydekker pointed out in defense of his belief that they belonged neither to the African nor to the South American species of Manatee, although it is conceivable that a specimen or two may occasionally be carried from Africa or from South America to St.Helena this surely could not occur regularly. [20]

As it happens, there is one notable feature mentioned in a number of the reports given here and elsewhere that on first sight greatly decreases the likelihood belonged to any species of manatee-known or unknown. Although they will rest on the surface of the water in shallow stretches when not feeding, manatees do not generally come ashore-yet according to several independant accounts, the St. Helena beasts have frequently been seen resting (even sleeping) on the sands or on rocks, completely out of the water, after the fashion of pinnipeds. Also, the large amounts of oil obtained from their carcasses is more suggestive of seals than of sirenians.

So are we to conclude that they were not sirenians after all, instead merely large seals or sea lions? Yet if this is all that they were, why did the islanders refer to them so deliberately as sea-cows? It is extremely rare for pinnipeds to be referred to anywhere by such names. In addition, as Lydekker judiciously pointed out, just because KNOWN sirenians do not normally come ashore voluntarily, this does not mean that there could not be an unknown distinctive species of sirenian that DOES (or did) come ashore under certain circumstances. [21]

And this is where we must leave the mystery of St. Helena's sirenian-that-might-be-a-seal-still unsolved, and quite likely to remain that way indefinitely, due to the tragic probability that its subject is extinct, lost to science before its identity had ever been established.

As a final comment, it is worth noting that there is at least one case on record that constitutes the exact reverse of this one, because it involves some supposed seals that were ultimately revealed to be sirenians. Sea mammals assumed to be seals had been reported from the red sea island of Shadwan-but as recorded in 1939 by Paul Budger, when the animals featured in these reports were finally investigated they proved to be dugongs [22] which are indeed native to the Red Sea.

REFERENCES.

1. Michel Raynal: *'Does the Steller's Sea Cow Still Survive?'* INFO JOURNAL No 3 (February 1987), pp. 15-19,37.

2. J Richard Greenwell (editor), *'New expedition identifies Ri as Dugong'.* ISC Newsletter 4. No 1 (Spring 1985), pp. 1-3.

3. Glover M.Allen. *'The former occurrence of the Dugong in Chinese waters'*, China journal 22 (February 1935), pp. 79-82; also Arthur de Carle Sowerby: *'The Dugong in Chinese Waters'*, China Journal 25 (1936), pp. 41-42.

4. Bernard Heuvelmans: *'Annotated Checklist of apparently unknown animals with which Cryptozoology is Concerned'.* Cryptozoology 5 (1986), pp. 1-26.

5. F.C.Fraser, *'Zoological notes from the voyage of Peter Mundy, 1655-56, (b) Sea Elephant on St. Helena'*, Proceedings of the Linnean Society of London 147 (1935), pp. 33-35.

6. G.C.Kitching, *'The Manatee of St. Helena'*, Nature 138 (4th July 1936), pp. 33-34.

7. John Masefield (editor), *Dampier's Voyages. Vol. 1.* (London: E Grant Richards, 1906), p. 526.

8. John Barnes, *A tour through the island of St. Helena* (London: J.M.Richardson, 1817), pp. 116-117.

9. Walter Henry, *Events of a Military Life, Vol 2*, 2nd Edition (London: Pickering, 1843), pp. 66-67.

10. Richard Lydekker, *'On the Supposed Former Existence of a Sirenian in St. Helena'.* Proceedings of the Zoological Society of London, (20th June 1899), pp. 796-798.

11. John Charles Mellis, *St. Helena: A Physical, Historical, and Topographical Description of the island.* (London: Reeve, 1875), pp. 86-87.

12. Lydekker, op. cit.

13. Ibid.

14. Theodor Mortensen, *'On the 'Manatee' of St.Helena'.* Videnskabelige Meddelelser fra Dansk Naturhistorish Forening 97 (19 August 1933),pp. 1-9.

15. Ibid.

16. Ibid.

17. Theodor Mortensen, *'The 'Manatee' of St.Helena'*, Nature 133 (17 March 1934), p. 417.

18. Kitching, op. cit.

19. Fraser, op. cit.

20. Lydekker op. cit.

21. Ibid.

22. Paul Budger, *'Sur la Pretendue Existance des Phoques dans la Region de I'lle Shadwan (Mer Rouge)'*, Bulletin du Museum National d'Histoire Naturelle (Ser. 2) 11, No. 5 (June 1939), pp. 450-453.

CROCODILE TEARS

What IS happening in THAT lake with THAT video?
The Editor aims to find out and fails miserably..

We have received so many letters about the brief items in the last two issues about the possible discovery of a large aquatic creature in New Guinea that we felt that it was time we printed a full resume of the story so far.

This matter has been discussed at length in the fortean press since Karl Shuker told a packed room at the 1993 Unconvention that Roy Mackal and a Japanese TV Team have claimed to have filmed a large unknown creature in a volcanic lake in New Guinea.

Everyone has quoted Bernard Heuvelmans in his 1986 : *'Annotated Checklist of Apparently Unknown Animals with which Cryptozoology is Concerned'* which includes:

'An unknown species of crocodile (or is it as has been suggested a surviving Mosasaur?) known as Migo, in Lake Dakataua, on the island of New Britain, in the Bismark Archipelago' [1]

The original reference cited by Heuvelmans is from Wilfred T.Neill in 1956 [2]

'New Britain, the largest island of the Bismark Archipelago is about 370 miles long. A rugged chain of high mountains extends from one end of the island to the other. Several peaks exceed 6,000 feet in height, some on the Gazelle Peninsula, reach 7,900 to 8,000 feet, according to recent surveys. The interior is not well known, and much of it was mapped for the first time during, and after World War Two. While serving with the U.S.Army Air Forces in the Pacific during that War, I once flew over New Britain. From the air I observed a number of crocodiles around the margins of upland lakes. Circumstances rendered it impossible to spend any time in investigation; but at one point the place passed so low over a lake that a crocodile was frightened into the water, and I could see it plainly. I also noted that the plane was at an altitude of approximately 1,400 feet.

Some weeks thereafter I heard a lecture on jungle survival, given by an officer who had been forced down into the interior of New Britain and had eventually made his way to safety. He mentioned having seen crocodiles about the lakes of the island; he thought that he had observed them as high as 4,000 feet but could not be certain of this. According to him, these crocodiles were shy, fleeing into the water at his approach'.

Neill continues to suggest that...

'...whilst a positive statement is not justified, I feel that the New Britain lake Crocodiles, probably are not C. porosus; they are much more apt to be either C. n. novae-guinae or an undescribed relative thereof'.

The first use of the name 'Migo' came in an article in a Japanese Newspaper in February 1972 [3] which claimed that:

'The chief of a research institute in Omata Town in Mie Prefecture said recently that he will survey Lake Dakataua of New Britain Island this coming fall in search of a monstrous creature rumoured to be inhabiting the lake.

Shohei Shirai, 38. the chief of the Pacific Ocean Resources Research Institute said that he had heard about the monster from some 15 natives from a small town called Talasea.

The natives said, Shirai added, that the monster, which they had named 'Migo', is about 10 m. long, has a head and a neck as long and slim as a horse and is grey in colour.

The natives also told Shirai that 'Migo' has sharp fangs and hair on the back of its long neck. Its huge back is round, Shirai, said that the natives added, its legs are as flat as those of a turtle and its tail, just like that of a crocodile, is rugged.

According to what the natives told Shirai, 'Migo', was first witnessed twelve years ago by a German hunting crocodiles near the Lake Dakataua. Some years later, an Australian patrol officer was said to have succeeded in photographing the monster.

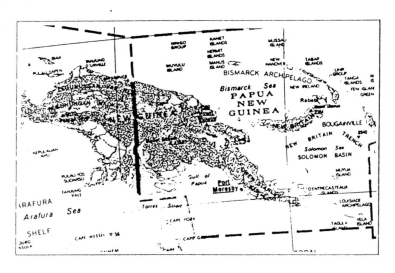

PAPUA NEW-GUINEA AND THE BISMARK ARCHIPELAGO

Lake Dakatua, on Williaumez Peninsula of New Britain Island is located about 50 km. north of Talasea. It is the largest lake in entire New Guinea, with a perimeter of approximately 32 kilometers.

Shirai was also told by many natives that 'Migo' is living between two small islands on the lake, and emerges from under the water several times a year, even in the daytime. Sometimes, the natives say, 'Migo', comes up to the shore

Shirai said that, all the accounts gathered 'Migo' quite looks alike a mosasaur.'

(I make no excuses for having quoted the above article in full but the information is otherwise unavailable. I am indebted to Bernard Heuvelmans for both this article, and the Neill and Heuvelmans articles.)

Bernard Heuvelmans himself wrote to me after reading the news item in issue two of Animals and Men (4). H suggested that if the animal did indeed exhibit the 'vertical undulations' that had been claimed then it would have to be a mammal, possibly the 'many finned' sea serpent whose existence he first postulated in 1965 [5]. I received several other letters including one from Animals and Men reader Mike Grayson, querying whether the 'mystery aquatic mammal of Lake Niu-Gini in New Guinea' and the mystery crocodile of Lake Dakataua on the island of New Britain are actually the same creature.

In December 1994 the plot got even more confusing. Fortean Times [6] which now described a lake monster called 'Migo' which is 'said to inhabit Lake Datakau'. (Note the small but quite possibly significant spelling change), on the island of New Guinea.

The article also described the famous video footage, that Karl Shuker had told us about in June. They describe a film which:

'clearly shows a very large aquatic animal at the lake's surface, with angular head, humped back and a long powerful tail thrashing from side to side. Dr Roy Mackal appears on the tape, declared that 'Migo' is a new sort of animal that he has never seen before'.

This sounds very exciting but the same day that the December issue of Fortean Times arrived on the Animals and Men doormat so did a long awaited letter from Canada [7]

Issue 19 of the British Columbia Cryptozoology Club Newsletter was very complimentary about us and about our publication. Its article on the creatures of Lake Dakatau/Niu Gini/Dakataua started off by quoting our news item from A&M 2 and then continues:

'Your editor was fortunate enough to receive a copy of this video, courtesy of Gary Mangiacopra and to view in the company of a japanese speaker. The program was shown on the 13th February 1994 on the NHK network in Japan. The host Nadaka Tetsuo, takes us on an explanatory adventure to Lake Dakataua, (not Niu Gini) on the island of New Britain, Papua New-Guinea. The Japanese camera crew is seen arriving in Port Moresby, interviewing an official of the Parks Service, who said that a careful survey had shown nothing unusual in the lake, but that natives still spoke of a strange animal. They all leave on Air Niugini eastwards towards the Willaunez Peninsula which juts north from New Britain like a clenched fist holding Lake Dakataua. After much filming (of the lake and each other), an indistinct remote object is sighted on the lake surface; Roy Mackal, author of 'The Monsters of Loch Ness' and other cryptozoology books is brought forward as an expert witness to assert looking at the telephoto video of the object swimming in the distance that 'it is not a fish, nor a crocodile; it is one (perhaps two or three), long, unknown animals'.

There are no distinct features visible. the animal would certainly satisfy your editor's first criterion for a worthwhile cryptid sighting: that the object must be unambiguously animate. It would certainly not satisfy the second criterion; that it should unambiguously not be a known creature. In spite of Mackal's opinion, there seems to be other possibilities to explain the moving objects: the marine fauna is rich in marine creatures and the available evidence certainly does not eliminate them all...'

(for those who did not read our news item in A&M 2 -our original information was that because of the volcanic nature of lake Niu Gini there was no endemic aquatic life and therefore the animals in the lake (whatever they

(are) were forced to surface more than would appear normal in order to feed off resting water fowl).

The B.C.Cryptozoology Club Newsletter continues:

...Nevertheless an elaborate explanation was put forward in terms of a zeuglodon, (a primitive whale); we are shown models of the zeuglodon, reconstructed from existing skeletons, swimming around the lake breaking the surface, flexing its squeaky jaws and entering the lake through a hypothetical tunnel from the nearby ocean Not convincing but nevertheless a very impressive effort. The Japanese team obviously put in a lot of money and effort in this expedition and they should be commended for their determination. It is certainly not by sitting at home, sitting in armchairs and reading books, that one discovers anything. Disagreements about interpretation should not thwart exploration, on the contrary, mystery should feed curiosity and further expeditions'

It must be said however that the two descriptions of the video are so different that it seems almost as if they are describing two different films. Both Fortean Times and we reported that the sightings took place in different lakes on the island of New Guinea whereas now it seems certain, that whatever the phenomenon actually is, it is in Lake Dakataua on New Britain which although it is politically part of New Guinea is geographically a completely different island.

What is also particularly intriguing is the way that creatures which were described in 1956 as a 'possibly unknown species' of crocodile, have by 1972 become 'monsters'. What is certain is that neither of the species tentatively postulated by Neill in 1956 as the true identity of the creatures of Lake Dakataua, neither of them even approach the size described in any of the post 1972 reports. I have not yet seen a copy of the video, and neither, as far as I know has anyone else in the United Kingdom. I have to agree with the editor of the British Columbia Cryptozoology Club Newsletter that the only way to solve mysteries is to actually go in search of the animals concerned, and I am sure that I join with him, and everyone else involved in eagerly awaiting the next stage in what will either prove to be the most exciting cryptozoological even of the century, or an embarrassingly wet squib.

REFERENCES

1. Bernard Heuvelmans: *Annotated Checklist of Apparently Unknown Animals with which Cryptozoology is Concerned.* 'Cryptozoology' 1986.
2. Wifred T. Neill: *The Possibility of an undescribed Crocodile on New Britain:* Herpetologica, Vol 12, pp. 174-176, 1956.
3. *'Many have seen Big Monster':* Mainichi Daily News, Tuesday February 1, 1972.
4. Bernard Heuvelmans pers. corr. September 8th 1994.
5. Bernard Heuvelmans: *In the Wake of the Sea Serpents)* (London; Rupert Hart Davis; 1965)
6. Edward Young and Ron Rosenblatt: *'What's new in New Guinea':* Fortean Times No 78, p.47 (December 1994)
7. *Almost too Good to be True:* The British Columbia Cryptozoology Club Newsletter.No 19, December 1994. p 2

LETTERS

The inclusion of a letters page has proved to be a great success, and it looks like this is going to be a regular part of the magazine. Thanks for the idea Dad! Opinions expressed are not necessarily the views of the editor.

Dear Animals and Men,

This summer has been rather a slow one in Denmark. I suppose it has been too hot for anything strange to happen - for anything at all to happen, as a matter of fact. Anyway, one thing did happen, that might be of interest. Please read the following summary and let your mind boggle (or do I mean boil?).

An Opera worth dying for.

In the beginning of August tragedy struck at the Zoological garden in Copenhagen. On Friday 5th August, the orchestra and the singers of the Royal Danish Theatre did their first sound rehearsals for their annual opera-concert. This took place in Sondermarken, a park right next to the Zoological Garden. Apparently the female okapi in the zoo was not an opera-lover. It became severely agitated and refused to enter the stable when the wardens closed at night. It didn't sleep all night, and when rehearsals resumed the next morning it went into a state of shock. The zoo's veterinarian tried all weekend to calm the animal down and save it, but to all avail.

It died on Sunday afternoon.

Source: Politiken 10.August 1994.

Best Wishes,

Lars Thomas,
Valby, Denmark.

THREE MILLION CHEERS!

Dear Editor,

I notice from various small references in your excellent magazine that you too are a devotee of classic children's literature. I wondered whether you and your readers have read Christina Hardyment's 'Arthur Ransome and Capt. Flint's Trunk' which discusses the background to Ransome's 'Swallows and Amazons' novels in great depth.

On two occasions Ransome seriously considered utilizing cryptozoological themes in books for this series which he later decided not to write. A friend of his, Margeret Renold suggested that the sequel to 'Coot Club' should feature 'the Death or Glories' looking for the Loch Ness Monster on the Norfolk Broads, and many years after, Myles North, the originator of the plot of 'Great Northern?' suggested the plot of a book tentatively entitled 'Coots in Kenya' in which:

The Coots-perhaps Tom and the Twins, come out with Mrs Barrable (to Kenya) to visit some friends who *have children. They are to hunt for the legendary Nandi Bear on the shores of Lake Victoria '......*

I hope these obscure little snippets are of some interest,
Best wishes,

Paul Nathan.
Bognor Regis.

THE MONSTER MASH (1)

Sir,

Referring to Mr Morgan's letter (A&M 3) I can name several instances of The Loch Ness Monster (something that could have been The Loch Ness Monster) being sighted before the 1930s.

a) Saint Augusta was said to have encountered it when he wanted to cross the Loch.

b) When General Wade's men were building the road south of the Loch his men mentioned seeing 'whales' the loch and another one mentioned Loch Ness being famous for its *'floating island'*.

c) In another instance a diver working on a sunken boat at one end of the Loch, sometime last century I think signalled to be pulled up quickly. When he got to the surface he mentioned seeing a large unknown creature.

d) Also, Loch Ness, in common with some other Scottish Lakes was meant to have had water spirits such the water bull (relatively harmless) and water kelpie/horse (extremely dangerous), inhabiting it. documentary in the 1970's had an interview with someone from the area who mentioned that as a child he a other children were warned not to swim in the Loch because of the water kelpie. Legends of these tv creatures went back centuries.

The two books where I obtained this information I am afraid that I no longer have. However one w published by Target and was written by Tim Dinsdale and the other was published by Scholastic Bo Services.

Yours faithfully

G.M.Stocker.
Royal Leamington Spa.

THE MONSTER MASH (2)

Dear A&M,

I am what you call a Monster Hunter but would not admit to being pro or anti Plesiosaur theory but keep open mind about the possibility of a living fossil, but the argument by Stuart Leadbetter must be the wo argument against a Plesiosaur that I have ever read.

I am afraid that the only part which is anti-plessie is being air breathing and the creatures diving ability. This could be overcome by some form of respiration unique to the creatures.

Now to Mr Leadbetter's views on their behaviour. I cannot believe that because of a picture he saw in a museum of two plesiosaurs fighting, that just because no-one reported such behaviour on Loch Ness then a plesiosaur could not be the inhabitant of the Loch. I think that we can agree that a picture of a reptile that is only known in fossil form must leave a lot to artistic interpretation.

Now to their breeding habits. Why does Mr Leadbetter expect creatures that live in virtually unchangeable conditions of light and heat to move on or into an alien habitat to mate. Could they not mate in their own habitat like us and most other animals.

As for the rearing of the young, I don't see why if live young are not born then eggs could not be laid in water enclosed in some kind of protective substance like frog spawn which could be hatched in the Loch.

Whatever the creatures are I think that we must keep a very open mind about them, and we must consider every possibility, even things that are not known to be acceptable to todays experts.

Lastly to the stomach contents of the fossil plesiosaur with the remains of the pterodactyl. Surely it would seem more likely that it was a corpse floating in the water and not snatched out of the air as Mr Leadbetter suggests. Very few animals live both in and out of the water.

I would like to finish with a quote from Mr Leadbetter:

'This assumption is very wrong and is highly misleading to the general public'. This is what his article is with its negative attitude.

We must keep an open mind to everything if we are ever to solve the Loch Ness mystery. This means not making judgements based in pictures in museums or things not fitting into already known categories or species.

This letter is not to tell Mr Leadbetter that he is wrong, but to urge him to have a rethink.

Yours

R.A.Carter
Huddersfield.

THE MONSTER MASH (3)

Dear Mr Downes,

I am writing to comment on Stuart Leadbetter's excellent article about the Loch Ness phenomenon. It is refreshing to find someone who accepts the concept of a 'long necked' creature without blindly believing in the principle of plesiosaurus survival.
Good work Mr Leadbetter.
Best wishes,

Stephen Nice, Colchester.

 This is the section of the magazine where we try to answer queries sent in by Animals and Men readers and attempt to help with ongoing research projects.

In issue one of Animals and Men, we printed an article about oddly coloured frogs which had been appearing in Cornwall. Just before Christmas we received an update from Mark Nicholson of the Cornwall Wildlife Trust.

'I'm still somewhat in the dark as to the genetic mechanism of the colour variation seen. It does seem odd that one frog without pigment should be orange, while another should be pink or white. It's also strange that some of each colour should have normal dark eyes while others have the red eyes expected of an albino. And what about Red Frogs - are they pigmented or are they pigmented albinos?'

Forty six records of unusually coloured frogs have been received by the Cornwall Wildlife Trust. Of these, sixteen were from Cornwall, twenty three were from other southern counties, seven were from the north of England and none at all were from Scotland.

This shows that although we have no idea what actually causes this strange trend amongst amphibians, one thing which is certain is that there is a definite bias towards this phenomena in southern counties.

'Albinism is a genetic defect which crops up in many animal species, and is present from birth, but there are also cases in which frogs have lost their normal colour through being deprived of light. One report described a whole colony of red frogs trapped in a drainage shaft, and a population of white frogs was once discovered in a boarded up air raid shelter.'

Some of these frogs have actually been grown in captivity from white or cream eggs and tadpoles, although it has been reported that some of these light coloured specimens suffer from spinal defects and other unspecified health problems.

Mark Nicholson concludes:

'If you see an oddly coloured frog, grab it! Keep it in an ice cream tub or similar, containing damp paper for moisture. In a cool place, your frog should be comfortable without food for two or three days while you contact an 'expert', to see if he or she would like to have a look.

If you can get your frog to me, he or she will be used carefully for some publicity shots and then returned without harm. If you are outside my area, I can put you in touch with a local contact interested in such things. We would also be very interested in obtaining spawn and tadpoles from such frogs'..

Mark Nicholson can be contacted on 0872 73939, or write to him at The Cornwall Wildlife Trust, Five Acres, Allet, Truro, Cornwall TR4 9DJ.

We also would be interested in both records and information and specimens of spawn and tadpoles of unusually coloured frogs.

HELP2

JAN WILLIAMS ASSURES ME THAT THIS IS NOT A CRYPTIC ESSEX GIRL JOKE!

Does anyone have information on two strange creatures found on beaches at Canvey Island, Essex, as referenced in 'Stranger Than Science' by Frank Edwards? He describes the first as two and a half feet tall with a thick brownish-red skin, pulpy head with protruding eyes, and *'feet and legs so arranged that it could walk if it chose'*. The second was found by Rev. Joseph Overs on 11th August 1954. It was 4 feet long and 25lbs weight, with two large eyes, nostril holes, gills, and thick pink skin lacking scales. It had two short legs with 5 toes arranged in a U-shape with a concave central arch.

I would be grateful for anything further on these or any similar reports.

HOW YOU CAN HELP THE CENTRE FOR FORTEAN ZOOLOGY

* We still need regional representatives in many areas. If you are interested drop us a line and we can send you a copy of our suggested guidelines.

* We are always interested in buying books on Cryptozoology, Hong Kong and its animals, Natural History, Folklore, The Occult, and Fortean subjects. Send us your lists and we will get in touch.

* We are still seeking specimens for our collection which will eventually comprise the CFZ Museum of Fortean Zoology.

* Carry on sending us your press cuttings. Jan Williams is in the throes of moving house at the moment but when she is settled we will be publicising her new address and fax number for the newsfile. We, at the main office will be getting a fax number, a mobile phone number and also an E Mail address within the next 12 months. Details of our Sightings hotline are in the editorial.

* We are always interested in purchasing any aquatic reptiles or amphibians especially the larger aquatic salamanders, and soft shelled turtles.

* We are planning a new feature on exotic pets. Could you let us know of anything really unusual that you see for sale in your local pet shops!

* We still want details of Fortean Pub signs and Comic books with a cryptozoological theme.

* We are looking for anecdotal evidence from ex colonial service workers about subjects of a cryptozoological and folkloric theme. We especially want stories on the subject of vampirism and were beasts from tropical africa and the east indies. For more details of our Colonial Service/Expat research project or for details of our other work please write to the Exeter address.

* By the way-a happy new year from us all

ERRORS AND OMISSIONS

There have been a number of, what we in the independent publishing trade call 'cock ups' over the past three issues and there are a number of apologies which are in order.

1. Because of an error by the printers the front page headline of issue 3 'Orobourous is alive and well and living in Eastbourne-see page 12' was omitted. This made the photograph of a bloke with a moustache grinning over a dead worm seem a little eccentric to say the least.

2. There has been a great deal of controversy following our publication of Stuart Leadbetter's article 'Near Lizard but not near enough' in Issue Two. Some of that controversy was caused by our printing that 'thousands' of sightings have been made at Loch Ness. This was our addition and in fact Stuart did not mention such a figure. God knows how it happened but we take full responsibility. Stuart will be answering his critics in an article in Issue Five.

3. We made another typographical error in the letters page of issue three. The letter about West African Scorpion Cults from 'A Retired Colonial Service officer' contained a misprint. The line "The Nightwatchman, known locally as the 'nightwatchman'" should, as all self respecting Gerald Durrell buffs will know have read "the nightwatchman known locally as 'the watchnight'". We are again sorry for our stupidity.

4. The electron microscope photographs of cat hair samples in issue three should have been credited to 'The National Museums of Scotland', but because the editor wasn't paying attention when the newsfile editor told him this they weren't. Thanks to Dr Andrew Kitchener for the photographs.

5. Tony 'Doc' Shiels took mild exception to my describing Samuel Beckett as a tedious hibernian playwrite. Sorry for any offense Doc, but I for one find your writings far more entertaining...

NERVOUS TWITCH

Our regular trawl through the weirder bits of bird lore with the nervous twitcher...who was that masked ornithologist?

A BEVY OF BUZZARDS

As you might expect, the winter weather has brought some unusual visitors to our coast.

In October it was reported that the number of Rough Legged Buzzards seen was approximately twice what would normally have been expected. Apparently a booming rabbit population has attracted hordes of the buzzards from the Arctic.

The birds were sighted from the Shetland Isles to as far away as Kent, with the main concentration being in East Anglia and South East Yorkshire. These birds dislike flying over water, in spite of their massive five foot wingspan, and so they crossed the North Sea at its narrowest point. *ITV Teletext 25.10.94. (Some of the birds were still around in January of this year).*

There has also been an influx of Asian Yellow Browed Warblers, turning up all over the place during January 1995 including Scarborough, North Devon and Norfolk. They were supposedly blown off course by the winter weather. *Birdline January 1995 C4 Teletext Greennews 3.1.95*

DON'T YOU JUST HATE IT WHEN THAT HAPPENS?

A rather tragic end to a very rare sighting of a Blyth's Pipit, usually found in Siberia, in Suffolk in November. It was only the third sighting in Britain this century, and the tiny bird was being photographed by keen bird watchers from all over the country when a Kestrel swooped down and flew off with it! *Daily Mail 18.11.94*

IS THIS THE END FOR THE CRESTED IBIS?

An extremely rare Crested Ibis, brought from China to Japan in the hope that it would breed in the spring, has sadly died. The two year old male which was on loan to a conservation group became ill very suddenly. This is a huge tragedy as there are only two Crested Ibis known to exist in Japan. *Newsround BBC Ceefax 13.12.94*

YOU GOT THE POWER

No 'Nervous Twitch' would be complete without more strange stories of bird behaviour. This one is no exception! An unknown bird caused chaos in May 1994 by dropping a Rosy Boa snake over a power station in the Morongo Basin, Southern California. A power line was short circuited leaving 4000 homes without power for two hours. I feel sorry for the bird-it lost its dinner! *Plain Dealer via COUDi May 13 1994.*

POLLY WANTS A **%^$&!

A foul mouthed parrot has been 'fired' from his job at the Isle of Wight Zoo recently. A Blue and Gold Macaw called 'Bluey' was part of a six parrot show until he told tourists where to go in no uncertain terms! Zoo managers tried to give him elocution lessons, but to no avail. It is thought that Bluey picked up his language from his previous owner, a sailor. I think that he should sue for unfair dismissal! *St. Louis Post Dispatch Aug 16 1994 vis COUDi.*

THE A-Z OF CRYPTOZOOLOGY

PART FOUR BY JAN WILLIAMS

BARABOEDAER BEASTS: Carvings on the 9th century Buddhist shrine at Baraboedaer, Jav depict tusked elephantine heads. Unlike Asian elephants, which have only a single cheek tooth, the carving bear four herbivorous cheek-teeth in each half jaw, comparable with those of mastodonts which supposed became extinct in Java during the Pliocene.

BIRDMEN: Flying creatures with man-like bodies and huge bat wings have been reported in Asia and th Americas. Near Vladivostok, the 'Letayuschiy Chelovek' or 'Flying Man' is said to reside in the Pid. Mountains. Described as humanoid in shape with webbed, bat-like wings, its howls and 'woman-like scream were frequently heard in the 1930s and '40s, and occasionally in recent years.

A bat-winged humanoid was seen flying over New York in 1877. Two six-foot-tall winged men were report at Pelotas, Brazil in the 1950s, and a man-like figure with bat wings appeared in a tree at Houston, Texas 1953. In 1969 a 'bird-woman' was seen near Da Nang, Vietnam, by members of the US Marine Corp Witness Earl Morrison described a black figure like that of a normal well-developed woman, possibly cover in fur, with flapping bat-like wings apparently moulded to the hands.

Many 'flying man' reports refer to silver suited humanoids, sometimes encumbered with machinery, and within the field of Ufology rather than Cryptozoology. Creatures akin to the Jersey Devil and Cornish Owlma will be treated separately.

BRAY ROAD BEAST: Animal resembling a werewolf seen on and around Bray Road, near Elkhor Wisconsin, USA. Witnesses described it as bigger and taller than a German Shepherd dog, with a long thic coat of silver-greyish-black hair, very broad chest, wolf-like head, pointed ears and golden-yellow eyes. It r and leapt on all fours and was also seen walking and running upright. Dog-like tracks, 4 inches wide and 4 inches long were found, and the beast was seen crouched on its haunches eating food with paws held palm upwards in human fashion.

BRITISH MYSTERY CATS: Reports of large cats date back to the early years of the twentie century, but have become both more numerous and more newsworthy in recent years. Sightings cover th length and breadth of the British Isles, though public attention tends to focus on specific areas. Famous cas include the 'Surrey Puma' in the 1960s, the 'Exmoor Beast' in the 1980s, and the 'Beast of Bodmin' - curre favourite of the tabloid press. The animals reported vary in size and appearance, ranging generally from 3-5 in length, and brown, black or grey in colour, sometimes showing spots or stripes. Physical evidence includ paw-prints, faeces, hair samples, territorial markings, and carcases of prey including rabbits, birds, deer, ar sheep.

Some photographic evidence clearly shows non-domestic cats, but debate continues as to the species involved. Free-ranging exotic cats have occasionally been shot in Britain; including leopard cats, Asian jungle cats, and clouded leopards; and a live puma was trapped in the Scottish Highlands in 1980.

Similar 'Mystery Cat' reports emanate from Europe, Australia and the USA.

BOOK REVIEWS

Escape from Extinction by Andrew Kitchener and Kate Charlesworth (HMSO Edinburgh/National Museums of Scotland 4.50 48pp.)

This is an excellent little booklet and unlike most contemporary childrens books on 'green' issues it is neither patronising or annoying! Written in an informative but easy to assimilate style this mixture of (presumably) Kitchener's writing and Charlesworth's excellent cartoons, this book presents a chilling catalogue of extinctions and near extinctions in the form of a comic book telling the story of a Phillip Marlowe styled private detective called 'RIP Dodo'..who is not unsurprisingly a Dodo.

This book is also recommended for connoisseurs of comic book art. The drawings are very reminiscent of the style of Pete Loveday's 'Russell' comics, with bold black and white pen and ink drawings and witty characterisation. Buy it for your children. and then keep it for yourself!

'Monsters of the Sea' by Richard Ellis (Robert Hale 429pp price unknown). I was unsure of this book at first. Subtitled 'the history, natural history, and mythology of the oceans' most fantastic creatures', much of the information within it is available elsewhere, and by the time I was about a third of the way through I was already comparing it unfavourably with about half a dozen book on the subject of Marine mysteries which I have within my own library. Suddenly, however, I realised that although I have a reasonably sizeable collection of books on Natural History, Cryptozoology, The Occult and a wide range of related (and unrelated) subjects, many people (in fact, probably most people) have not, and what is old information to me is new and exciting to most people. I then started to read this book with a new and less pompous eye and I was very pleasantly surprised.

Written in a warm and engaging style, laced intermittently with a gentle but incisive wit this book collects together a veritable treasure trove of information about Sea Monsters, Whales, Giant Squids and Octopi and Sirenians. The section on sharks is particularly interesting, and all in all I think that whereas I would probably not recommend this book to a professor of marine biology, it makes a useful, entertaining and informative addition to the libraries of most cryptozoologists including that of your humble editor who is using it as an object lesson in how not to get too big for his size 12 boots!

PERIODICAL REVIEWS

*We welcome an exchange of periodicals with magazines of mutual interest although because we now exchang
with so many magazines, as of the NEXT issue we shall only include in our listings those magazines who hav
published an issue which we have recieved during the previous three months*

BIGFOOT RECORD. Bill Green, c/o The Bigfoot Centre. 21 Benham St, Apartment F. Bristo
CT06010 USA This free news service for bigfoot buffs is bi-monthly and has a refreshingly informal style

DRAGON CHRONICLE. The dragon trust, PO   Box 3369. London SW6 6JN. A fascinatin
collection of all things draconian which now appears four times a year

NEXUS 55 Queens Rd, E. Grinstead, West Sussex RH19 1BG. Intelligent look at the fringes of scienc
Well put together and a must for paranoid conspiracy buffs..

NESSLETTER Rip Hepple, 7 Huntshieldford, St Johns Chapel, Bishop Auckland Co Durham DL13 1R(
Rip Hepple is a genuine original. This magazine has been appearing regularly for many years and cannot
reccomended highly enough.

CREATURE RESEARCH JOURNAL, Paul Johnson, 721 Old Greensberg Pike, N   Versaill
PA15137 USA. An intelligent look at the interface between Cryptozoology and UFO research

TRACK RECORD, Bigfoot Research Project, PO   Box 126, Mt Hood, Oregon 97041USA. Excelle
for anyone with even the most passing interest in North American Manimals.

DELVE, Gene Duplantier, 17 Shetland St, Willowdale. Ontario. Canada M2M 1X5. Intriguing and eccentr
collection of forteana and general oddness.

BIPEDIA. Francois de Saare. CERBL BP65, 06202, NICE. CEDEX 3. FRANCE. A magazine about Initi
Bipedalism, scholarly and concise.

TEMS NEWS, 115 Hollybush Lane, Hampton, Middlesex, TW12 2QY. An engaging collection of qu
fortean odds and ends from veteran UFO buff Lionel Beer, who also runs Spacelink books and is compiling
Crypto booklist. Anyone who can send a Christmas card co-addressed to my pet pigeon is OK by me.

TOUCHSTONE and PEGASUS, Jimmy Goddard. 25 Albert Rd. Addlestone. Surrey two n
UFO/Fortean mags. Well produced and collated.

THE CRYPTO CHRONICLE, 50Green Lane, Worcester. General Crypto Mag with a bigfo
bias.

ANIMALS, Freepost Sidcup, Kent. The magazine of the British Zoos Supporters Club. Hig reccomended

DEAD OF NIGHT. 156 Bolton Road East, Newferry, Wirral, Merseyside, L62 4RY. An amusing and intelligently put together Fortean magazine. Issue three includes a fine section on The Pendle Witches. One of the most entertaining section is the media reviews bits where fortean TV is dissected with wit and aplomb.

CRYPTOZOOLOGIA, Association Belge d'Etude et de Protection des Animaux Rares, Square des Latins 49/4, 1050 Bruxelles, Belgium. A French language magazine published by the Belgian society for Cryptozoology.

THE BRITISH COLUMBIA CRYPTOZOOLOGY CLUB NEWSLETTER, 3773 West 18th Avenue, Vancouver, British Columbia, Canada. V65 1B3. Excellent and well put together, and they were very nice about us in their last issue.

ENIGMAS, 41 The Braes, Tullibody, Clackmannanshire. Scotland, FK10 2TT A Fine 'mysteries' magazine with a UFO bias.

PROMISES AND DISAPPOINTMENTS 42 Victoria Road, Mt Charles, St Austell, Cornwall, PL25 4Qd England. Kevin McClure has always been one of my favourite writers in the field and it is good to be able to report that this magazine on 'non human intelligence' is everything one would hope it would be.

FROM OUR FILES

Part two of our rundown of recent Bigfoot reports.

Woody Woodworth was a 0000quarter of a mile from Wildcat Mt Road, seven or eight miles from the junction with Kitzmiller Rd. on September 2nd 1994 early in the morning. He was checking the movement of an elk herd that returned to the area every seven days to feed. From the next canyon he heard a high pitched whistle, quite loud that lasted for 20 seconds or so. Very familiar with wildlife sounds he thought this whistle was peculiar, and not an elk or a cat. The whistle set dogs from nearby homes to barking crazily for about five minutes. (WESTERN BIGFOOT SOCIETY 22.9.94)

"Bigfoot is 20 miles S.E from Mollada Oregon The first time we saw our Bigfoot was memorial day weekend 1993 on the saturday night at about 10.00. We heard something in the bushes circling the camp. The next morning we went out looking for tracks. My kids went out first, they came running back, saying 'Mom we found a huge footprint in the mud'. Boy did they? It was 17" x 9", a real good print. Then we got to looking and found prints of all sizes......the trees started moving up high....About that time I saw a big huge thing run out of the trees and run off. About ten minutes later I saw the huge thing run back into the trees. I knew it was a bigfoot..That night my husband Leroy went behind our tent to the rest room about 9.15 p.m. He heard something big in the trees and close to him. He shined his light on it. It was the Bigfoot. It was about 50 feet from him and brown in colour. After that we all packed up and went home. We went back camping all summer and have seen him and his eyes a lot. There is a family of them. " Sharon Jones (THE BIGFOOT RECORD) Mrs Jones also saw the same creatures during the summer of 1994, over the weekend of July 1st It will be interesting to see what happens this year!

Typeset by Poultrypower   ISSN: 1354 0637

Issue V
April 1995

Issue V April 1995

Our first anniversary, and wow were we proud of ourselves? With hindsight this issue marks the end of the initial phase of *Animals & Men*. The magazine had started to get an identity of its own, and many of the features which are still to be found in the magazine today were already in place by the fifth issue. The controversy over the Migo video continued, and with hindsight it is difficult to see why no-one wrote to us complaining "Enough of the Migo Video Already" like they did a few years later when the ongoing arguments about whether or not there were Wolverines in the UK began to get nasty.

At the end of our first year we were able to look back with a certain amount of pride and self satisfaction on what we had achieved. Re-reading the magazines now for producing this compilation I am still proud. I would like to take this opportunity to thank my ex-wife, my adopted daughter, Jane Bradley and Jan Williams for all that they did to get the magazine off the ground. Jane is dead, my ex-wife and I don`t communicate any more and Jan Williams has gone off to do her own inimitable thing. Only Lisa my daughter is still involved at the time of writing (November 2001) and that is only on an ad hoc basis of manning the photocopier and answering the telephone. But I can truthfully say that if it hadn`t been for those four women the CFZ as we know it today would never have existed.

Animals & Men

The Journal of The Centre for Fortean Zoology

Lake Monsters-Loch Ness and Lake Dakataua;
Mystery Cats; The Hairy Hands of Dartmoor;
and much more.....

Incorporating "The Crypto Chronicle".

Issue Five   £1.75

CONTENTS AND CREDITS

This issue of Animals & Men was put together by the following band of Animals and Men:

Jonathan Downes: Editor and Fall Guy.
Jan Williams: Newsfile and Catfish.
Alison Downes: Ornithological Administratrix.
Lisa Peach: Art, Typing Tea and Ferrets.
John Jacques: Sole Representation.
Graham Inglis: Video.
Dave Symons: Software jockey
Nigel Smith: "SHUT UP NIGEL!"

Regional Representatives

LANCASHIRE;   Stuart Leadbetter.
SUSSEX: Sally Parsons.
CUMBRIA AND LAKELANDS: Brian Goodwin.
HOME COUNTIES: Phillip Kibberd
EIRE   Tony 'Doc' Shiels.
SPAIN: Alberto Lopez Acha.
FRANCE: Francois de Sarre.
MEXICO: Dr R.A Palmeros.
SCOTLAND: Tom Anderson.
WEST MIDLANDS: Dr Karl P.N.Shuker.

Consultants

SURREALCHEMY   Tony 'Doc' Shiels.
ZOOLOGY: Dr Karl P.N.Shuker.

Advertising Rates by arrangement.

The Centre for Fortean Zoology
15 Holne Court
Exwick, Exeter.
Devon EX4 2NA

0392 424811

Contributors this issue:
Roy Kerridge, Jan Kingshott; Dr Karl P.N.Shuker.
Stephen Shipp, Stuart Leadbetter, Eric Sorensen,
Mike Grayson, Nick Morgan, Andy Stephens,
Suzanne Stebbings

4 ISSUE SUBSCRIPTION RATES
UK/EIRE £7.00
EEC £8.00
EUROPE Non EEC £8.50
REST OF WORLD: £10 (surface Mail)
REST OF WORLD £14 (Air Mail)

Payment in UK Currency, Cheque drawn on UK bank, IMO, Eurocheque. Cheques payable to A&J DOWNES or THE CENTRE FOR FORTEAN ZOOLOGY

CONTENTS

ANIMALS & MEN is published four times a year and is typeset and assembled by diverse poultry using an antiquated AMIGA A500, Pagesetter 2, D Paint v.4, and Penpal. Oh for a 486.

THE GREAT DAYS OF

Dear Readers,

With this our fifth issue, the magazine is just about a year old and we are now ready to move onto a new and more exciting plane.

We have commenced the first stages of our expansion programme. The more astute amongst you will have noticed that the cover price has risen by 25p an issue, and that the UK subscription rate is therefore a pound more a year than it was three months ago. This is because, starting with this issue we have added eight pages and are now forty pages long. We eventually intend to be about seventy pages each issue with a cover price of about two pounds fifty! The new rates will not effect existing subscribers until their present subscription has expired.

Craig Harris, the founding editor of our friendly rivals, 'The Crypto Chronicle' has decided to call it a day, and he has donated his considerable archive to The Centre for Fortean Zoology. 'The Crypto Chronicle' is now incorporated within this magazine, and all subscribers to 'The Crypto Chronicle' will have the balance of their subscriptions transferred to 'Animals & Men'. Subscribers to both magazines (and there were quite a lot of you) will have their subscription to 'The Crypto Chronicle' added to the end of their existing subscription to this magazine, and articles submitted to 'The Crypto Chronicle' for publication will now be published by 'Animals & Men'. Craig himself, although mostly retired from Cryptozoology has joined our editorial team as 'Bigfoot Consultant'.

Also new to our team are the legendary fortean and surrealist Tony 'Doc' Shiels whose self appointed designation as 'Surrealchemist in Residence', is one with which we concur one hundred percent, and Dr Karl P.N.Shuker, probably the UK's most eminent Cryptozoologist as 'Zoology Consultant'. Both Karl and 'Doc' have been helping out behind the scenes for some time and it is a great pleasure to be able to welcome them officially to the team.

The A-Z of Cryptozoology has been held over for this issue, partly because of Jan Williams' ongoing problems with moving house, but mostly because of the two pages of obituaries which we felt the need to include in this issue. Assuming that noone else dies normal service will be resumed with the next issue. Jan still hasn't got a permanent address at the moment, so if anyone wants to write to her please do so care of the editorial address.

I would like to include a special 'Thank You' to Steve Browning, the antipodean D.J on Gemini Radio in Exeter who has had me on his show as his special guest on a number of occasions this year. His good humoured support and encouragement is much appreciated.

My very best wishes until next time.
Best Wishes,

ZOOLOGY ARE NOT DONE

NEWSFILE

Compiled and Edited by Jan *"Don't talk to me
about Estate Agents"* Williams with bits from
The Editor.

MYSTERY CATS

Cornwall

Deer farmer Stephen Pattle is convinced his herd is being preyed upon by a big cat which has been seen several times in the Galowras area, west of Mevagissey. Mr Pattle discovered the carcasses of seven young deer on his farm near Polmassick in January. Only the heads, legs and feet remained.

Mevagissey resident Dave Brewster reported a puma-like animal on the road from Tregony Hill to Gorran. He said *'the creature's fur appeared to be bright red, probably accentuated because of the bright daylight'.* (*Cornish Guardian 2.2.95*)

Devon

Sue Hatcher was taking her four-year-old daughter for a pony ride down a steep-sided lane near Buckland St. Mary when her labrador dog flushed what she thought was a deer from the top of the bank 20 feet above them. The animal leapt down the near-vertical bank and bounded across the lane about 10 yards in front of them, with the dog in close pursuit.

To her astonishment, Sue realised it was a large, sleek, black cat the same height as the labrador, but longer-bodied with a thick black tail. The cat jumped into a tree on the other side of the lane, and Sue stood underneath it for several minutes, looking up at the animal, before realising this might not be a sensible policy and retreating towards a nearby cottage. She noted that the cat's head was the size of a small football, and it had greeny-yellow eyes. The pony took little notice of the cat and was more concerned by Ben, the labrador, who was chasing about in the undergrowth.

Sue said *'If someone had told me they'd seen a big cat before this I would have been sceptical. But it was definitely a cat - I was so close to it - and Ben was only feet from it and was a clear point of reference as to size'.*

Panther-like cats were reported a few miles away in the Bishopswood area in January of this year, and Terry Cox of Greendale, near Ilminster, watched a strange black animal through opera glasses as it stalked through fields at Herne Hill on 2nd March. Two weeks previously he had observed the same animal apparently following exactly the same route. (*Chard News? 8.3.95*)

Further south in the county, Tim Holmes was 'gobsmacked' by an encounter with the Beast of Salcombe Regis - centre of a major catflap in Spring 1993. He was driving near Tipton St. John on 30th January when he caught a glimpse of the animal. He got out of the car, leaned over the hedge and saw a black cat 'like a

Jaguar' and at least two feet high, in the field. Large prints were found. *(Sidmouth Herald 4.2.95)*

Cambridgeshire

Trudy Bristow and David Brown saw a large cat-like animal dart across the road in front of their car in the early hours of Sunday 12th February, near the village of Haddenham. They described it as slightly smaller than a labrador, thin and black with a very long tail. *(Ely Standard 16.2.95)*

Rutland

A *'black panther'* and a lynx-like cat were reported in the villages of Ketton, Knossington, Preston and Barrowden, in and around the Vale of Catmose, in January of this year.*(ITV Teletext 20.1.95)*

Clwyd, Wales

Police were called to the Graig Park Country Club at Meliden, near Prestatyn, in February, following sightings of a *'panther'* in the hotel grounds. Receptionist Kathryn Jones was among the witnesses. She saw the animal lying on a concrete surface about 100 yards away and described it as *'the size of a Labrador dog, jet black and with a long tail'*. *(Daily Post 1.3.95)*

Tayside, Scotland

A large black cat was seen leaping across a road and into undergrowth close to the village of Colliston, near Arbroath, on January 6th. The motorist who reported it said *'It was black, much bigger than a Dalmation, but what struck me was the speed at which it moved. There was a lot of power in its rear legs and it was gone in a split second'*. (Actually, she didn't say it was bigger than a Dalmation, but I'm sick of typing 'Labrador'.) Arbroath Police searched the area.

Colliston is within 10 miles of Tannadice where a big cat was reported in November 1994 and January of this year.*(The Courier and Advertiser 7.1.95)*

Grampian, Scotland

An unnamed turkey farmer in Alves, Moray, claims to have shot a *'black panther'* which raided his bird pens in February.

In March Banffshire's Deputy Lord Lieutenant, Dr David Clark, photographed huge *'cat-like'* pawprints in a bunker at Banff's Duff House Royal golf course. He said *'The prints really were unusually large - about 5.5-6 inches across - and definitely feline . . . It looked as if the beast leapt into the bunker after a roe deer'*.

Dr Clark, a former medical lecturer at Aberdeen University, is a firm believer in mystery cats, having seen one in late 1994 on the Huntly - Kildrummy road. *'A large black cat with a long curved tail leapt out of a pine wood and ran along a dyke for 60 yards before disappearing back into the trees'*. (Aberdeen Press and

Journal 16.3.95)

Ecologist Doug Mortimer of the Grampian Badger Survey Group stated that a roe deer carcase found in woods near Pitcaple bore *'all the classic signs of other big cat attacks'*. The remains were unearthed on March 14th by Doug's dog 'Jan' (no relation!), who also found a stash of meat from the kill buried in the ground beside the skull of another deer. *(Aberdeen Press and Journal 16.3.95)*

Enfield, Middlesex.

A series of well publicised sightings of a mystery 'cat' during the summer of 1994 were consigned to the 'oh well' file when the animal in question proved to be a rather effeminate looking fox. Interestingly, the photograph of the animal finally printed by the newspapers looked very much like a jaguarundi, although its vulpine identity is not in question. *Enfield Advertiser June 8th. 15th. 22nd 1995 Via COUDi.*

Hillsboro. Ohio, USA.

Sherrif Tom Horst of Highland County. Ohio is coordinating the search for a mystery beast which appears to be living off small animals and road kills in the area. A partially 'eaten deer carcass has also been found. Several witnesses have seen the animal but although one witness has reported a tan and white striped 'tiger'. most of the reports refer to a creature that appears to be a puma. The only question of real interest is. whether it is an escaped pet/zoo/circus animal or possibly an Eastern Cougar. a subspecies of f.concolor thought extinct. outside Florida for many years. Columbus Dispatch Nov 27 1994 via COUDi

Vermont. USA.

Another possible population of the Eastern Cougar has been reported in Vermont where cats have been seen near the town of Craftsbury in a rural. forested area in the northern part of the state only 30 miles from the Canadian border. Mr Ronald Regan (no relation) of the Vermont Department of Fish and Wildlife described it at *"Exciting News"*. CRYPTOZOOLOGY NEWSLETTER Dec 1994 via COUDi.

Indonesia.

This isn't really a mystery cat but a farmer was recently killed in southern Sumatra by one of the worlds rarest felids..a Sumatran Tiger. There are only a handful of these animals left in the world which I don't suppose made the farmer feel any better. *Teletext world news ITV 9.3.95*

..and in the end..

A final word on mystery cats for this newsfile must come from Johnny Morris whose TV show 'Animal Magic' was essential viewing for animal loving children in the sixties and seventies: *"Well, what's wrong with them? They knock off sheep occasionally. but so do dogs. Its something we have to accept! I wish them the best of luck. I don't think that they have a very easy life in this country'.* C4 TELETEXT 14.9.95

Right on Johnny!

NEW AND REDISCOVERED SPECIES

GILBERTS POTOROO *(Potorous gilberti)*

The rodent sized Gilberts Potoroo which has been presumed
etinct for 125 years has been rediscovered by accident at Two
Peoples Bay, 250 miles South East of Perth, Australia. 'They
are the most beautiful creatures that I have ever seen with
their long noses and their incredibly soft skin' said Elizibeth
Sinclair, a zoology Student who caught the first two specimens,
a young male and an adult female. Soon after three more were
caught. The first two specimens and two of the others were
kept to start a captive breeding programme whilst the third was
fitted with a radio transmitter and released back into the wild.
*BBC CEEFAX TELETEXT Newsround 1.3.95, Westfalenpost 2.3.95 Die Welt 28.2.95. Picture: Engraving
by John Gould courtesy Dr Karl P.N.Shuker.*

SPIDERS IN THE BOG

Spiders usually turn up in the bath, but scientists from Liverpool Museum discovered a *Gnaphosa nigerrima*
spider at Wybunbury Moss, an 'Ice Age' bog near Nantwich, Cheshire. The spider was previously believed
extinct in Britain, though it survives in parts of continental Europe.*(Daily Mail 20.1.95).*

Another new species of spider is described in the December issue of The Cryptozoology newsletter. Researcher
Margaret Lowman, climbing through the forest canopy in Belize has discovered a new species of spider with
an amazing ability to 'shoot' its prey. The spider grasps a thread of its web, pulls it back like a boawspring, and
then 'snaps' it at a passing insect.

EIGHT ARMS TO HOLD YOU..

Another unknown species of octopus has been spotted. About 15 inches long and almost completely
transparent, the mollusc was sighted by the submersible 'Alvin' 1000 miles west of Guatamala at about 12, 000
feet. The animal caught the scientists attention because it was attempting to mate with another, much larger
octopus and they were both males. Scientist Janet Voigt speculated that '...deep sea octopi meet so rarely that
males will go for anything they bump into!' CRYPTOZOOLOGY NEWSLETTER Dec 1994 via COUDi.

GENETICS

JURASSIC PARK?

Michael Chrichton's best selling fantasy would appear to have come a few paces closer to fruition. 'Cotton like' substance on the inside of the shell of a fossilised dinosaur egg found in a field in Henan, contained amino acids but although the scientists of Beijing University managed to partially isolate some of the DNA, even if Chrichton's cloning experiments ARE possible, (and at the moment noone seem quite sure), not enough DNA was isolated to even attempt such experiments.

A month or so earlier scientists from Brigham Young University in Utah, USA announced that they have extracted the DNA from a fragment of Cretaceous period bone found in a coal mine. '*I am confident that we have a DNA sequence that belongs to a cretaceous-period bone fragment. Based on the circumstantial evidence we believe that it is a dinosaur*', said microbiologist Scott Woodward who lead the group.

Meanwhile in Montana a second group of scientists claim to have extracted genetic material from an unusually complete and well preserved skeleton of a six ton Tyrannosaurus rex discovered in 1990.

'*We have done it three times*' says dinosaur expert Jack Horner at Montana State and the Museum of The Rockies. '*We know that ours is 65.million years old but it is still unclear whether it belongs to the dinosaur or to some fungus or some bacteria or something else!*'. *Die Welt 17.3.95, Columbus Dispatch 1.2.95*

THE BUTTERFLY BALL

Two species of butterfly extinct in the UK for over three quarters of a century may reappear. The Large Copper Butterfly and The Chequered Skipper became extinct with the mass destruction of much of Britains hedgerows, but still exist elsewhere in Europe.

Geneticists from '*British Nature*' hope to combine the DNA from preserved museum specimens with living insects from Europe and then reintroduce the beautiful insects to their old habitats. There are three subspecies of The Large Copper in Europe and although the British

The Large Copper   The Chequered Skipper
Lycaena dispar   *Carterocephalus palaemon*

subspecies *L d.dispar* became extinct in 1848 there have been sporadic and relatively unsuccessful attempts to introduce the smaller Dutch species to a fen near Huntingdon where a colony has been maintained intermittently for some years. C4 TELETEXT GREENNEWS 27.3.95

MYSTERY HOMINIDS & PRIMATES

DEBBIE GOES APE

Debbie Martyr has just returned from her latest expedition in search of the elusive Orang Pendek of Sumatra. Martyr, who claims to have seen the creature on three occasions describes '*an intelligent biped standing up to four feet tall. with silky, reddish coloured body hair. The face is bare with a heavy brow and almost human nose but the head and neck is gorilla like*'. She says that the animals actively avoid contact with humans and feed off ginger plants, termites, fruit, freshwater crabs and nesting birds and have even stolen the 'lunches' of researchers. Ms Martyr however is of the opinion that the creatures are intelligent apes rather than relict hominids. '*Bild*' *March 7.95, BBC Wildlife 1995.*

BIG FOOTPRINTS

A massive operation involving Trekkers, Wildlife experts, jungle tribes, policemen and even units of the Malaysian Army has been mobilised to search for an 8 foot tall hominid named 'bigfoot' (sounds familiar?) in the dense jungle surrounding Tanjung Pia in Johore province. Footprints have been found, but as we went to press it appeared that 'Operasi Kaki Besar' (Malay for...you guessed it, 'Operation Bigfoot'), was unsuccesful in obtaining more concrete evidence in favour of these mystery beings which the Johore tribesmen claim have been sent into Malaysia by unspecified 'evil forces'. *Rocky Mountain News Jan 13 1995 via COUDi, Columbus Dispatch 22.1.95 via COUDi*

WAITING FOR THE MAN

The intelligent and exciting research carried out by Chinese researchers into the Yeren or Chinese Wildman has been perverted a little recently when a number of newspapers worldwide, excitedly claimed to be printing a photograph of 'Son of Wildman' the putative offspring of a human girl in a remote Chinese village and one of these elusive mystery hominids. The photograph, which we make no apologies for reproducing here, without copyright clearance is nothing more than a picture of an oriental man in his late teens or mid twenties suffering from Microcephaly, and has no real relevance whatsoever to the main body of mystery hominid research. We are printing it purely to close this rather unwhoselsome sub-chapter of the history of cryptozoology and also as a heartfelt rebuke to journalists, editors and even scientists who should know better for using a photograph of a severely impaired human being in a crass attempt to sell newspapers.

The 'real' research in China continues apace with several new sightings, a new body dedicated to the mystery, 'The Committee for the Search of rare and Strange Creatures', (formed by a group of scientists from the Chinese Academy of Science), and even a martyr to the cause!

Wang Guan Xiang, a 40 year old forestry worker saw a Yeren when he was ten years old: "I was walking home from school at three P.M when I saw him just ahead-he looked like a big, tall man but was covered in long red hair..I told my mother but she worried that I was telling lies and asked my Uncle to look at the spot. He found a footprint next to the rock where I had seen the wildman standing".

The martyr is another Forest ranger, Yuan Yu Hao, who has also seen the creature on a number of occasions and has become so obsessed with capturing a specimen that his employers recently docked him two months wages for neglecting his job in favour of wild man research. *Brisbane Sunday Telegraph 15.1.95 Brisbane Sunday Mail 8.1.95 via COUD i and UK Daily Mail December 1994.*

WILD CHILD

A 'wild child' found two years ago in rural Romania and placed in a home in Bucharest remains 'feral' and continues to suckle the bitch which succoured him, a news agency has repoorted. The child, named Sorin, who is about nine years old speaks no human words but communicates with the dog (with whom he still shares his food) by making barking sounds. BRISBANE COURIER MAIL 24.7.94 Via COUDi

RHESUS NEGATIVE

Three Rhesus Macaques escaped from Woburn Safari Park. Bedfordshire, on 17th March. The monkeys remained within the park boundaries for several days, then moved out into the surrounding countryside. By the weekend of the 25th they had crossed the M1 motorway, and were heading for more densely populated areas. At dawn on Sunday one of the macaques was shot in a tree at Westoning, and a second, which had been running through gardens and over rooftops in the town of Flitwick, was shot on Monday morning. The third was enticed into a garage by a householder acting on the advice of Safari Park staff and was recaptured safely.

Chris Webster, Managing Director of Woburn Safari Park, said he and the rest of the staff were concerned and upset by the deaths, but there was no alternative. They had tried to recapture the monkeys, and had considered using tranquillizer darts, but this had not been practical. Macaques are listed under the Dangerous Wild Animals Act, and once they moved into built-up areas there was a possible risk to the public. Police and RSPCA officials agreed shooting was the only viable option.

DUTCH BABOONS CLIMB A TREE...

Two hundred Baboons in Emmen Zoo in Holland all climbed up the same tree for no apparent reason. Last summer one animal started to scream and they all climbed the tree and refused to come down. *BBC TELETEXT 20.7.94*

MORE BABOONS...

Foreign seamen smuggling rare species into the UK pose a real problem say customs officials in Plymouth, who cited the recent case of a Maltese seaman who smuggled in a West African Olive Baboon and offered it for sale in the city. *ITV WESTCOUNTRY NEWS TELETEXT 27.1.95*

THE BEAST OF BALA

What seemed for five minutes like it was going to be the most exciting crypto news story for many moons fizzled out again just as we were going to press. 7.30 PM Wednesday April 5th, a Policeman driving on the A494 between Bala and Llanuwchllyn saw an animal chasing 30-40 sheep. The sheep were terrified and climbing on top of each other. The officer threw a stone and a stick at the animal which ran away. The Policeman was concerned that the sheep would be injured and went and told the owner, and the policeman and the farmer, armed with a shotgun followed the animal into a field, saw it running towards the flock of sheep, and shot it. The animal was described as about 4ft long, black and white with 'a badgers head' and the tail of a monkey.

It turned out to be a Ruffed Lemur, an endangered species, and a creature that normally eats nothing larger than sweet fruit and nesting birds. As we went to press its origin was uncertain but it had been announced that it had escaped locally. *BBC TELETEXT and various radio reports 6.4.95*

THE WIZARDS OF OZ

A lost tribe of pygmy Aborigines could be living in the north Queensland jungle claims Australian amateur historian Frank 'Salty' O'Rourke. When he was a boy he had been told stories about these mysterious little men: 'Old fellows used to say watch out when you go into the forest for those pygmies..they reckon they were in there and so small and quiet that they would disappear when they saw the white man coming'. Mr O'Rourke has gathered an impressive body of evidence to support his claims and he even claims that these people were photographed in the 1880's. There have only, however, been two reports of 'lost' aboriginal tribes being 'discovered' in the last thirty years, the most recent being in 1984 when nine Pintubi nomads arrived at the Papunya outstation west of Alice Springs. BRISBANE COURIER MAIL. 17.10.94 via COUDi

FRESHWATER AND MARINE MYSTERIES

JAWS!

A Great White Shark is suspected in the fatal attack on diver James Robinson, (42) near San Miguel Island 40 miles off the coast of Santa Barbara, California. The states last shark fatalities were off Malibu in 1989. *USA TODAY 12.12.95 Via COUDi*

TURNING TURTLE

A record number of sea turtles were washed up dead on the Texas coast last year according to experts who blame off-shore dredging operations. *TELETEXT ITV 9.3.95*

THE 'NESSIE' WITH THE GOLDEN HAIR

A large aquatic creature described as *'having a head as large as a bull and a dragon like body covered in flowing golden blonde hair'*, has been reported from Tianchi Lake on the mountainous border between China and North Korea. The sightings have, apparently continued intermittently for the last century and photographs and even video footage has been taken. After the saga of Lake Dakataua the editor is far less sceptical than he used to be about such things and awaits more news with interest. *WATERBURY REPUBLICAN-AMERICAN 10.9.94 via COUDi*

JAPANESE MEGAMOUTH

The seventh Megamouth shark (*Megachasma pelagios*) has been washed up in Hakata Bay, Kyushu, Japan. This specimen, a female measures 4.8m and weighs 790 kg. The specimen is in a deep freeze at the Marine Museum, in Fukuoka. The species was first seen in 1976 when a dead specimen was hauled up in Hawaii, and it wasn't scientifically described for another seven years. Only two living specimens have ever been seen. *BBC WILDLIFE Feb 1995 and Dr Karl Shuker.*

PIRANHAS IN THE HOLY LAND.

Yaakov Ezri, an Israeli fisherman, caught three mysterious fish in the sea of Galilee. A local 'expert' identified them as Piranhas. These voracious South American fish are kept worldwide as popular, if slightly macabre pets and have been accidentally (or possibly even maliciously) introduced into parts of Europe bordering on The Mediterranean. The three fish were bought for more than $100 dollars each by souvenir hunters in search of a novelty. They were, presumably, not too pleased when the fish turned out to be the equally exotic, and closely related (but not so media friendly) Pacu..a harmless vegetarian. Although local experts speculated that the fish would be unlikely to survive the temperature drop in the winter one wonders what the effect on the Galilean ecosystem would be if these unusual fish became established there? *COLUMBUS DISPATCH 18.12.94, DETROIT NEWS 18.11.94 both Via COUDi*

OTHER NEWS

DUMBO STRIKES BACK

Walt Disney Inc has taken extreme measures to stop fake copies of its toys being sold in India. It has hired two elephants to crush 20, 000 fake Mickey Mouse toys in Dehli as a symbolic warning. *NEWSROUND BBC CEEFAX 23.3.95*

HOLY HERMAPHRODITE GOATS!

A Palestinian shepherd is making a considerable income from the milk from his goat! Israelis and Arabs are queuing up to to drink the milk because they believe it is a cure for impotence. The goat is male and has sired more than fifty kids, but he has one teat which gives two glasses of milk a day. Shepherd, Mufid Abdul Chafer is charging twenty one ponds per glass! *WEIRD BUT TRUE ITV TELETEXT 11.2.95*

FUNKY DUNG

Two totally trivial news items which caught your editor's attention for no apparent reason. Rochester City Council recently announced that each week one and a half tonnes of dog excrement were deposited on the streets of their fair city. Sounds Divine! Maybe we should all go to Boysie Idaho. London artist Sally Matthews used eight buckets of cow dung spread on a cow shaped steel and wire frame for her latest life sized work in an exhibition entitled 'With Animals'. *AUSTRALIAN COURIER MAIL 25.7.94 via COUDi*

URBAN JUNGLE

Complaints from neighbours prompted environment officials to investigate Vincent Pace's house in Syracuse, New York. The small house was crammed with 74 exotic animals and birds. An African lion, Bengal tiger, black bear, wallaby, and monkeys were roaming free in the property. Pace has been charged with unlawful possession of protected wildlife.*(Mail on Sunday 15.1.95)*

FLAMING PETS

'Our policy is humans first, hamsters second' said fire officer Tony Reid after two fire engines loaded with firefighters rushed to a blazing house in Far Cotton, Northamptonshire to rescue a three-month-old hamster. Dusky the hamster was asleep at the time, but they poked him to see if he was all right, and he wasn't even warm. Snakes apparently come third on the list in Northants. Firefighters rescued four large pythons - one 13 feet long from David Vine's burning bedroom in Romany Road, Northampton. Two tarantulas and a scorpion also survived the blaze. Mr Vine's mother said her son had kept 'weird animals' for several years. *(Northampton Chronicle 22.3.95)*

Newsfile Correspondents: Alan Beattie, Dionne Jones, Alan Pringle, Steven Shipp, Karl Shuker, Tom Anderson, COUDi., Wolfgang Schmidt.

Boars and Pumas

by
Roy Kerridge

Most English people, however ardently they may speak of conservation, feel a secret relief that dangerous wild animals in this country have been wiped out a long time ago. Even amidst the wildest Northern Hills, (it is believed we may walk freely without having to fear wild boars, bears and wolves. Our non conservationist ancestors have, with bow and arrow, granted us this freedom. Now, for the first time in centuries these certainties are beginning to fade. Rumours of wild beasts returning mysteriously to moorland and mountain are causing many a head to turn nervously whenever the bracken rustles.

When a wild boar, nicknamed 'Bonnie' by the local press, escaped from a farm into the hills of County Durham, headlines proclaimed the return of Boar Hunting to Britain.Garbled reports in southern papers suggested that police marksmen were closing in on a giant sheep ravaging wild boar. Sergeant Eddie Bell, of Consett Police Station, had been named in such a report, and I took him to be the leader of the hunting party. So up to County Durham I went, to meet Sergeant Bell in his home town of Stanley, where he lives with his wife Patricia, not far from the Blue Boar Inn.

The Bells, Eddie and Patricia, were about to move house when I arrived, so I sat among packing cases, drinking tea and listening to fascinating tales of wild beasts at large. Eddie proved to be a big, genial man, round faced yet rugged. Although the boar story proved not as exciting as I had hoped, Eddie Bell's account of Pumas and other big cats more than made up for this. Police reports of big game on the loose had been sent to him from every part of Britain, and he kept them in a battered file stained by banana sandwiches from his 'bait box'. (Geordie for lunch box). Meanwhile Eddies expertise on animal matters has spared the Durham police from mounting a costly boar hunt.

'The farmer who claimed that he had seen the boar attacking his sheep based his description of the animal on a TV Film he had seen of warthogs in Africa. He described a warthog and when I told him what a female wild boar looks like, he didn't know what to say. For a start Bonnie weighs less than the sheep she is supposed to have savaged, and her teeth are not capable of tearing flesh, as a male boar's tusks might do. In Germany where wild boar farming is commonplace, female boars feed in the same fields as sheep. Dogs, probably lurchers were the real culprits. A police hunt for a harmless animal like Bonnie would have been a real waste of money. Mr Pinder, the farmer who lost her, simply went along with a pheasant shooting party, in the vain hope that Bonnie would be flushed out of hiding by the guns'.

(It seemed odd to reflect that Bonnie was not only a 'female boar' but a 'tame wild boar'. However, I suppose that many wild ducks are really drakes, and that wild ducks in parks are tame).

Vague plans for capturing Bonnie were still under discussion (drugged apples were one idea - a bit like Snow White), but as she did little harm, I felt that she might as well remain in the woods as a tourist attraction. More alarming were Eddie's files on escaped big cats. Call me squeamish but I have a horror of wild leopards. Records seem to prove without a doubt that black panthers (as black leopards are known), lurk in English woods. Writer Auberon Waugh has seen one running across a cricket field in Somerset, to name only one witness.

Fortunately for the friendly people of County Durham, Eddie believes that most *'big cat sightings'* locally are of pumas. A puma is slightly smaller than the average leopard, and is russet brown in colour, with a white and black muzzle, large black rimmed ears, a white throat and a long, thick black tipped but not tufted tail. Its natural range covers the whole american continent from Alaska to Patagonia. Although supposedly extinct in the Eastern states of the U.S.A., individuals appear enigmatically every ten years or so. Pumas only attack humans if trapped, wounded or cornered, and usually prefer rabbits or deer to farm stock. They are easily tamed and the introduction and sudden suppression of the puma as a pet shop animal has caused the cat to become part of Britain's wildlife.

I remember seeing an enchanting puma cub in a Weymouth pet shop at the height of the 'Surrey Puma' scare. Young pumas have spots which fade on adulthood.

Tough, wealthy young builders and men of action, in the early 'seventies, began to buy big cats as pets, a trend which alarmed the government. The Dangerous Animal Act of 1976 was an attempt to control matters by introducing licenses, 'vetting' owners, laying down standards of cage construction and so on. Many families appear to have responded by driving the family puma, leopard or jaguar to a lonely spot and turning it loose. I was incredulous at such folly, but Eddie assured me that it happened.

'Supposing a man grew fond of his puma, and couldn't afford to comply with the new regulations. He may have felt it was better to turn it loose than to have it put to sleep', he complained, with something of an animal lovers pity in his voice.

Eddie's file showed that in the early 'eighties pumas in County Durham were reported in the populous semi-industrialised eastern part of the county, near the sea. Now, most reports come, far more infrequently from the wild and mountainous west. It seemed as if released pumas had gradually made their way further and further from the scene of their release from captivity into wilderness country. At first they might have scavenged for food, but now they had learned to hunt rabbits and roe (a small deer), and could survive independantly of man.

'There's so many rabbits lying squashed on the roads that a puma could live on them easily without hunting at all' Eddie told me. *'I could live on them, if I had to.*

I estimate that in the hills west of here eleven to fourteen pumas are living wild within an area of six hundred square miles. Roe Deer are increasing at a great rate, and in the same area there may be twenty thousand deer! These deer are culled frequently. A deer census has been held but I think that it only shows a third of the true numbers. When a helicopter hovered just over a wood, more deer ran out into the fields than any census taker would have believed possible. Roe Deer like broken farmland.

Just across the border in Northumberland, in Keilder forest, there are supposed to be two thousand roe deer, but I believe that there are really six thousand there. Each year there is an .attempted cull of eighty percent of the deer. In other words, if you have four thousand deer in your wood, you must shoot three hundred and twenty a year to keep the numbers stable, and stop them from destroying their own neighbourhood.

For many years now, natural predators of deer have been wiped out. Now the puma is taking over the role. A large puma could live very well on seventy to ninety deer a year. experiments with captive pumas in large enclosures show that zoo bred animals can learn to hunt almost overnight. It seems that as deer are the natural prey of a puma, wild pumas will stick to what they know and ignore sheep'.

I wondered if there had been many cases of sheep killed by pumas

'Well, round here, a sheep was killed by a big cat at Bowburn, to judge by the evidence. West of Stanley, in the hills, a sheep could vanish and the farmer wouldn't know that it was gone. Of course, every big cat reported is not a puma. Larger cats would certainly kill sheep. I estimate that there must be about two hundred wild pumas nationwide'.

According to his files there are other species loose as well..

'I have had reports of lions and even a cheetah, but that's a bit far fetched. Apart from pumas there are Indian Jungle cats, leopards, leopard cats, lynxes and a Bengal Tiger'...

'A What??' I gasped..

'Yes, in Sutherland, north east Scotland there is a solitary Bengal Tiger living wild. People who own private zoos or keep exotic pets, very seldom report it if an animal escapes. They keep quiet in case of trouble. You say you're staying at the Neville's Cross Hotel, Durham City? There was an African Crested Porcupine living wild there for ages. It survived being knocked down by a car, and was eventually captured by a man from the Ministry of Agriculture.

On another occasion a well known zoo decided to send two male timber wolves to an exhibition at the museum in Newcastle. The wolves travelled up in a van which was parked overnight at the Town Moor. In the morning when the driver got there, he found the back of the van open and the wolves gone! No one has seen them since!

Baboons escaped from the Lambton Wildlife Park, and began throwing stones at cars on the motorway. Those animals were caught but of the two Nilghai (a large Indian Antelope) that escaped from Flamingoland, Yorkshire, one was shot and one may still be free'.

Of the wild cats on Eddie Bell's list, the Indian jungle cat and the leopard cat pose no threat to human life. They are not much larger than a domestic cat. Jungle cats are brown, with tufted ears and short tails and have been reported from the Welsh Borders. One was found dead near Ludlow in Shropshire.

(EDITORS NOTE: Another specimen was killed by a car in Hayling Island, Hampshire. The stuffed remains of the Shropshire animal are now the property of 'Animals and Men' contributor Dr Karl P.N.Shuker).

Leopard cats also from India, are small and unalarming. These attractive little animals have been shot in Scotland.

(EDITORS NOTE: The Bengal Leopard Cat (Felis bengalensis) is widely distributed across Asia where it is often kept as a house pet and has hybridised with domestic 'moggies', as well as being hunted for food in Southern China. A new breed of domestic cat currently in vogue amongst the cognoscenti also has some F. bengalensis in its bloodline. Feral specimens of this charming creature have been shot in Cheshire, on Dartmoor and on the Isle of Wight, as well as in Scotland).

Our native Scottish wildcat once lived across Britain.
Pockets of native wildcattery may have remained in Wales and on Exmoor. It seems that Scottish Wildcats, feral (gone wild) domestic cats, jungle cats and leopard cats may all be breeding with each other in the wild.

Odd looking hybrid cats are constantly being reported. Many are black, and I put forward the idea that Mothe Nature has decided to settle on black as a catch all colour for hybrid cats of various multi coloured backgrounds.

'Perhaps escaped BIG cats, like pumas and leopards are breeding' I suggested. So many reports of big cats describe black animals, and black panthers are rare in captivity.

'No, I think that nearly all reports are of Pumas' Eddie replied. There is no known case of a melanistic (black mutation), puma.

(EDITOR'S NOTE: Not quite true-but statistically close enough).

Bodger, my Bull Mastiff is a brown puma colour. If you see him close by in a field by moonlight he looks black At thirty yards he's invisible. I've watched him under car headlights and unless he's directly in front of the car, he STILL looks black. Even under street lighting he looks dark, so I think that many so called 'black panthers' are really pumas which are not so dangerous'.

As Eddie spoke his own cat Samantha, leaped onto a packing case and flattened her ears wildcat fashion.

'She's a cross between a domestic cat and a Scottish Wildcat', Eddie said calmly. 'Near here, Consett and Stanley there have been reports of big cats that appear to be lynxes. That's puzzling as Lynxes are seldom kep in captivity'.

A lynx is a jungle cat writ large, though not as large as a puma, it seldom attacks man and a full grown shee would probably be too much for it. Nobody seems quite sure whether Lynxes survived in Britain into historic times. References in old books to 'the catamount' might refer to the Lynx or to the scottish wildcat. (I America the Puma is often called 'The Catamount' or 'Mountain Lion').

Eddie and I agreed that Lynxes might have survived in Britain unnoticed until now. William Cobbett, author o 'Rural Rides' (1830) saw a strange wild animal as a boy in England that in adulthood he recognised at a lynx He travelled to North America where lynxes were common, and saw the same species of animal there.

At long last, Eddie handed me his precious file, and I had a look for myself. The file opened in 1986, the yea of 'cat fever' in Britain, with a Mr Dawkins of Edinburgh's report about seeing a black panther late at nigh near the city.

The second item was altogether more amusing.

'24th September 1986. Woman from Bowburn reported hearing an animal roaring at rear of a hedge next to a field. She said it sounded just like a tiger roaring. It was a field full of cows. Believed to be the sound of a cow mooing'.

'Until I started this file I thought that people could at least tell a cat from a dog', Eddie remarked. 'Now doubt if people can tell an elephant from a frog'.

Three reports of big cats in County Durham itself seemed most convincing. At Melsonby a puma with three cubs was seen by a man described as a 'proper countryman'. who knew all about animals. Near Beamish, lynx had been seen by a professor of biology. On August 25th 1992 a biology teacher and her daughter saw a puma hunting rabbits along the edge of a railway line and watched it for quite a time.

Now utterly convinced of the puma's future place in books of British wildlife, I asked Sergeant Bell if he had ever seen one in the wild. To my surprise, he had not, but he had made a plaster cast of a fresh pug mark in the clay at nearby Wingate. (All readers of books on big game hunting will know that a big cat's footprint is called a pugmark). The print had been identified as that of a puma. A bulldozer had destroyed most of the prints by the time he had arrived.

My interview was over, but as an extra treat Sergeant Bell took me into a back room where he kept a delightful zoo of little disneyish animals-chipmunks, opposums, flying squirrels and bright eyed spiny mice from Arabia. Before leaving County Durham I called at Stanley Taxis and asked Michael, a young driver to give me a tour of puma country. A gifted conversationalist, Michael told me of roe deer he had seen running across the fields, but he knew nothing of pumas. We drove through market towns, along scenic forest roads and into the river Wear at the ford near Stanhope.)

What a country! All the best qualities of the Cotswolds and of the Highlands combine to make County Durham a holidaymakers dream. But I was disappointed in one thing. We drove all the way through Hamsterley Forest and didn't see so much as a hamster. Perhaps I'll spot a puma next time!

Witness Reliability in Mystery Cat Sightings: A Cautionary Tale.

by J.B.Kingshott BSc (Hons) M.A ARSM

The worldwide mystery cat phenomenon has a common denominator present in every single sighting, and that denominator is the obvious presence of one or more witnesses to that sighting. Much of the evidence for the presence of mystery cats comes from the written or oral evidence presented by the witness, based upon their cognitive recollections of the incident itself. In considering this fact we must be aware of the dangers of accepting witness testimony as indisputable fact without real evidence. Just because a witness says that a particular fact was true does not mean that it actually was. Am I saying that all witnesses to mystery cats are hoaxers? Of course not. A hoax can be defined as a conscious decision to deceive for humourous or mischievous purposes. [1] While hoaxers do permeate the field of mystery cat studies, as they do in any field of unexplained phenomena, the majority of reports come from genuine people who have actually seen an unexpected and unexplained animal, and often need much cajoling to relay the facts for fear of ridicule from peers. Why then, should we be sceptical of their testimony? The following discussion should explain this more fully. I am not dismissing reports of mystery cats, as it is a fact that they do exist and are physically very real, but I am introducing the concept of caution to the reader.

Is there such an entity as 'the reliable witness'? If you were to ask one hundred people to list variable professions that they believe to be reliable witnesses, included near the top of that list would be the police officer. Should we therefore consider police officers to be unshakable in their views of mystery cat incidents? As a Police officer myself, I have taken the opportunity of talking to colleagues about their own unreported sightings of large felines. When working the night shift I have often had the opportunity of being double crewed in a panda car. In this situation topics of conversation are wide and varied and invariably turns to stories of the unexplained. Police officers are out and about at all sorts of strange hours and a conversation with any of them will bring forward a torrent of stories about strange goings on that have been witnessed. An example would be where former PC's Cliff Waycott and Roger Willey encountered the famous 'flying cross' UFO in Hatherleigh, Devon, in October 1967.[2] Whether you actually believe in UFOs or not is irrelevant, as the point is that it was a strange occurrence, it did actually happen, and the principal witnesses were police officers.

Of the ten members of my shift four people (not including myself) had seen what can only be described as mystery cats, some on numerous occasions. As police officers we are often required to be moved to various stations around Devon and Cornwall. Consequently in more rural stations, the opportunity arises for night patrolling in out of the way places. It is here that such sightings seem to occur. These sightings, although often amongst the most interesting go largely unreported for fear of the unrelenting ridicule expected from colleagues. What sort of sightings am I talking about?

Perhaps the best sighting came from my tutor constable, whose name I will withhold for the reasons outlined above. His sighting occurred on an unclassified section of road near the village of Kenn just outside Exeter. He was driving his police car down the road when he noticed something moving in the outer limit of his headlights. Thinking it was a dog he slowed the car down and continued to approach the animal. As he got closer, he realised that it was not moving in a 'dog like' manner, but was loping along like a cat. It continued to move along the edge of the road in front of the car until it was about twenty feet away. By this time it was well within the illuminated area provided by the headlights. He watched as the creature turned its head towards him and looked at the car, which by now had stopped. He described the creature as follows:-

'It was definitely a big cat with a shaggy coat that was dark brown or black in colour with lighter patches underneath. It had small ears and the eyes shone green in the headlights. It was about five feet long and had an enormous curving tail, the end of which kept twitching. The head seemed quite small for the body and the legs were stocky with large feet. It watched me for about ten seconds and then casually walked up into the hedge'.[3]

Another sighting was made by a police officer from Exeter known as Jock. This sighting which occurred near the village of Whimple is remarkable principally due to the close proximity of the witness to the cat and the behaviour of the cat itself. I have not interviewed Jock myself, but my Dad, at the time a Sergeant at Heavitree Road, did.

'I was driving along the road when I saw a bloody great cat by the side of the road. It wasn't the least bit surprised at the noise from the car or the light from the headlights. It was brown in colour, of stocky build and had a comparatively small head, a long tail and big feet. It wasn't frightened and started to walk towards the car. I killed the engine and just sat there. It came across the front of the car and started to walk down the offside. I was in a Ford Escort and the head was visible above the bonnet. It walked up to the drivers window and sniffed at it. It had black patches around its mouth and the colour of its head seemed to be a lighter brown than the body colour. It looked straight at me and then walked off behind the car. When I had recovered from the shock I turned around and it had gone'.[4]

These are just a couple of the many sightings by police officers that I am collating. Other sightings have been made from all over Devon, and I am just scratching the surface because being stationed in one particular place

I do not get the opportunity to meet many officers from the more rural regions. However unreported police sightings are still drifting to me, the latest being reported to my Dad (now an Inspector in Camborne), on the 25th October 1994.

As to analysing such sightings, I have not really covered much ground, due to the small number of sightings I have collected as yet. From this small number I find that approximately 75% of the sightings refer to black cats and that the remaining 25% refer to brown cats. This agrees favourably with the reported frequency of such cats in North Devon collated from a much larger survey by Trevor Beer [5]. However such a distinction based on so small a number is hardly methodologically sound! It is the quality of the sightings that interest me rather than the quantity. Many people see fleeting glimpses of animals running across fields and assume them to be big cats, but police officers are usually described as 'reliable observers', and the comparatively higher incidence of close range sightings is interesting.

As to the eternal question of what they are, it is hard to say in most cases. Some, such as the sighting by Jock described above, point quite strongly to the ubiquitous puma, but what of the others? When reading through the descriptions of the cats as provided by eye witnesses, a researcher can just about reach a conclusion as to the animals possible identity, when a physical characteristic that the witness insists upon throws your opinion out the window. Does this mean that the United Kingdom is populated by several unknown species of bizarre cats? I would suggest that it does not and discrepancies arise due partly to the nature of witness observation as a phenomenon and partly due to misidentification of accepted though alien species.

In police work, the nature of witness sightings has important connotations in witness trials. Several people can see exactly the same incident and the people involved. Each witness will state categorically that what they describe is what they have seen, but they can't all be right. Similarly, if only one witness is present that description may not necessarily be correct with regard to the actual incident. These unconscious discrepancies, though not purposefully designed to deceive, can have a bearing on the reliability of that witness in a criminal trial, where all a defence barrister has to do is to introduce an element of reasonable doubt. This is an important point to bear in mind when considering mystery cat sightings. Add to the above the usual emotional reaction of shock, fear or excitement upon seeing a misplaced creature, often on a dark night, sometimes at quite a distance, sometimes for a brief moment and you have considerable room for error. Also, the replaying of the incident over and over again in the witnesses mind will gradually alter the facts from what was seen to what was believed or perceived to have been seen. Therefore, the witness may believe absolutely in what he is describing to you, but this does not automatically mean that it is an accurate rendition of what he actually saw. If a criminal case depended on such observational conditions, a defence barrister would shoot the witness down in flames.

Having said this, however, it does not mean that all reports are wildly inaccurate. Many may be perfectly valid and the descriptions given may be incredibly accurate. It is important to bear these points in mind when considering the validity of witness evidence. It is also important for researchers not to accept those sightings that confirm to known animals whilst dismissing those that don't as witness error. With this in mind are police officers more reliable as witnesses than other people?

Police Officers witness events just like everyone else and are subject to the same psychological discrepancies when considering witness testimony. However, we, (police officers) tend to have more experience and a degree of training in observational techniques, so are often described as 'reliable witnesses'. This is generally true, but the mind of a police officer is designed the same as anyone elses (contrary to popular belief!), so it is open to the same perceptual difficulties outlined above. An example would be the insistence by a certain Bodmin Police Officer, who has declared himself a 'big cat expert', that the big cats he regularly sees on Bodmin Moor are Pumas, when all the evidence, including the black colouration of the cats and expert testimony, points to the fact that they are not pumas at all. This illustrates another important point. That of witness prejudice. i.e You see what you want to.

If a person were to go out looking for a black panther on Exmoor, and see a dark coloured animal run onto woodland, he will be more open to the interpretation of a panther sighting than a more commonplace explanation. In other words he could have convinced himself that what he saw was a panther, almost before he saw it. If he were with a similar minded friend, they would effectively convince each other that they had seen a panther. Dr Karl Shuker identifies this problem in his excellent book *'Mystery Cats of the World':*

'Such excitement and interest (not to mention apprehension), (OCCUR,) that after a time any animal seen is automatically identified at the mystery one concerned' [6].

This is an automatic human reaction and some researchers suggest that most big cat sightings are simply misidentifications of feral cats [7], either consciously as in the infamous Sun photographs [8], or unconsciously as in the Surrey Puma sightings of the mid 1960's [9]. When considering some, but by no means all, amateur big cat investigators, it seems evident that little objective researching is undertaken and they are clearly open to such interpretations. This phenomenon can also be used to consider the animal kills commonly attributed to various *'Beasts'*. As soon as a sheep or a foal is killed everyone starts shouting 'its the Beast of Exmoor/Dartmoor/Bodmin/Tedburn etc!'. How many carcasses are actually scientifically examined and proved, not suspected, but proved beyond reasonable doubt that the kill is attributable to a big cat, and not a more commonplace native predator.

Allied to this is the power of suggestion when attempting to identify alleged mystery cats. How often have you heard a witness state categorically, *'It was a Puma, a Black Puma'?* Very few of these witnesses have any qualifications or experience in zoological identification, so could not tell a puma from a jungle cat, and many probably couldn't tell a puma from a dog. The identification of a *'black puma'* is a common one, and appears to stem from media misrepresentations during witness questioning, resulting in a misinformed opinion of identity. This is seen over and over again when the media are involved, and in one case the television crew told the witness to say that it was a cat when she thought it was a dog. However, the black puma has become the standard explanation for mystery black cat sightings, although as Dr Shuker states:

'Though variable in colour, only a single black puma has ever been officially documented. Hence it is highly unlikely that melanistic pumas could be the large black cats sighted in Britain' [10].

Having said this, so called 'experts' from local zoos and wildlife parks continue to categorically affirm that the large melanistic cat seen on Bodmin Moor last year was a *'female black puma'* [11].

This illustrates the problem when examining the method used by the researcher to elicit the required information during the interview stage. There are many differing techniques used in interviewing suspects and witnesses but the most useful for mystery cat sightings would be successive free recalls of the incident without questioning. Because there is no questioning the interviewer cannot colour the recall by suggestively implanting false information. Once this has been achieved, indirect questions such as *'What can you tell me about its head?'* are used instead of the more direct *'Did it have big ears?'*. This enables the witness to give a detailed description of what he saw without suggestive interruptions from the interviewer. By using the Cognitive Method of interviewing, the witness is allowed several recall stages enabling successively more detailed recollections of the event. Therefore a truer representation of the sequence of events in question will be presented.

be presented.

In conclusion, the presentation of witness evidence, be it by police officers or other people, should be considered cautiously when attempting to identify the presence of large cats in rural Britain. By no means dismiss as fanciful all reports of large cats, as there are many reliable reports each year, but beware of the pitfalls of taking witness testimony as fact without supporting evidence of whatever kind.

Copyright by J.B.Kingshott BSc (Hons) M.A ARSM Exeter, November 1994.

The opinions expressed in this article do not reflect any official police viewpoint and are simply the views and opinions of Jan Kingshott based on experience and research.

REFERENCES.

1. The Concise Oxford English Dictionary, Oxford University Press, 1976, p.510.
2. CHAPMAN, R: Unidentified Flying Objects, Mayflower Paperbacks, 1970, pp. 13-22.
3. Interviews with author, March 1994.
4. Interviews with Brian Kingshott, October 1992.
5. BEER, T: The Beast of Exmoor:Fact or Legend?, Countryside Productions, 1986 (?), p.13.
6. SHUKER, Dr K.P.N: Mystery Cats of the World: From Blue Tigers to Exmoor Beasts, Robert Hale pub., 1st Ed, 1989, p. 53.
7. BRIERLEY, N: They Stalk By Night: The Big Cats of Exmoor and the South West, Yeo Valley Productions, 1989.
8. The Sun newspaper, story and photographs by Robert Kellaway and Colin Shepherd respectively, Saturday 30th October 1993 pp. 1-2.
9. BURTON, M: Animals, vol 9, December 1966, pp.458-461.
10. SHUKER, Dr K.P.N: op.cit., 0.56.
11. From BBC South West TV Programme 'The Search for the Beast' first broadcast in November 1993 on BBC2.

CROCODILE TEARS II

Just when you thought it was safe to go back into Lake Dakataua.........
we finally get a copy of the video and everything we wrote in the last
three issues goes out of the proverbial window!

The recent revelations that a Japanese TV crew had managed to film what is apparently a large, long and apparently unknown species of animal in Lake Dakataua on the island of New Britain in the Bismark Archipelago, off the coast of New Guinea has been rocking the cryptozoological world to its shaky foundations. We first printed the news item in issue two and since then each issue has revealed progressively more about what is undoubtedly the most exciting piece of cryptozoological news for many years, if not ever. One morning we received a video cassette containing the original Japanese TV programme from our sole Japanese subscriber, Tokuharu Takabayashi. We transferred it over from NTSC to PAL at Exeter University, and when, after so many months of anticipation we finally saw the video we were astounded.

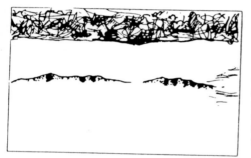

Your editor is a sceptic. He has usually found that the best way to survive within the jungle of truths, half truths, rumours and lies that makes up so much of cryptozoology, is not to believe in anything until he has to, and he was quite expecting, especially in view of what we wrote in issue four to see a video consisting of an unimpressive and amorphous blob in the middle distance, and he was mildly looking forward to writing a sarcastic 'put down' to that effect. What we actually saw was something far more exciting

For copyright reasons we cannot print pictures direct from the film but we are hoping to get permission to include such pictures in a future issue. In the meantime you will have to make do with an artistic impression of a still from the video from our resident artist Lisa Peach. For a full analysis of the video we sent it (with our hearts full of trepidation because we all know what happens to fortean evidence in the post) to our Zoology consultant, the eminent cryptozoologist Dr Karl P.N Shuker...

The Migo Movie: A further muddying of murky waters
by Dr Karl P.N.Shuker

Quite a while ago, Japanese cryptozoologists received the opportunity to make up their own minds concerning the possible identity of the *migo*, when a Japanese TV documentary was screened that charted the now famous Japanese expedition of January/February 1994 in search of Lake Dakataua's mystifying water monster. So far, however, no portion of that documentary has been broadcast in the U.K. Thanks to the kindness of Jonathan Downes, who recently loaned me a videocassette of the programme sent to him by a Japanese correspondent, I thus became the first zoologist in Britain to view this elusive *migo* movie.

Inevitably, much of the documentary's dialogue was in Japanese, but the visuals were sufficiently self explanatory for this to be of little hindrance. After arriving in New Britain and reaching Lake Dakataua, the expedition's team interviewed local eyewitnesses, sailed upon the lake, and succeeded in filming the *migo*, sent divers into the lake and also into the nearby sea (it was suggested that the horseshoe shaped Dakataua may be connected to it by underwater channels), unsuccessfully attempted to lure the *migo* using dead chickens, lowered a cage into the lake and also some sound recording equipment, and exchanged views as to the *migo*'s identity with the expedition's scientific consultant, Prof. Roy Mackal, who recounted his views in English (Regrettably, however, much of his account was lost to all but the most gifted of lip readers - due to the programme's misguided decision to employ a Japanese voice-over translation, instead of visual Japanese subtitles, for most of Roy's scenes).

Throughout the documentary, the identity promoted by the team was that of a mosasaur, a huge sea-dwelling lizard related to today's monitors, but which officially died out over 60 million years ago. Sadly, its candidature was not assisted by a woefully-inadequate model - impressive in close-up 'head and shoulder' shots, but with an impassively inflexible body that showed neither the inclination nor the ability to perform any natatory undulations. **(Personally I thought that it looked like a clockwork newt! Ed)**

Excluding some footage that showed little more than a blurred hump, the *migo* movie comprised two separate sections. The longer section, lasting for approximately five minutes and shot at a distance of approximately 0.7 miles, portrayed what Roy referred to in the film as three different body portions of a very large, long animal, travelling through the water. The most anterior portion was an indistinct head, staying out of the water throughout the footage. Behind this was a smaller portion that could have been a neck. Somewhat further back, but maintaining a constant distance from the 'neck', was a third body portion, taking the form of a large, flattened hump. This hump seemed to be actively propelling along the 'head', 'neck', and whatever body portion (perpetually hidden beneath the water surface) linked the hump to the 'neck' - every few minutes the hump submerged, then swiftly bobbed back up again. This section of footage also included some close-up shots - intriguingly, these gave the impression that the dorsal surface of the large, flattened hump was serrated, but this may well have been an optical illusion.

Shown earlier in the documentary was a much shorter piece of footage, lasting just a few seconds, but which to my mind was much more impressive. When I forwarded it frame by frame, it revealed what appeared to be a section of the *migo*'s body rapidly emerging from the water in a vertical upsurge, and bearing two slender projections resembling dorsal fins or spines, before submerging again - followed immediately by the momentary vertical emergence of what may have been a tail, with two horizontal, whale-like flukes. Regardless of the precise identity of the body portions in view, however, it was abundantly evident that the object being filmed here was not only animated, but also animate - alive.

Nevertheless, in my opinion, the *migo* is not a mosasaur, nor indeed anything of reptilian nature. The cardinal cryptozoological rule in classifying water monsters focuses upon the direction of body flexion (undulation) - horizontal or vertical. Reptiles, amphibians and fishes flex horizontally - only birds and mammals flex vertically. (There is one notable exception to this rule - judging from the shape of their vertebrae as preserved in fossil form, the long-extinct sea crocodiles or thalattosuchians could probably have undulated vertically, but for reasons elucidated a little later, a thalattosuchian identity is not among the front runners for the *migo*.) Their anatomy suggests that mosasaurs swam via horizontal, snake-like flexions of their long body and their laterally-flattened, vertically-finned tail - movements very different from those of the vertically undulating *migo*.

Following his return to the U.S.A. after the end of the expedition, Prof. Mackal corresponded with me regarding his own views as to the identity of the *migo* - which he terms the *migaua*. He has also very generously provided me with much background information concerning it for inclusion within my forthcoming book, 'In search of Prehistoric Survivors' (due for publication later this year and surveying a wide range of mystery beasts that may be undiscovered modern-day descendants of 'officially' long extinct animals).

According to Roy, the migo, or migaua was over 33ft long and travelling at a speed of 4 knots. On film, he ruled out the possibility that it was a crocodile or any known type of fish and within his letters to me he opined that it was an evolved archaeocete, i.e. an archaeocete that has continued to evolve beyond the form acquired by the most recent species known from the fossil record. Archaeocetes were primitive cetaceans (whales) that officially died out around 25 million years ago, and included the overtly serpentine zeuglodonts, such as the famous 70 ft long *Basilosaurus*. Their skeletal anatomy indicates that zeuglodonts propelled themselves through the water via a series of sinuous vertical undulations. They may have sported one or more dorsal fins, and a small pair of horizontal flukes on their tail. Evolved zeuglodonts constitute the most popular, and likely, identity for many serpentine water monsters currently on file, including *Ogopogo* of Canada's Lake Okanagan, the monster of Lake Flathead in Montana, and British Columbia's '*Cadborosaurus*' sea serpent.

Judging from their dentition, zeuglodonts were carnivorous - but this raises a problem, at least on first sight, when attempting to reconcile the migo with this identity. The TV programme included an interview with an English-speaking Papuan official - who commented that during a detailed investigation of Lake Dakataua in 1974, a visiting wildlife researcher discovered that it contains no fish of any type. This remarkable fact was also mentioned in Roy's letters to me - so if the migo is a zeuglodont, what is it feeding upon? As Roy disclosed, the answer is quite simple - namely the vast abundance of waterfowl that settles upon the lake's surface. The necessity to remain near the surface in order to seize these birds presumably explains why the migo is seen more often (and filmed more easily!) that comparable lake monsters elsewhere around the world - which undoubtedly feed predominantly upon fishes rather than waterfowl, and therefore do not need to frequent the upper levels of their watery domains so regularly.

Like Roy, I consider it feasible that the migo is indeed a modern-day archaeocete - and from the film evidence alone, a zeuglodont is a likely candidate. As readers of earlier '*Animals & Men*' installments regarding the migo will have realised by now, however, it is precisely when everything seems to have become relatively straightforward with this animal that events become increasingly complicated again. When he sent me the videocassette, Jonathan Downes also enclosed some information sent to him by his Japanese correspondent, Tokuharu Takabayashi, which he permitted me to draw upon here.

Mr Takabayashi notes that in October 1978, Lake Dakataua was visited by Japanese cryptozoologist Toshikazu Saitoh, who learnt from natives inhabiting the nearby village of Blumuri that the lake monster was known as masuli, masalai, and masuli (all translating as 'spirits'), and was first seen during the summer of 1971, by five different eyewitnesses. According to their accounts, the creature has a total length of about 30 ft, a relatively small head with long pointed jaws resembling a crocodile's and containing many sharp teeth, a long neck, a burly but streamlined body, a slender crocodilian tail, and two pairs of flippers (of which the front pair is noticeably larger than the hind) that resemble those of a marine turtle.

Interestingly, the overall image conjured up by this description recalls that of the 1994 team's favourite migo identity, the mosasaur - until, that is, one final feature attributed to the beast by its eyewitness is added to the picture. For according to them, the monster of Lake Dakataua is covered with short black hair. Mosasaurs were true lizards, and, like them, were covered not in hair but in scales - as attested by several well-preserved fossil specimens. Even allowing for the effects of continued evolution spanning the 60 odd million years between the most recent fossil species and the present day, it is not likely that a 20th Century mosasaur would have evolved a hairy pelage. The same also applies in relation to the prospect of a modern-day thalattosuchian as the identity of this mystery beast - though the pen portrait of the *massali* offers little encouragement for this solution anyway.

There is, however, one type of creature that fits the description of the *massali* and for which the possession of hair would not pose a problem. Arachaeocetes include the earliest of all cetaceans - and as cetaceans descended from quadrupedal land mammals, the first of these archaeocetes must have had four well-developed limbs. Until recently, no fossils of these 'missing links' had been found, but in 1994 one such species was finally documented.

Unearthed from river deposits in Pakistan's Kuldana Formation that are roughly 52 million years old, the fossilised remains belonged to a long-snouted species of very early cetacean approximately 9ft long, with a streamlined body, lengthy tail that probably lacked flukes, and two well-developed pairs of limbs. Moreover, the structure of its vertebral column implied that this was very flexible dorsoventrally - i.e. it could undulate vertically.

This radically new species was formally dubbed *Ambulocetus natans* - 'swimming walking whale' - because there is good reason to suppose that it was able to swim effectively in the sea, but also to move around on land rather like modern-day sealions. It is likely that as cetacean evolution progressed, the hind limbs of *Ambulocetus*'s descendants became ever smaller (for today's cetaceans possess only the merest vestige of hind limbs), and there would have been a stage during this evolution when cetaceans remarkably similar to native descriptions of the *massali* existed. So is this the identity of the *massali/migo* - not an evolved zeuglodont, but a morphologically-conservative, pre-zeuglodont archaeocete?

Even the monster's name, let alone its identity, is no longer as straightforward as once thought. After all, the usage of *massali* and similar names in preference to *migo* could be dismissed as nothing more dramatic than differences in local dialect - were it not for the comments of another visitor to Lake Dakataua. Japanese explorer-writer Atsuo Tanaka, who stayed at Blumuri in September 1983. Confirming to Mr Takabayashi that the local names for the Dakataua water monster were *massali* and *rui*, he stated that *migo* was actually the native name for a three foot long species of monitor lizard! Moreover, according to Tanaka, many of the villagers do not believe that anyone has seen a monster here or that it even exists.

Tanaka's own opinion is that any sightings that may have been made here are of a crocodile (perhaps an unknown species, but more probably either the New Guinea crocodile *Crocodylus novaeguineae* or the larger saltwater crocodile *C. porosus*), or a dugong.

So where does that leave the *migo*, *migaua*, *massali*, *rui* - or whatever else we may wish to call it? According to Roy, the region's provisional government is very keen for further expeditions to take place, and for the capture of a living specimen. Judging from the extraordinary extent of contradictory evidence presently on file, it seems likely that this is the only hope for ever uncovering the truth concerning the enigmatic denizen of Dakataua.

EDITORS NOTE

So here the story rests....for the time being. We shall bring you more information as and when we get it.

THE CASE OF THE HAIRY HANDS
by Stephen Shipp

The tale of the Hairy Hands is perhaps one of Dartmoor's most famous mysteries. It could well have been worthy of Sir Arthur Conan-Doyle, with his famous fictional detective Sherlock Holmes investigating this strange occurrence. However, this is not fiction, and many people have suffered as a result of their appearance.

In the autumn of 1921 it produced the headline in The Daily Mail, 'Hairy Hands on Dartmoor'. Reports of this strange apparition have been around for centuries with horse drawn travellers fearing their presence, pony traps being turned over, cyclists having their handle bars wrenched from their hands, horses shying, cars and coaches crashing and so on. These events have all taken place along or close to an ordinary stretch of the B. 3212 road just outside of Postbridge and toward Two Bridges. They have sometimes resulted in fatalities as you will read.

These hands, though not exactly an animal, are included in this magazine as they might once have belonged to some unusual hairy creature. It has been speculated that wild bears once roamed Dartmoor-so could they be something to do with it? Or perhaps they are the apparition hands of a prehistoric person haunting the spot? This kind of spectre is fairly unusual-as although there are cases of ghost hands they are always reported to be without hair.

The accounts for this century begin in June 1921 when a Medical Officer for Dartmoor Prison was riding his motorcycle along the B.3212 from Two Bridges to Postbridge. With him were two small children in his side car. As he drove down the hill to where a small bridge crosses the East Dart river (SX 647 789), he called to the children to quickly jump clear. This they somehow did and landed unharmed on the grass verge whilst the motorcycle swerved off the road and crashed killing the doctor instantly.

This crash may have been accepted as being an ordinary road accident except for what happened to another motorcyclist on August 26th of that year. A young army officer left the house of a friend to visit some other people a considerable distance away. His route took him along the same stretch of road where the crash, described had occurred. An hour later he returned to his friend's house in a dazed condition with his motorcycle badly damaged. When he was eventually calmed down he said that as he went down the hill towards the bridge, he felt a pair of rough, hairy hands close over his own on the handle bars forcing the motorcycle to veer off the road very near to the spot that the doctor had been killed. He remembered nothing else until he regained consciousness.

Three years later, in 1924, a woman witnessed a hairy hand at a place about one mile west of the spot where the two accidents had happened. She and her husband were asleep one moonlit night in a caravan near the ruins of the Powder Mills (Sx 628 767). Suddenly she was awoken with the strange feeling that something horrible was close at hand. As the woman looked up to the little window at the end of the caravan, she saw a strange shape on the other side of the glass. Moving closer, her heart beating fast the shape became clear- it was the fingers and palm of a very large hand with hairs on the joints and back of it. This phantom hand was clawing its way up the window which was open a little at the top. Despite her fear, she was able to make the sign of the cross and pray very hard. The hand then slowly sank down out of sight and the feeling of terror passed.

One account, undated, talks of a young man driving his car from Plymouth to Chagford one evening. He never arrived there, and his overturned car and dead body were found close to the location of the previous crashes. No satisfactory reason for the accident could be determined.

More recently, a doctors car suddenly stopped with no apparent mechanical failure at the same point where the motorcycle accidents in 1921 occurred, and in 1979 at this spot yet another doctor ended up with his vehicle in the roadside ditch after an unknown powerful force seemed to take control.

To end on a personal note, the author and his then future wife Frances, were driving along the B.3212 from Moretonhampstead to Two Bridges. They had just gone over the bridge at Postbridge and were climbing the road hill when the car suddenly pulled to the left and bounced off the grass verge and back onto the road again. Frances, who was behind the wheel and is a safe driver couldn't explain why it had happened. It was only months later, when reading about the Dartmoor legend did we realise that this was the stretch of road haunted by the hairy hands and only yards away from where all the previous crashes were reported!

The map references given are for Ordinance Survey Landranger 191 (1:50,000)

REFERENCES

BARBER S. & C. Dark and Dastardly on Dartmoor (Obelisk Publications 1988)
BORD J. & C. Alien Animals (Paul Elek Ltd 1980)
BROWN T. Devon Ghosts (Jarrold 1982).
COXHEAD J.R.W. Legends of Devon (Western Press 1954).
PEGG J. A visitors guide to Dartmoor (John Pegg Publishing 1983)
PEGG J. After Dark on Dartmoor (John Pegg Publishing 1984)
ST. LEGER-GORDON R. The Witchcraft and Folklore of Dartmoor (Robert Hale 1965)

The B3212 looking towards Postbridge

'Near Lizard but not near enough'; An Addendum
By Stuart Leadbetter

(In Issue two we printed the original article, which Stuart wrote on the subject of his particular theories about the Loch Ness phenomena. This provoked an enormous response in our letters page both for and against his theories. Here, Stuart answers his critics...)

In the letters submitted by Nick Morgan and Martien Mannetje in Issue 3 Mr Morgan considers my statement that whatever lives in Loch Ness "has a body form easily mistaken for a Plesiosaur" to be incorrect, and to a certain degree and after much deliberation I agree. I have now come to realise that there does not exist a creature which possesses an exact match with the body form of a plesiosaur, but I believe that there does exist one which has a partial similarity, and this is mentioned by Mr Morgan in his letter : The Sturgeon.

This theory was first formulated right at the beginning of the whole Loch Ness saga by Rupert T.Gould in his book 'The Loch Ness Monster and others' (1934). On pages 136 and 137 Gould suggests that a partially submerged sturgeon showing only the bony plates on its back, would appear as a multi humped sea serpent with a long neck and small head. (There is a drawing on page 136 to demonstrate this).

Although I agree with Gould's basic premise there are parts of it that I disagree with. In the drawing on page 136, the snout of the sturgeon does appear to be substantially longer than the snout of any sturgeon I have ever seen, and I don't think that the bony plates on the back would look like anything other than bony plates, but these observations have not diminished my belief in the 'Sturgeon-as-Nessie' theory because I have come across some information which could explain the 'Upturned Boat', aspect of the Loch Ness sightings and I think that individual variability or even the possibility of a sub-species of sturgeon could explain some of the reports of head and neck sightings. Let me explain further.

In their book, 'Freshwater Fishes', P.S.Maitland and R.N.Campbell on page 90 state that the series of bony plates covering the sides and backs of sturgeons become smoother and sometimes disappear altogether as a fish grows older. Not only is this conducive to giving the appearance like that of an 'Upturned Boat', but older sturgeons are usually larger sturgeons, and if they really do exist in Loch Ness, an area untouched by intensive fishing and fairly free from pollution, then there are likely to be some sizeable specimens present. I am quite comfortable for this explanation for the appearance of large humps on Loch Ness because sturgeon of twenty feet or more were common in the Danube and the Volga during the 19th Century, but as they were over fished the size plummeted.

I am not comfortable though with the hypothesis I have developed explaining the sightings of apparently serpentine heads and necks on Loch Ness.

To make the snout of a sturgeon into a believable explanation for the sightings of head and necks on Loch Ness, it would either have to be longer than is the norm, due to individual variability in body form and size present within any species population, or either be the adaptation of a previously undescribed sub-species of sturgeon. Both conditions are known to exist in other species but I have to admit that the possibility of a new sub-species of sturgeon, separate from the other known sub-species of sturgeon is pure speculation. (There is a way that fellow members could help me make this hypothesis a little more solid if at all. Apart from searching for evidence and photographic records on captured sturgeons myself, if anyone reading this article has any information regarding records from which snout lengths of captured sturgeons can be gleaned please send it to the journal for publication).

Moving on to Mr Mannetje's letter. He questions my statement that 'In all the thousands of sightings not one describes Nessie plucking a bird from air in mid flight'.I still stand by this statement and may I take this opportunity to point out a glaring error that has been committed by the editor of this journal and which was seemingly attributed to me. This is the use of the word 'thousands'.

(SEE APOLOGY IN ISSUE FOUR P 26. Ed)

In my original manuscript I wrote that I considered myself to be familiar with the vast majority of the Loch Ness sightings and I am well aware that the total number falls well short of being in the 'thousands'. In my opinion the people who are responsible for the spreading of this patently false piece of information are Nick Witchell and Roy P. Mackal.

Talking of sightings, it makes me wonder why Mr Mannetje bothers assembling his collection of Loch Ness reports. What does he hope to achieve by doing so? In previous years I had the idea of compiling my own computer database of Loch Ness sightings but I scrapped the idea after some serious thought- what's the point of compiling all that information if you're not even sure that the stories from which it comes from are based on fact? How could you check the reports from many years earlier for accuracy when you had no witness address to go on? and even if you did have the witnesses address the person in question would probably be long since dead. In my view if Mr Mannetje uses his collection of Loch Ness reports for research purposes he should only do so with the clear knowledge that the data being processed may be highly flawed and unverifiable.

(EDITORIAL NOTE: If I have learned nothing else from my time a both a journalist and a cryptozoologist, I can tell a story which will not lie down when I see one. This one will run and run. Its now over to you...Comments please!)

Readers in the Westcountry may be interested to know that The Editor, (under the aegis of the Devon County Council Adult Education Department) will be giving a series of summer school lectures on the subject of Cryptozoology. Titled "Still on the Track of Unknown Animals" these lectures, at St Luke's High School, Exeter will feature video clips of our ongoing researches and are aimed at the novice and the expert alike. The dates currently confirmed are.

Saturday May 27th
Saturday June 17th
Saturday 22nd July
Saturday 26th August

For more details telephone 01392 424811

NERVOUS TWITCH

The Nervous Twitcher takes her regular look at all thats most wierd in the world of our feathered friends...who WAS that masked ornithologist?

CRIME AND PUNISHMENT

Several tales of stolen and smuggled birds have filtered through in the last few months. A man was caught at an unnamed airport recently trying to smuggle 10 fighting cocks and two brood hens.Some of the birds woke up from a drugged sleep and started to crow loudly, giving the game away. The chickens had been hidden inside a large shipping carton by Florante Pascua, a Philippino-American from Guam. *ITV TELETEXT 18.3.89*

Two very rare yellow shouldered Amazon Parrots recently reared a brood of four youngsters. The two birds, Ken and Barbie, had been separately kidnapped from their native Venezuala and smuggled out. Barbie was picked up at Heathrow customs and Ken was found in Amsterdam. The happy couple have now set up home at Paradise Park, Hayle in Cornwall, where they will play an important part in a breeding programme designed to help the species survive. *DAILY MAIL Jan 12.95*

A blue fronted Amazon was stolen with personal possessions from a house in Hale, Cheshire. The owner Julie Rollings, sent out a desperate plea via a newspaper advertisement for his safe return but heard nothing for nine days. Then one day she had a strange 'phone call from a woman who told Julie to be at the car park of the George and Dragon pub in Altrincham at a certain time. *'Be there and you can have your parrot back'* she said, *'but no questions asked'*. Eventually a taxi turned up and the sole passenger was Silver, her lost parrot! It sounds like a plot from a bad B Movie but at least it had a happy ending! *Daily Mail 23.2.95*

SOCK IT TO ME MAMA

A ten day old vulture called *'Bert'* is currently being reared by....an old sock! He was abandoned at an early age and zoo keepers at Whipsnade are using the makeshift puppet to help feed Bert and to make him think that it is another vulture. *BBC TELETEXT NEWSROUND 23.2.95*

WHITHER SHALL YE WANDER?

I can't think of many worse things than slicing off your own finger with a chisel, but one of them must be when the finger you've just sliced off gets eaten by your pet geese! That's exactly what happened to handyman David Bidmead from Crawley when he was doing a spot of DIY. *Northampton Chronicle 22.3.95.*

DON'T BE SILLY

Is this an urban myth, a practical joke or real life? The *Daily Mail* reported in 1993 that hundreds of tiny wooly jumpers had been knitted by volunteers to help save oiled seabirds. People, it is claimed, believed that the jumpers would help soak up the oil and keep them warm. Apparently the RSPCA were inundated with them. If this story had appeared on the first of April I could understand but it appeared on the 20th February. Any thoughts?

LETTERS

As has been the case since the editor's father first mooted the idea of a letters page last summer the crypto post bag has been overflowing with your missives on all subjects Crypto not to mention Zoological.

EASY AS A B C?

Dear Sir,

Regarding cats: Zoologist Dr. Ingvald Lieberkind in his Danish Encyclopaedia 'Dyrenes Verden' from the mid sixties lists the following big cat crossbreeds:

Lion/Tiger
Lion/Leopard
Lion/Jaguar

and between the domestic cat and:

Felis chaus
F. Silvestris
F.s.ocreata
F.s.ornata
F.s.cafra
F.lynx

The latter fits some descriptions of Alien Big Cats (ABC's). Other than that he also listed a cross between Puma and Leopard (two different genera).

It seems that cats are in general so close genetically that 'anything goes', and this fact could for the moment be a necessity in a thinly spread population. Some of this offspring should be considered sterile though, but we just might be so lucky as to watch a 'species' in the making; nature working from scratch. A topic for future investigation would be an independent library of hair types for reference purposes. A zoo would probably be helpful. The library should contain pictures of hair types, including individual variation, protein profile and possibly DNA profile. Considering the interest from the police in this matter they will help.

By the way: We should not expect to keep the big cats forever. The moment the ABC's (or should we say the BBC's) get their official confirmation we could lose them. England can live with in the region of 5, 000 people killed in traffic per year and (multiplied from Denmark) more than 100, 000 dog bites, but man is an irrational animal. The moment a threat is perceived from ABC's, real or imagined, the devil is loose. This problem has to be dealt with along the way. My feelings are therefore mixed with worry, but that must be the eternal problem of cryptozoology. Personally, regarding ABC's, the British fauna needs a medium sized or big predator, whether cat or wolf. Some purists may argue but the present state of the ecosystem with nothing bigger than a fox or a badger is un-natural.

Eric Sorensen
Denmark

LOCH'ED IN COMBAT?

Dear Mr Downes,

The letter from G.M.Stocker (*A&M4 p 22*), concerning pre 1930's sightings of the Loch Ness Monster sent me hunting through my bookshelves, to try and find further details. I would like to comment here on Mr Stocker's statement that *"when General Wade's men were building the road south of the loch his men mentioned seeing 'whales' in the loch"*...

I found the following account in '*The Loch Ness Story*' by Nicholas Witchell (*Penguin Books 1975*). Witchell states that in 1964, a 'correspondent in New Zealand' (unnamed) claimed to have come across a book published in 1769, which told of *"two leviathan creatures"* being sighted by the road builders. *"It was thought that these might have been one of the whale variety or some huge, unknown sea species which had made their way through some subterranean passage and grown too large to return."*

Witchell then goes on to say that attempts to trace this supposed book had been unsuccessful, so unless someone has found the hoary tome in the twenty years since Witchell wrote the story of the early 'whale' sightings must be taken cum grano salis. Can any reader of '*Animals & Men*' shed any light on this matter?

Turning now to your article '*Crocodile Tears*' (*p.17*), this has proved very useful in untangling the Migo/Migau/Unknown Crocodile mess in New Britain. It is now clear, thanks to your reprinting of the original sources, that we are looking at two quite separate cryptids on that island, which until now have been conflated.

Firstly we have the account by W.T.Neill of animals that were quite clearly crocodiles, spotted around 'upland lakes'. These reptiles probably constitute a new sub-species or even a new species of the Crocodylidae. The animal reported specifically from Lake Dakataua, on the Williaumez Peninsula, and called 'Migo', is a very different kettle of fish.

Migo is said to have a 'head and a neck as long and slim as a horse' with 'hair on the back of its long neck' and a round back (i.e its back appears as a single hump, rather than several vertical undulations). This description matches very well the type of 'sea serpent' named 'The Merhorse' in Heuvelmans' classic "*In the wake of the Sea Serpents*". Certainly one would hardly expect to find hair on the nape of a crocodile - or a mosasaur for that matter - so if Migo is real, it must be a mammal. Perhaps New Britain will be the next Vu Quang, with several unknown species awaiting the intrepid zoologist?

Keep up the good work,
Yours sincerely,

Mike Grayson.
London.

EDITORS NOTE: I think that it is more than possible that there are at least three new species of animal to be discovered on the island of New Britain. A new species of crocodile, an aberrant monitor lizard, and most importantly a surviving pre Zeuglodont Archaeocete. I am just wondering how long it will be before anyone else picks up on the similarity between the 'Rui' mentioned in Dr Shuker's article in this issue and the 'Row'

described by 'Cannibal' Miller from nearby New Guinea and included in Heuvelmans'
'On the Track of Unknown Animals'.

LOCH'ED IN ONCE AGAIN

Dear Sir,

Without wanting to earn myself a reputation as a blinkered sceptic on the issue of the Loch Ness Monster
G.M.Stocker's letter (A&M4) does require further comment.

Turning first to the historical records. If General Wade's men had sighted 'whales' in the loch this would have
given very strong support to the theory of the 'monster'. Unfortunately there is no evidence that there were
any such reports. This reference is supposed to have come from a book published in 1769 but as far as I am
away this publication has never been located.

The 'floating island' is more interesting and comes from Richard Franck's book 'Northern Memoirs'. Of the
supposed earlier evidence of this creature this reference does at least have the merit of actually existing.
Franck, incidentally thought that the phenomenon was caused by mats of floating vegetation (whilst other
writers have identified it with the crannog of Cherry Island at the south-western corner of the loch). It is
interesting too that the most famous example of a 'floating island' was actually in Loch Lomond which has
not sustained any tradition of 'monster' sightings.

The third example given by G.M.S.; the diver being frightened by a creature ...'like a huge frog" is another
example of a supposed earlier sighting that was not made public until after the 1933 flap.

Turning to the legendary examples given in the letter. The whole subject of folklore traditions is highly
complex and whilst it is interesting that St. Columba (not St Augusta) performed his miracle with a monster
at, or near, Loch Ness this legend should be seen in the context of stories designed to show the power of the
Christian faith and shouldn't be taken simplistically as prima facie evidence of a physical creature.

Similarly the Kelpie tradition is so widespread, including waters that could never have sustained a 'monster',
that its link with the Loch Ness creature is at best tenuous. There are other equally convincing explanations
for the creation of this legend including, as illustrated in G.M.S.'s letter, their use to frighten children away
from swimming in what are potentially deadly waters.

Yours faithfully,

Nick Morgan,
North Yorkshire.

Midnight Books
SPECIALISTS IN SECONDHAND BOOKS ON THE UNEXPLAINED

To receive our latest book catalogue, simply send four first class stamps (or if overseas,
two International Reply Coupons) to:

Midnight Books
Frances and Steven Shipp
The Mount, Ascerton Road
Sidmouth, Devon, EX10 9BT

HELP

This is the section of the magazine where you, the reader can help us
(and vice versa) with ongoing research projects.

FUNKY FROGS

In Issue One we printed an article about the multi coloured frogs which have recently been appearing across the south of Britain and in Issue four we printed an update with an appeal for information about sightings. 'Animals & Men' reader Andy Stephens, of Bristol wrote in...

"When I was a child I used to go and stay with my Aunty and Uncle who lived in Uplowman near Tiverton in Devon with my brother. During these stays we would fish in the canal near Halberton for tench and perch. Often for the tench we would throw in a rake head on a piece of string into the canal to clear weed. During the 1960's I was doing this one hot day. As I emptied the weed onto the bank I was startled to see a creamy white frog jumping out of the pile.

I was extraordinarily keen on reptiles and amphibians in those days and it was undoubtedly a white or cream coloured version of the common frog. I could not say what colour its eyes were. I realised this was something unusual and I tried to catch it. I was pretty fast and I got both hands round it. As I raised my hands it slipped out and leapt into the water never to be seen again. I do recall that my brother who is three years older than me thought that I was making it up, (he was fishing further up the bank). That's older brothers for you!

That place on the canal is a magical place for me, right where a bridge crosses it. A few years ago when on a business trip (once again on a very hot day), I took a detour on the way home just to go there. It was as quiet as the grave except for the buzzing of flies. Then a shrill ripped through the air and I immediately recognised the sound of a raptor or bird of prey. Slinking through the fields nearby I entered a field of nearly mown cereal and there amongst the stubble were two magnificent buzzards who were soon joined by a third. I watched them for fifteen minutes or so and I felt like I had never grown up. I love that place!"

PINBALL LIZARDS

In issue one we printed a letter from reader Suzanne Stebbings who had a query about some unusual lizards in her collection that she appeared to have bred 'by mistake'. She writes with an update:

"You may remember the mysterious lizards that hatched from Lacerta viridis eggs. The babies looked like G. galotea. They both eventually died. The latter from a black leg disease, that infected a number of lizards. The baby did grow to resemble a brown version of L.tulineata".

These mysterious baby lizards are a real puzzle. SOMEONE out there must have some ideas as to what and why they were?

We are still looking for the following pieces of information to help us in our research:

- 'Big Bird' sightings post 1977.
- More oddly coloured frogs. Photos and specimens of same.
- Comic Books and pub signs with a Cryptozoological theme.
- Live specimens of soft shelled turtles and larger aquatic salamanders (mudpuppies, sirens, amphiumas etc) or correspondence with people who have kept them.
- Books, magazines etc on Hong Kong and its wildlife.

OBITUARIES
"There is a farm called misery but of that we'll have none"

GERALD DURRELL (1925-1995)

In my life I have been unlucky enough to meet most of my personal heroes. I have ended up working for two of them but in every case they did not live up to my expectations. I never, however met my first, and greatest hero, Gerry Durrell who died of complications following a liver transplant operation on the 30th January this year. I have known of his serious illness for the last year because ever since we started I have been sending each issue of Animals and Men to him at Jersey Zoo, and I have been exchanging letters with his assistant John Hartley who said repeatedly kind things about us but said that *'Gerry was too ill'* to read the magazine. This has been my greatest personal disappointment since we started because if it hadn't been for Gerald Durrell I wouldn't be who I am today.

My mother read me extracts from his books when I was a small child and as soon as I was old enough to read them for myself I devoured them avidly. His most popular book 'My Family and other Animals' (1956), provided me at an early age with my two most enduring role models, Gerry himself, and his almost sociopathically eccentric elder brother Larry. For many years I was determined to be either an investigative (if slightly anthropomorphic) analytical field zoologist (and burgeoning zookeeper), or an eccentric and irascible writer surrounded by an ever changing bevy of ridiculously highbrow friends.

Gerald Durrell.   Picture Copyright Jersey Wildlife Preservation Trust

Gerald Durrell made a number of highly acclaimed TV series, including most recently 'The Amateur Naturalist' and 'Durrell in Russia', but for me it was the sheer good natured amateurishness of his earlier B&W TV appearances in the 1960's which encapsulated the character that we had all come to know and love from his books. In the field of Cryptozoology he wrote the forwards to perhaps the most important two books on the subject, to have been published in the UK; 'On the Track of Unknown Animals' by Bernard Heuvelmans (1956) and 'The Lost Ark' by Karl Shuker (1993). For many years he had been inferring that he would write something on the subject himself and all of his many fans within the wider sphere of Forteana are disappointed that now this will never happen.

I haven't even attempted to detail his work as founder of Jersey Zoo, his work as a conservationist and within the field of Animal Behaviour or his work as founder of the mini university attached to the zoo which now trains'people from all over the world to work within their own countries conserving their own natural heritage. Many people have written all that over the past three months. I would just like to say that the world will be a poorer and a less exciting place without him.

JANE BRADLEY 1961-95

The first four issues of this magazine were defined by the cartoons and graphic design of Jane Bradley. She was also our Scottish correspondent and had been responsible for gathering some of the silliest and most eccentric news stories to grace our pages. She also thought out the silliest and most cerebral campaign slogan of all time with 'SOLIPSISTS UNITE'. She was killed whilst hitch-hiking on the M5 on the 5th February this year. She was an extremely talented artist, and surreal humourist but as is the case the spark which produced this 'wild' talent also caused her to suffer from severe depression, psychological and behavioural problems. She had been undergoing treatment for these illnesses and had been making considerable progress, when the news of the suicide of a close friend in Edinburgh threw her already unstable emotions into a turmoil and she left the residential centre where she had been living and itchhiked towards Scotland. Unfortunately, she never made it! She left a two year old son called Bal who lives with his father. Whenever anyone dies the same platitudes are trotted out, but in her case one at least is true. There will never be anyone quite like her again.

Many of Jane's cartoons were wry self portraits, and this picture, that she drew on a visit to the Editor's beast filled abode seems an appropriate memorial.

OTHER ABSENT FRIENDS.

In the first three months of this year we have also lost popular animal author and vet James Herriot, Satirist and actor Peter Cook, and the irreplaceable Viv Stanshall. We wouldn't be who we are if we did not remember them in these pages: ...."because we know of one, that's really much more fun ".

BOOK REVIEWS

FOLKLORE AND MYSTERIES OF THE COTSWOLDS by Mark Turner (Robert Hale pb 191pp 6.99)

This excellent little book does just about what the title implies but unlike so many others of its genre it does it well. Most of the material is broadly fortean in nature but it covers several 'black dog' sightings in considerable depth as well as a particularly interesting 'monster' episode in Aston Magna, Gloucestershire where a 'bear' like creature preyed on local pets during the early eighties. There are several other ghostly bear stories in the book and these taken together shed a possible new light on the recent sightings of a brown bear near Oxford (SEE A&M 2).

I would, however, have liked to see illustrations and proper maps as the one sketch map that is included is barely adequate for its task.

THE GOOD GHOST GUIDE by John Brooks (Jarrold 288pp 8.99).

This is a workmanlike gazetteer of over a thousand British Ghost sightings and haunted sites and as such contains a number of animal ghosts of interest to readers of this magazine. It contains yet another folk story to explain the ghostly monkey of Athelhampton Hall in Dorset, and a number of ghostly bears and black dogs and even a werewolf that is new to me.

There is a comprehensive index, a glossary and some excellent maps. However, suprisingly whereas it is doubtless an excellent reference book, unlike my own favourite in this field (Andrew Green's "Our Haunted Kingdom" from 1973), it fails to imbue the reader with any sense of excitement, interest or involvement which is a great pity.

STRANGE STORIES AMAZING FACTS (Readers Digest 608pp)
STRANGE WORLDS AMAZING PLACES (Readers Digest 432pp)
EXPLORING THE SECRETS OF NATURE (Readers Digest 432pp)

Unfortunately Readers Digest didn't actually send me the books I wanted to review, which were the two on which our own Dr Karl Shuker had acted as consultant. Each of these (especially 'Strange Stories Amazing Facts'), have something to recommend them to the amateur fortean zoologist but the more serious student will probably have most of the source material already.

These are strange books. Probably the best way to describe them is as the literary equivalent of a Transatlantic Corporate fast food restaurant. Everything is stunningly presented in bite sized chunks which look and taste great but in the end do little to satiate your hunger. (Would it be churlish to also say that too much of either makes you slightly bilious?...yes it probably would!)

Great pictures though!!!

PERIODICAL REVIEWS

We welcome an exchange of periodicals with magazines of mutual interest although because we now exchange with so many magazines we only include in our listings those magazines who have published an issue which we have recieved during the previous three months

BIGFOOT RECORD. Bill Green, c/o The Bigfoot Centre, 21 Benham St, Apartment F, Bristol, CT06010 USA This free news service for bigfoot buffs is bi-monthly and has a refreshingly informal style

DRAGON CHRONICLE, The dragon trust, PO Box 3369, London SW6 6JN. A fascinating collection of all things draconian which now appears four times a year

NEXUS 55 Queens Rd, E. Grinstead, West Sussex RH19 1BG. Intelligent look at the fringes of science. Well

NESSLETTER Rip Hepple, 7 Huntshieldford, St Johns Chapel, Bishop Auckland Co Durham DL13 1RQ. This magazine has been appearing regularly for many years and cannot be reccomended highly enough.

BIPEDIA, Francois de Sarre, CERBI, BP65, 06202, NICE, CEDEX 3, FRANCE. A magazine about Initial Bipedalism, scholarly and concise.

TEMS NEWS, 115 Hollybush Lane, Hampton, Middlesex, TW12 2QY. An engaging collection of quasi fortean odds and ends from veteran UFO buff Lionel Beer.

TOUCHSTONE and PEGASUS, Jimmy Goddard, 25 Albert Rd, Addlestone, Surrey two neat UFO/Fortean mags. Well produced and collated.

DEAD OF NIGHT, 156 Bolton Road East, Newferry, Wirral, Merseyside, L62 4RY. An amusing and intelligently put together Fortean magazine. Issue four has an article on 'black dogs' and a long round up of absurd items of fortean zoology. One of my favourite magazines.

CRYPTOZOOLOGIA, Association Belge d'Etude et de Protection des Animaux Rares, Square des Latins 49/4, 1050 Bruxelles. Belgium. A French language magazine published by the Belgian society for Cryptozoology.

ENIGMAS, 41 The Braes, Tullibody, Clackmannanshire, Scotland, FK10 2TT A Fine 'mysteries' magazine with a UFO bias.

PROMISES AND DISAPPOINTMENTS 42 Victoria Road, Mt Charles, St Austell, Cornwall, PL25 4Qd England. Kevin McClure is the editor of this excellent magazine on 'non human intelligence'

THE BRITISH COLUMBIA CRYPTOZOOLOGY CLUB NEWSLETTER, 3773 West 18th Avenue, Vancouver, British Columbia, Canada. V65 1B3. Excellent and well put together, and they were very nice about us in their last issue.

FROM OUR FILES

I have a particular interest in the winged entities that have been reported occasionally worldwide over the past couple of hundred years. These are apparently completely different to the 'big bird' sightings which often occur in the same places. These sightings often come in chronological spates, (although not always in the same geographical area), and it has been many years since the last well attested outbreak of this, possibly the most bizarre of fortean quasi-zoological phenomena. The most well known of such creatures are 'Owlman' (Cornwall during the late 1970's) and 'Mothman' (USA during the mid 1960's), but these apparitions have occurred everywhere from Vietnam to Surrey.

The latest 'winged thing' was reported from Washington State in the Pacific Northwest of the USA in April 1994. The Pacific North-West is one of the more prolific window areas for fortean zoological phenomena, and is famed for its Bigfoot sightings and for the mysterious falls of poisonous jelly reported in A&M4. This latest outbreak started when 18 year old Brian Canfield was driving home to the isolated settlement of Camp One from the nearby town of Buckley at 9.30 in the evening. The engine of his pickup truck died and the dashboard lights fell dark and the vehicle stopped suddenly. His headlights were still functioning and they lit up the shape of a nine foot figure descending from the sky to the road in front of him. It had blue tinted fur, yellowish eyes, the feet of a bird, tufted ears and sharp straight teeth. Its wings were folded and attached to its back and broad shoulders.

"It was standing there staring at me like it was resting, like it didn't know what to think", said Brian, *"I was scared, it raised the hair on me. I didn't feel threatened. I felt out of place"*.

The newspaper report goes on to describe Brian in terms which make him seem almost saintly by comparison to the usual media representation of young people from that part of America, and stressed that not only had he never had any paranormal experiences before but he didn't take drugs, or drink, play 'Dungeons and Dragons' or listen to heavy metal

"BATSQUATCH"

music. Although it doesn't sound like he would be much fun at a party his description of the apparition was clear and succinct: *"Its eyes were yellow and shaped like a piece of pie with pupils like a half moon. The mouth was pretty big. White teeth. No fangs. The teeth were like a wolf"*.

The general consensus of opinion both amongst his family and his friends and of the reporter from the TACOMA NEWS TRIBUNE who carried the story on the 24th April 1994. (Thanks COUDi), is that young Brian saw something but noone is prepared to say quite what. They have given the creature the stomach churningly twee name of 'Batsquatch', but noone, as far as I can make out have equated this latest apparition with the well attested 'winged things' of previous years. The last word, I think should go to Brian himself:

"I'm really not into this stuff. It boggles my mind really hard core. I really can't explain it. It's weird, definitely wierd. I don't like it. Usually this stuff happens to someone else".

We at Animals & Men await further developments in the skies above Washington and Oregon with great interest.

JANE BRADLEY
1961-95

As Glastonbury Festival looms on the horizon–even the
cryptids are getting in on the act....

ISSN 13540637 TYPESET BY CHICKEN
POWER